Dogs on the Runway

Roger Thyer-Jones

Queen Anne's Fan

First published in 2012 by Queen Anne's Fan
PO Box 883 • Canterbury • Kent • CT1 3WJ

© Copyright Roger Thyer-Jones 2012

ISBN 9780 9547 1509 0

The names of some places and persons have been altered for reasons of privacy and security. The author has tried and failed to find the owners of the copyright in some of the material quoted. He would be pleased to insert an acknowledgement in future editions.

A CIP record of this book can be obtained from the British Library.

Set in New Baskerville 11 on 12pt.

Printed in England.

LIST OF CHAPTERS

PREFACE & ACKNOWLEDGMENTS

What right do I have to openly discuss my memoirs and share my emotions, secret thoughts, conduct, behaviour and career with family, friends and strangers? Was it ego that prompted me to write about my life? I hope not but I don't know.

Jonathon Swift said, 'the latter part of a man's life is taken up in curing all the follies, prejudices and false opinions he has contracted in the former part.' I believe that reviewing my life experiences, my early mistakes and letting go of my previous emotional anchor-weights has helped me understand myself better. Testing experiences and suffering have forced me to look within myself. Often I have not liked what I saw. But most importantly, I am prepared to keep trying to learn from others, polish my character and find ways in which to give back my experiences in a positive and enriching manner.

This book is not my work alone. Thank you to Drina and Michael Parker for your editing work. I have learned so much from your knowledge and skills over the last twelve months. You pulled no punches.

Martin Lloyd, you have given me encouragement, wise words, tempered with a gentle humour, and an insight into the arcane world of publishing which has been invaluable. Besides this, you are a dear friend and I value your friendship.

Michelle, my wife and friend, has supported me throughout the project and chided me when I have been chronologically challenged. I love her dearly. My sons, Gareth, Alex and Andrew have taken an interest in my work and fed me encouragement. I am indeed a lucky man.

Nothing of worth is ever achieved without the help of others and I am particularly grateful to my close friends, John and Elaine Doust, Mike and Pat Knight and Nick and Sue Westfold and Alp and Elaine Mehmet who have never ceased to keep me firmly grounded. You are all dear to me. My brother-in-law Peter has shared many a guitar thrash (and whisky) with me over the years, helping me to keep my perspective on life.

Derek Beadle, you were my first boss and mentor. You are a bard whose love of poetry and language has inspired me.

I have had the privilege to work and train with so many extraordinary people in the world of immigration, intelligence and martial arts and so many of you have contributed to my development in some way or other. I would particularly like to thank Jun Shihan Tony Robinson, Branch Chief of Seido Karate in Jamaica for his love and friendship. Roger and Roxanne Blatz and Jesse Horowitz, you have put up with me staying in your New York apartments during my many visits to our Seido HQ for training and promotions and I really appreciate your kindness.

Finally, if you get the privilege to become a student under one master in life then cherish that opportunity. My fighting master, Kaicho Nakamura, founder of the World Seido Karate Organisation, has encouraged and supported me for many years and I deeply appreciate his wisdom and guidance. I wish his son and successor, Nidaime Akira Nakamura every success in steering our Seido organisation into the future.

Osu!

1
FATE

'Don't you dare die on me,' I shouted at Richard. Dave was on the floor at the side of me, pumping Richard's heart. 'Don't you dare die on me,' I shouted again before putting two more breaths into his mouth.

Damn those dogs on the runway. I knew that Richard had to get to London. The connection to London would have been tight to make without the delay. Damned dogs. We would have to run with our hand baggage to make the flight. Dave and I were fit but if you are in your late fifties, overweight and your idea of exercise is walking to the bar to order another pint, then running is not a good idea. I really hoped that the stewardess would have responded to my request and have asked the pilot to radio ahead. If Lufthansa knew that we would be a few minutes late they might just keep the gate open for us. In my heart I somehow knew that this wouldn't happen but I had told Richard not to worry. He was red-faced and anxious. He had to get home and be there for his wife's operation. He had told her that he would be by her side. She was relying on his word.

I exchanged looks with Dave sitting on my right. We both knew that unless a miracle happened then it would be highly unlikely that we would make the connection. All I could do was reassure Richard. He seemed a bit calmer after my reassurance.

At last the dogs were caught and we were off. We all relaxed and, once we were airborne, Richard ordered a large gin and tonic. After all, it had been a very successful trip in the most trying of circumstances. We had wrung a commitment from the Bosnians to arrest a major criminal who operated illegal entry and drugs networks, as well as dealing in the awful trade of body parts. This was something to be celebrated. We were tired – travelling, presentations, negotiations and socialising had all taken their toll. Richard had been tireless in supporting our aims. He was very well-connected and knew whom to approach to get the job done. He could be testy at times but had a self-deprecating sense of humour and a knack of putting people at ease. He was a born diplomat and was highly focused. A fondness of drink might have got him into trouble but he handled it well and I had never seen him act unprofessionally.

Yes, it had been a good trip.

'Ladies and gentlemen, we shall be landing at Munich airport in twenty minutes time.'

I opened my eyes and became fully awake. I had been dozing pleasantly. I looked at Richard, who was staring intently ahead as if he could see the airport. His face was quite red. He looked at his watch, stared ahead and then peered at his watch again. Dave met my gaze. I said that as soon as the plane landed we should grab our hand luggage and run for the check-in desk. Once there, we would be able to manage the situation. We would have just fifteen minutes. We had no idea how long it would take and the stewardess had been unable to tell us. I told Richard that all he needed to do was to follow us at a brisk pace. He was not to run. We would do our very best to get him on to the plane.

Bump. The wheels of the airplane touched the tarmac. The engine noise reduced as we left the main runway and turned towards the gate for disembarkation. I could almost feel Richard's anxiety but I didn't want to look at him. We came to a halt. We were in the front row of business class so I knew that we could be the first off the aircraft. As soon as the seat belt signs were extinguished, all three of us sprang out of our seats, opened overhead lockers, grabbed our hand luggage and headed for the exit. I almost knocked over one of the stewards as I ran out on to the enclosed gangway that led from the aircraft. I still had no idea from where our Munich flight was due to depart. I looked frantically for signs. I couldn't see any indication but Dave grabbed my shoulder and pointed. Richard was behind us so I turned and pointed to the sign. He nodded.

We ran.

Our gate was about ten minutes away. It would close in five minutes.

We ran.

Sweat dripped from my forehead and into my eyes. Passengers on either side passed me in a blur. Dave was at my shoulder. We ran up an escalator and saw the Lufthansa desk. There were no passengers waiting there.

Bad sign.

One young man, smartly dressed in his dark Lufthansa ground staff uniform, stood behind the desk. Dave and I slammed down our tickets at the same time.

'Our flight from Sarajevo was delayed.' I said. 'I asked the pilot to radio ahead to say that we would be a few minutes late. Did you get the message?'

'No sir. The gate is now closed. No more passengers can board the flight. *Nein.*'

I tried to calm my breathing. I needed to persuade him to let us on the plane.

'We have a colleague coming behind us. He must get on the flight.' I explained the situation.

'*Nein.*'

'Look, even if we two cannot go, you must make an exception for Richard.'

He was implacable. In a clipped English accent, he said, 'The flight is now preparing for take-off and the captain will not accept any more passengers. *Nein.*'

I pleaded with him to reconsider but deep down I knew that my request was useless. I thought that he was taking some pleasure in his *'nein'* but that might have been just the state of mind I was in.

I turned away from the desk as Richard came up behind me, red-faced and out of breath. I caught him by his jacket as he tried to move forward. I told him that it was useless. We would have to get a flight the next day. The gate was shut. I was very sorry. He pushed me out of the way with an abrupt motion. He dropped his hand luggage and strode, bristling with anger, towards the check-in. I looked at Dave who shrugged his shoulders as if to say that we could not have done more. I heard Richard arguing with the ground staff representative and demanding to speak to the manager. His voice was raised. I turned slowly and saw Richard walking towards me. He had a glassy stare and I sensed that something was wrong.

'Richard,' I said. 'Richard.'

He brushed past me and collapsed, falling forward and hitting his head against a stainless steel rubbish bin. He crashed face down to the ground.

2

WINSTON REBORN

With a pen stuck in my mouth, and a face like a wizened walnut, you would have thought that my impression of Winston Churchill was a bit unconvincing. You would have been right.

My mother was a nurse at the time of my birth on 4 April 1949 and already had one boy, my brother Mike, then aged seven. What she really wanted now was a girl, not a Winston look-alike. In fact, my mother was so small that the other nurses barely knew that she was pregnant and she certainly made no fuss about it. She was two weeks overdue when I popped out and, because she was then a children's nurse, she was well known to all in the maternity ward.

She was celebrated in the children's ward as being the only night nurse who could get the whole ward full of babies to shut up. I asked for her secret once and she told me that a tiny drop of water and sugar does the trick, and if that doesn't do it, just a single drop of brandy works even better!

So, she must have been solely responsible for a generation of London-born babies yearning for a glass or two of brandy to get off to sleep, or cooking sherry if brandy wasn't available. Still, it has fuelled distillery profits over the years since, and what's the loss of an odd liver or two balanced against a decent night's sleep? Anyway, she was up and about shortly after the birth and waltzing about the ward with me jogging on her shoulder. I weighed in at about 4 lb at birth, barely the size of a decent pumpkin, and apparently had the look of a skinned rabbit about me. So picture me as this sorry creature with a pen in my mouth, reducing the ward to tears. I am inclined to think that my mother (I am sure that I called her that at birth as she felt that it was somehow more dignified than being called 'Mum') would have swapped me for any girl available, but presumably they were a bit short that night.

So, with that start to life, I clearly needed feeding up and I think that I was fed full cream milk, sausage, egg and chips and Yorkshire pudding during the first months or so, in order to ensure that at least the weighing scales jumped when I was plonked on them.

It's hard to remember details of my early days, even my birth is a bit hazy, but I can remember being left out in the garden for 'fresh air' for weeks at a time. At one point I was almost swallowed by a tortoise that somehow got into the pram. I can just about recall it licking my face as I gurgled happily, rain water slowly filling the pram.

The only reason I came in from the garden at all is that I floated out of the pram and into the kitchen where my mother noticed I needed changing. She also adopted the tortoise as a pet. Incidentally, that same tortoise became a garden resident and stubbornly refused to leave its garden lair until several years later.

I left all sorts of offerings outside its shell: grass, bacon rind, snails. But all to no avail. Finally, I picked up the shell and, finding it a bit light, looked inside only to find that that there was nothing there. What a swizz ! All that time I thought I had a pet and all I had was an empty shell. Now there's a point for reflection if there ever was one.

We lived in Greenwich. The flat we lived in was enormous and you could fit a bowling alley into the hallway. The full address was, 50 Crooms Hill, Greenwich, London SE10. It was right next to the park and one of the directors of Millwall Football Club, Bill Neelan, lived next door to us in a house within a walled garden. Poor old Bill. Every time

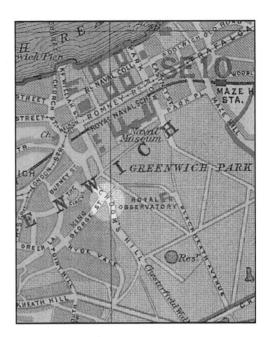

50 Crooms Hill
Greenwich

(Bartholomew 1939)

Millwall lost a home game the 'fans' would come around looking for his Jaguar car and then trash it. He used to have to hide it before games.

The entrance to our house was in King George Street. Our local church was called 'Our Lady Star of the Sea'. It was a Catholic refuge with a nunnery just up the hill where unspeakable practices must have taken place. Well, you would think that, wouldn't you? I've seen *The Devils*.[1] Why on earth did my mother send me to the nuns at such a young age? Mother Margaret Mary was my own personal nun trainer and I had to go to see her every week. She was a kindly red-faced person who wore glasses. She had no body that I could see and I often wondered if she actually had legs as when she walked she seemed to glide along, a bit like a Dalek.[2]

Apart from encouraging me to have St. Michael as my patron saint, I have absolutely no idea of the purpose of Mother Margaret Mary. She did prepare me for my 'confirmation' which seemed to consist of a load of mumbo jumbo totally unintelligible to a youngster. This is a Catholic ritual, akin to a coming of age ceremony, that binds you further to the church.

I can't recall any unspeakable practices being done to me but I think I attended the convent for a couple of years. Maybe I was given a potion to wipe out the memories of satanic rites with nuns dancing around a vegetable of human dimension or something. (Now I'm just fantasising. Steady).

Chris Difford of the group Squeeze,[3] and his family lived up the road and Chris wrote a song, funnily enough, with the title *King George Street*. In later life I really enjoyed the music Squeeze produced – great lyrics that tell a story. In fact *Cool for Cats,* written by Chris, is still high on my list of great songs and has a real south London feel to it.

I loved Chris' mum, Mrs Difford, who was from Coleraine and had black hair and twinkling eyes. She used to give me sweets when I was a kid and lived in a prefab – the technical name for low cost housing – with her husband, Sid, and their sons, Lewis, Leslie and Chris. Lewis was about my brother's age. He was a very calm lad and a terrific swimmer while Leslie was anything but. He would fetch a right hander at anyone who upset him even though he had a hole in the heart.

When I was younger, I never understood what was meant by a hole in the heart. I imagined that you could see right through the hole which must be about two to three inches wide. Leslie's heart defect didn't seem to affect either his ability to punch or to play football. He didn't complain about it at all and I felt it was something that I wouldn't mind having if it would make me a better footballer.

I recall my first act of law breaking. Mrs Difford was a generous woman who used to give me sweets when I visited. One day I went to the prefab to see her and no-one was in.

I knew that the Diffords hid the key to the door under a stone so I quickly found it and opened up the door. I must have been only about six years old. I knew that I was doing something wrong but the lure of sweets drove me on. I found the green tin that held the temptation and helped myself to a few sweets. After all, Mrs Difford would have given them to me anyway. But, already, as a fledgling Catholic recruit, guilt was rising slowly through me and I knew that God was watching. The sweets quickly started to lose their appeal and I replaced the lid securely, or so I thought, and put the tin back. I then locked the door and returned the key to its hiding place.

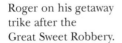
Roger on his getaway trike after the Great Sweet Robbery.

Of course, a six-year-old was no match for the vigilance of the Difford family and somehow – was I under surveillance at the time? – word came down to my mother that I might be the culprit. Mother kept a twig in the kitchen which she called the 'rod' and if I was naughty she used to eye it and even on occasion wave it about a bit. I was never actually beaten with it but the thought of that evil bit of stick hitting my legs made me cringe.

Hence her looking lingeringly at the 'rod' during her interrogation about the 'break in' reduced me to a wreck. I promptly confessed. If I did something I shouldn't then she would nearly always tell my father and you didn't really want him on your back. So a double whammy loomed and it was suggested that I hot foot it back up to 'Ma Diffs,' as she was affectionately known, and apologise.

I vaguely remember dragging myself up the street to face my executioner and apologising to Ma Diff who gave me a bit of a dressing down and a hug while the rest of the Diffords eyed me suspiciously. I really didn't like Leslie doing too much eying especially with that big hole he had in his heart that might prompt a punch or two. No more sweets for me. Funny how as a boy I never thought of the right or wrong of stealing. I simply acted on self interest.

Ma Diff was a great character and very friendly with my mother even though there was a north versus south divide in their homeland. Sadly Ma Diff ended up as a recluse suffering from agoraphobia which I suspect was connected to the tumour she had on her face. My mother encouraged her to go to the doctor when it was just a small mole but she didn't and it just grew bigger and bigger until finally it killed her. She was a sad loss.

Ma Diff and Sid lived in Blackheath at just about the time that Squeeze were emerging as a band. Chris used to compose upstairs in his bedroom with Glenn Tilbrook and Jools Holland who had a Rolls Royce. Jools Holland sometimes offered my mother a lift back home in his Rolls but she never accepted. Ma Diff always knew that Chris had talent and Sid did too. Apart from the usual parents' sniping about 'getting a proper job', they supported him during the early days when the band was establishing itself. The Diffords always were a lively family.

Now picture 50 Crooms Hill, our home. You entered through an enormous green door facing onto the street. It led into a glass cupola with a flat on the left and iron stairs leading up to our door straight ahead. Our door was also green and seemed immense to me as a child. It had a big brass knocker. Under the iron stairs was the basement. God, that place would make Dracula shiver. You went down wooden stairs to a creaky door next to a filthy window.

Our coal was kept in one of the rooms in the basement which was a warren and had been used as some sort of chemical storage space during the war. The whole building had originally been a school. It had been designed by Sir Christopher Wren so it was of historical interest. The servants' quarters were down below. My brother Mike told me that one of the servant girls had been found hanging by her neck in one of the rooms. He was clearly trying to cheer me up for when I was on coal duty.

I hated that damn place. Once the fire in the enormous lounge started to go down, Mother or Dad would eye the empty bucket and it would be either my or my brother's job to hop down and get the coal. I could barely lift the scuttle and my heart would sink if Dad told me to fill up.

Imagine yourself on a cold winter night, lighting a pathetic candle stub with a shaking hand. Clutching the coal scuttle and iron shovel and setting off down those dark stairs. The door would always creak and as I entered the first room, the shadows thrown by the candle would half light up dark corners. My first few steps would be tentative and I sometimes tried to whistle but soon stopped as I thought it might alert any horrors waiting to get me. Fear coursed through my young blood.

I wish Mike hadn't told me about that hanging rope as I swear that I could sometimes see a dark stained rope eerily swinging across an old beam.

The coal was held in a bunker behind a thick oak door with iron fixings. You had to leave the first room, open a door and then open the coal door. The candle light would flicker, caught by hidden currents and by now I would be so aware of every sound that I could hear a mouse breathe.

I would jam open the big oak door with iron fixings and then make a beeline for the coal.

Next came the difficult part of the task: I had to put the candle down on the shelf as I couldn't shovel with one hand. I didn't like doing that. What if the flame went out? Anything lurking in the pit could get me. So, shovelling furiously, I would try to fill the scuttle to the top in order to avoid having to make a another journey to the cellar.

The trouble was that once the scuttle was full, I couldn't actually lift it as well as hold the shovel, pick up the candle and get out of there. Often, I simply tipped half of the coal out on the floor in order to be able to carry it. Rather self-defeating.

Once, the worst thing happened to me. In my darkest dreams it should never have happened. Never. The door shut behind me with a bang and the candle blew out just as I was shovelling the coal into the scuttle. I stopped dead. I could hear my heart thumping and desperately willed it to shut up as clearly whatever was in the pit would hear it too. I stood still for what seemed ages just waiting for the touch of some scaly claw on my shoulder.

In fact Coleridge[4] must have experienced the same fear:

> Like one that on a lonely road
> Doth walk in fear and dread,
> And having once turned round walks on
> And turns no more his head,
> Because he knows a frightful fiend
> Doth close behind him tread.

I fumbled slowly in my pocket for the box of Swan Vestas matches, guaranteed to light under any circumstances. Not when you open the box upside down and all the matches fall out. Now I had no matches and I could hear strange scuttling sounds around me. My heart was beating so loudly now that any self-respecting monster, even a totally deaf one, would hear me.

Gingerly, I squatted down and felt for a match. Success. I slowly scraped it against the side of the box, assured of a light, but it broke in half with a sharp crack. I felt as if I had been in the room for an eternity. I fought back the tears that were brimming in my eyes. Steady the Buffs. I felt the ground with my hand again and this time scooped up a handful of matches.

Just imagine my joy when I actually succeeded in lighting the match – it must have been how Gandalf [5] felt in lighting up the Mines of Moria with his magic staff. I saw the candle stub and grabbed it like the Holy Grail. Shaking hands lit it and once again the shadows danced around the room making me feel elated.

Then I felt sick. I had to get out past whatever had closed the door and I knew that IT must be awful what ever IT was. So, with the scuttle in my left hand and the shovel inside it, I walked to the door holding the candle. It was then that I thought that a demonstration of assertive behaviour would probably scare the pants off any monster so I shouted out, 'Here I come!' or some such battle cry, pulled open the door and rushed through the room towards the stairs and safety. It was a pity that I dropped the coal scuttle on the way out with lumps falling all over the place but no matter, I bounded up the stairs like Linford Christie[6] at his best and into the light.

Saved. I walked back into the lounge and put the coal scuttle down. Dad said, 'What have you been playing at? There's not much coal. Give it here.'

Mercy, perhaps there is a God after all. I watched him walk off holding the scuttle while Mother told me to wash my face and hands.

My character was developing as I faced and dealt with my childhood terrors but the twin horrors of royalty and rice pudding lurked close by.

NOTES FOR CHAPTER TWO

1 – This refers to Ken Russell's 1971 film based on Aldous Huxley's non-fiction book of 1952, *The Devils of Loudun.*

2 – The Daleks are a fictional extraterrestrial race of mutants from the British science fiction television series *Doctor Who.*

3 – Squeeze are a British band that came to prominence in the United Kingdom during the New Wave period of the late 1970s, and continued recording successfully in the 1980s and 1990s. They are known in the UK for their hit songs *Cool for Cats, Up the Junction, Tempted, Labelled With Love* and many more.

4 – A poem, *The Rime of the Ancient Mariner* by Samuel Taylor Coleridge.

5 – *The Lord of the Rings* Trilogy by the English writer and poet JRR Tolkien.

6 – Linford Christie OBE, born 2 April 1960, is a former sprinter from the United Kingdom. He is the only British man to have won gold medals in the 100 metres at all four major competitions open to British athletes.

3

THE WELSH CONNECTION

It's funny how so many people love the Royal Family. I mean, just what is it that makes them so attractive? For centuries they have abused their position and power, suppressing the lower classes, being haughtily indifferent to the middle classes and positively supporting the upper classes through patronage.

Even today, Great Britain cannot really be called a meritocracy as the class system is like a serpent with suffocating coils of privilege and wealth. The inheritance tax was meant to split the great estates and move us forward as a nation, but all that happened is that hidden forces kept the Queen's great wealth intact, exempting her and her dynasty from taxes, thus maintaining the status quo.

Like many of us, although it almost chokes me to say it, I admire the Queen and even Prince Phillip as consummate professionals in terms of consistency of image.

So what is my link to the Royal Family, apart from the entrance to our flat being in King George Street?

Mother liked to get out of the house and decided that anything to do with royalty must be character-building for me. Once or twice a week, we boarded a number 53 bus in Greenwich and went to see the changing of the guard in Whitehall or soldiers marching up and down at Buckingham Palace. Why Mother had any time for the Royal Family is a mystery to me as her family in Ireland is from Donegal – Lisahully to be precise, if you can find it on the map.

The whole history of the British persecuting the Irish impacted on every Catholic family and our Irish family was no great lover of the English. My mother's family, however, liked my father as he was Welsh and shot foxes. Incidentally, he nearly shot Mother once when he mistook her for a fox – another mystery as yet unsolved in our family.

But how are the Royal Family and my loathing of rice pudding linked? Through the Welsh, of course. Prince Charles is the Prince of Wales and Wales is where my grandmother came from. She was the one who made me eat rice pudding.

How I hate rice pudding, especially the skin! It makes me shudder just to think of it. During some of the school holidays, I was packed off to stay in Weston-Super-Mare to stay with my Aunt Josie, who owned a hairdressing salon, and Uncle Roy. Nana, as she was called, was my Dad's Mum and also lived with Aunt Josie.

Uncle Roy was a chef and had hands like hams. Shaking hands with him was sure to bring tears to your eyes and his hearty slap on your back nearly made you spit out your front teeth.

He traced his family in Plymouth back to sea captains and was as hard as nails, having grown up fighting in the back streets. Amazingly, he carved out a career for himself as a top chef working at some of the best hotels in London, after serving his apprenticeship in Paris. The fact that he was a regimental sergeant major in the Second World War gives you a clue about how he ran his kitchens.

Back to rice pudding. After dinner we always seemed to have that damned pudding and it was always put in front of me in a china bowl. Nana used to say, in the voice of a Welsh grave digger, something that sounded like 'Eatyorreecepuddeenwiththatluvlyskin–vereegoodforyou Roger'. Shortly after, as I sulked, she would address Aunt Josie and say, 'What's wrong with him, wasting loveley food like that?' The whole family would glare at me. Yes, mealtimes were a real pleasure.

When we think of Wales many of us think of choirs, coalmines, short tubby men, grim-faced women, Shirley Bassey[1] and possibly rain. All I can think about is Nana. My grandmother was probably the most grim-faced woman ever to be born in Wales. Her nose seemed to be enormous to me, as a child. It was big and hooked and gave the impression that she was being dragged forward by its weight. Often you could see a drip or two at the end of the nose and this feature hypnotically drew you into staring at it. As Nana grew older and her body shrank, all you could see was a nose on legs, walking unsteadily. An unkind portrait but there was no love that I saw.

She inevitably dressed in sombre colours and if she did say anything it was always critical. I can never actually remember her smile, although she did once produce something resembling a death grimace: I hid in the closet in my aunt's hairdressing salon in Weston-Super-Mare and waited until I heard Nana coming down the stairs and, as she neared the bottom, I jumped out shouting 'Boo!' or some such thing. I was aged about seven or eight.

I recall being slightly surprised as she clutched her bosom (what there was anyway – who knows what lurked under those widow's weeds?) and staggered backwards muttering. My Aunt Josie, a dowager sort of a woman, rushed out of the salon and seemed to be trying to revive Nana.

She survived, but I was in the doghouse for weeks and all I got from her was dark muttering. She was bloody-minded like most of the Welsh, and once she got an idea into her head no amount of earthquakes would shift it. I suspect 'Chapel' does that for you with all that fire and brimstone on Sundays dished up by some dark-clothed preacher ranting on about the torments of Hell.

On the other hand, Nana's husband, my grandfather,

was a lovely kind man. I was actually with him when he had a heart attack in Weston. I recall sitting on a bench near the seafront when he suddenly keeled over. A crowd was around us in minutes: I was taken home and my grandfather was taken away. He died later. Maybe my grandmother had been different with her husband when she was younger but I got the impression that she ran his life.

Later, when I was about fourteen years old and staying with my Aunt Josie at Weston, I decided to spend my birthday money on a pair of shoes. But not any pair of shoes; winkle-pickers. And not any winkle-pickers, but black suede ones that were about a yard too long for me – I had to stuff cotton wool into the ends of them to make my toes fit. Come to think about it, those shoes looked a bit like Nana's nose.

I could hardly walk in my winkle-pickers and Nana threw a fit when she saw them. No amount of my eloquent logic would convince her that, at a stroke, I had not joined the ranks of the chain wielding Teddy boys[2] tearing up cinema seats. Funny how Teddy boys seemed to become milkmen or ambulance drivers later in life, recognisable by their swept back hair and love of fancy waistcoats.

Again, the whole Weston posse ganged up on me demanding a return of the shoes. The fact that I was crippled walking in them and nearly broke my ankle at every step was neither here nor there as I would not give them up. A telephone call was made to my mother in London for her to put pressure on me but to no avail. Eventually they left me alone.

I wore the winkle-pickers for only about two days anyway. I grew tired of tripping up whenever I wore them. My game plan was that girls would find me irresistible in my winkle-pickers but they must have made me look like Coco the Clown. Who wants to go out with Coco, except perhaps another clown?

Years later, relations with Nana the Nose reached their lowest ebb. At the age of about eighteen, I sported a wispy growth on my chin that almost resembled a beard. I have no idea why I chose to have facial hair other than that I wanted to save the razor blade money – my Welsh side coming out. When I visited Weston, I went to kiss The Nose and she recoiled as if stung by a jelly fish. Waving an old crone's finger in my face and in a quavering voice she asked, 'Whaaaaaaat's that?' I gave her my best smile and said that it was a beard. I asked her if she liked it.

Without a word, she marched out of the front room and later, using Aunt Josie as an intermediary, as international relations seemed to have broken down, declared that unless I shaved off the beard she would never talk to me again.

I could have jumped in the air with glee. Not something that I am proud of now, of course, but thanks be to the deity, she never said another word to me again and you won't be surprised to learn that I kept the beard. I never again had the dread of trying to kiss her while at the same time desperately avoiding the drips from the end of her nose. The result? Happiness. Strange, the little things that cheer us up when we are young.

I never really did find out why my mother was so keen to send me to Weston. I even went to school there for a few months when she was suffering from a back problem. I had no friends there and was often lonely wandering about the seafront with nothing to do. I climbed rocks just for the thrill of it and, especially now, can see how dangerous this was for me. I didn't care at the time. But they say that what doesn't kill you makes you stronger so in some way, Weston played a part in my foundation, perhaps giving me the backbone to later stand up for myself in so many different ways but starting with the 'Bully Boys'.

NOTES FOR CHAPTER THREE

1 – Dame Shirley Bassey, DBE is a Welsh singer who found fame in the late 1950s and has continued a successful career since then worldwide.

2 – The British Teddy boy (also known as Ted) was typified by young men wearing clothes that were partly inspired by the styles worn by dandies in the Edwardian period, styles which Savile Row tailors had attempted to re-introduce in Britain after World War II. The subculture started in London in the 1950s, and rapidly spread across the UK, soon becoming strongly associated with American rock and roll. Originally known as Cosh Boys, the name Teddy boy was coined when a 1953 Daily Express newspaper headline shortened Edward to Teddy. 'Teddy boy' style featured tapered trousers, long jackets and fancy waist coats.

4
THE BULLY BOYS

I grew up in Greenwich. My first primary school was called James Wolf Primary School. Everyone I knew from my street and surrounding area went there. It was not far from Greenwich Church and quite close to The Mitre which was my Dad's favourite pub. His previous pub of choice had been The White Horse but Mother hated that place and I suspect that the God she prayed to answered her prayers, finally gave in and had it burnt to the ground.

We thought Dad must own shares in the brewery. If he did, he must have stored them in his liver. His favourite drink was 'Worthington E' which was a strong bitter. He later told me that I should watch my step drinking it but, judging from the times he came home and fell over entering the hall, he failed to watch his.

Dad was a policeman. In fact, a detective. More about that later. He had a strange sense of humour. Whilst drinking with one of his pals who owned a corgi dog breeding farm, the pal happened to mention to Dad that he had a winning dog whose breed was impeccable but who gave a bad name to the words 'barking mad'. The dog was virtually uncontrollable and bit anyone who came near.

Consideration was being given to putting the dog to sleep. Now Dad could spot an opportunity when he saw one and clearly saw himself as the hero returning home with a pet for his boys. He ignored the fact that this dog bit anyone who came near it and one day arrived home with the dog. I recall that we all hid in the kitchen as the dog rampaged up and down the hall, Mother suggesting to 'Daddy' as she called him, that it might not be a great idea to keep the dog.

Dad was not one to let a mere dog beat him. He had faced razor gangs in Chinatown, London, at the age of nineteen and dealt with marauding Swedish seamen, legless on vodka. He took off his coat, removed his tie and rolled up his sleeves. It was a tactic that he used later on me to good effect. He opened the door to the lounge and invited the dog, now known as 'Sandy' after his honey-coloured coat, to enter, assisting him with a kick up the backside.

The door shut. All you could hear were barks, growling, shouting and furniture crossing the room. Didn't that sound like the piano stool? I thought I heard middle C as the dog hit the piano.

After what seemed like an age both staggered out clearly with a new-found respect for each other and Dad said that the dog was fine now. I was far from convinced and went nowhere near him and Mike shot out the door as fast as he could. Before setting off for the pub, Dad instructed Mother to feed Sandy on chicken as he liked that. Chicken! Chicken was a luxury in those days. We had it only on Sundays. I thought that this must be some royal animal.

Sandy stayed with the family until he died at an old age. We had to have all his teeth taken out but even then he used to chase the postman and try to bite him. He never really achieved pet status but merely tolerated us. Dad used to take him for a walk in Greenwich Park at about 5 o'clock in the evening, heading down through the park gates and crossing the main road to The Mitre pub.

He would usually give up calling Sandy who sniffed his way endlessly from tree to tree but would eventually cross the busy main road and waddle into the pub where he was fed and watered. They would come back home together but how the dog wasn't run over is still a mystery to me.

My life seems to be just full of mysteries. For example, why did our cat, Paddy, get hit by lightning on a stormy night and blow up? What had he done to deserve that? There were bits of him all around the garden.

Well, I got older; it was inevitable I suppose. My best mate in King George Street was Howard Norman, a blond haired lad who lived up the road. His dad was a capstan worker who was a betting man with the ability to work out the most astonishing combinations of bets – all to no avail, sadly. David Buckingham, who visited his Nan in King George Street but lived in the flats near Creek Road down by the river Thames, was also my friend.

The Bowens, Pat and Ken Bowen and their children Ken and Elaine, lived up in Hyde Vale and I would spend many a happy hour in their company at their house which was a magnet for all the local kids. Pat made great cheese and tomato sandwiches at anytime of day and her Yorkshire personality and hospitality were legendary. In her kitchen, she had a yellow American fridge, the size of a butcher's freezer, and it was always stuffed with goodies. I thought they must be rich as they owned the local grocery shop and Ken drove a big car.

There was a basement in their home which was a kids' paradise and we had many crazy times there. Sometimes the atmosphere was electric – especially when Ken and I, training to be self taught electricians, rewired the light switch so that when switched on, it was live. I can still hear big Ken's shouts of fury as he hit the switch and with hair standing on end was thrown across the room. Well, in our eyes it had worked well, but he just didn't see the funny side of it. I don't think he ever really liked me much after that.

We local kids had our own football league and we were joined by John Doust from East Greenwich. John eventually married Pat and Ken's daughter, Elaine, thoroughly confusing us all as we didn't think he thought much of her when we were young. Later on in life our families proved to be the greatest of friends.

We played football almost nightly in Greenwich Park. We just threw down some coats at each end of the 'pitch' and the four of us kicked lumps off each other pretending to be our favourite players: Bobby Charlton, Georgie Best, Eusabio, Pele, Alf Ackerman. Who? You Millwall fans – all one of you – will remember Alf who took legendary free kicks.

Ken and I supported Millwall and John and Howard supported Charlton so the rivalry could get intense. At that time, most of the kids just got along with each other or at least left each other alone. There wasn't much bashing up going on as we knew each other from school and I think that is a real strength of local schools which mix kids and backgrounds.

Kids really only assume the prejudices of their parents and most people at that time were too focused on how to pay the bills and have money left for a pint, or a port and lemon, to worry much about class divides.

However, I do recall personally being the subject of much bashing. There were two kids who lived in the local flats, Harry and Robin, whose dad was a copper too. For reasons I can't explain, every night after school they used to wait for me and then taunt me, push me around, and punch me. You get the picture.

Harry was a real handful and I knew that I wouldn't stand a chance in a fight against him. Before anyone was doing karate or kung fu in this country, I once saw him throw a kick to a kid's face that just about knocked the other kid out. I couldn't work out how he did it. On the other hand, Robin was a bit of a fat boy and I suspected that his courage came from having Harry, the enforcer, at his side.

It was so bloody sapping to be sitting in class trying to concentrate on drawing swastikas on Howard Norman's leg and listening to Mr. Ford drone on about adding up when all I could really think about was the prospect of getting beaten up again.

I would never tell my parents but that dreaded feeling in the pit of my stomach would come on about 2 p.m. and I would try to think of ways to evade my tormentors. Sometimes I out-thought them and hopped over the back fence and went home the long way round. What I never thought of doing, was asking my friends, the Diffords, to help out. Leslie was still at school then and would have been only too happy to let one fly but I just felt that I was on my own.

Fear. It builds and builds and can destroy you. Over the years I have learned how to handle and control it. Make it my friend. Use it to intimidate others when I need to, but no-one, and I repeat no-one, can run away from it without it destroying them. Cus D'Amato, the legendary trainer of Mohammed Ali said that 'The hero and coward both feel the same thing, but the hero uses his fear, projects it on to his opponent, whilst the coward runs. It's the same thing – fear – but it's what you do with it that matters.'

I finally thought of a plan. I would challenge Robin to a fight whilst acknowledging that Harry could kick lumps out of me. I would ask Harry to referee. I thought that this was a stroke of genius and just couldn't wait for school to end. Of course I felt sick to my stomach, wanted to wee, and my mouth felt as dry as sawdust, but I was determined.

We Thyer-Jones' have coal dust in our veins – my great-great-grandfather was a coal miner – and we are not going to be intimidated by a couple of bully boys. How I used to dream of being some boxing hero capable of not only bashing up my two tormentors but also able to bash up all those people I disliked in the world, including Monsignor who ruled up in our church. All he did was glare and shout at you if you got your catechism wrong and he refused to answer my simple question when I asked him why the church was so cold. He snorted, his jowls quivered, his body mass shook, and he told me to shut up.

Afternoon came. There they were, the smirking pair. I walked up to Harry with my well rehearsed pitch – rehearsed some ten thousand times at least, with slight variations of the aggressive tone I would deploy. 'Now listen, Harry, I know you can bash me up no trouble but I don't think he can – gesturing toward my target – and anyway there's no fun in bashing me. (Not too sure about that line, but it popped out.) So how about you refereeing a fight between me and him? OK?'

Now Harry looked at Robin and there must have a been something in him that didn't much like Robin anyway, probably because his dad was a copper and lived on their estate. Coppers were not universally liked.

'Awright,' he said. 'Get going then!'

With that, I turned and flung myself at Robin punching him in the face for all I was worth. Months of pent up agonies flowed out and the lump fell to the ground with me on top of him, still punching him. To be truthful, I was rather enjoying it and thought that I might make a decent living of it if I could get the work. At least I wouldn't have to do geometry.

True to our agreement, Harry did nothing. Suddenly I was lifted up by the back of my coat and an adult stood me up. He then shouted at me! Can you bloody believe it? All that time of my taking hits and this idiot was shouting at me to stop being a bully and leave the kid alone or he would report me.

Now if there is a God in the world then surely this interfering man would have been struck by a lightning bolt or at least been confronted by a plague of frogs/locusts? But nothing happened. I wiped the spit from my face and saw there was a bit of blood on my shirt – I liked that as it was a sort of battle flag – and walked over to Harry who had returned once the man had left.

'What now, Harry?'

'Nuffin, I s'pose,' he said.

'I'll bash Robin again if he tries to hit me but I'm still not good enough to fight you.'

I thought that this clever flattery would stop Harry giving me another bashing. Amazingly, it worked.

At 2 p.m. the next day I felt all those damn butterflies, wanted to wee, and went into the usual fear cycle. I left the school but there was no bashing up party. I even walked home looking behind every hedge to see if I would be jumped on but nothing happened.

Nothing happened the next day. It got better. I saw that Harry was letting Robin stay by himself in the playground. I exploited this to its fullest, wandering over to Harry with an, 'awright, have a marble,' a ploy which seemed to satisfy him to such an extent that he said, 'Yer, thanks.' Peace seemed to have arrived at last and now I could really concentrate on drawing swastikas on Howard Norman's legs. Why? Well, for some unknown reason that we could not work out, it used to drive Mr. Ford crazy. Ah, the ignorance of youth.

Bullying in life just never stops. It can be oral, written, electronic or physical. It's all the same, and needs the same tactics to confront it, once you have identified your tormentor. But first you have to acknowledge it and face down your own fears. Then try to get some sort of support network around you to confront the cause of your distress. We are strong when we rely on each other and the bully always wants to isolate his victim and then intimidate him into silence.

I faced my fears alone and, on reflection, I think, that made me stronger. I was certain that whatever life threw at me, I would always stand up for what I believed in. But fear comes back to you in so many different ways. How did I feel later when I thought that my Dad was dying?

5

Dad's Dying – Dial 999

Fear keeps leaping out at you when you peer back into the past. At the age of about seven, how do you react when you think your Dad is dying? Dear Reader, imagine that it is 5.30 p.m. and I am alone in our flat as Mother is in the flat upstairs with Uncle Fran and Aunty Molly. I am probably galloping up and down the hall slapping myself on the thigh and pretending to be Robin Hood or the Lone Ranger. There is a banging on the door and I walk down the long hall in order to answer it. I turn on the light near the front room on the way. The light does not really illuminate the front door which has two vertical panes of glass in it. I am little and it is difficult to see, but peering through the glass I can make out that it's Dad standing there. I open the door to greet him.

He takes one step forward and then falls flat on his face on the floor. He gives a groan. I drop to his side, desperately trying to turn him over and crying out his name. He suddenly makes an effort to turn over and rolls over on his back. He groans again. I am convinced that he is dying and yell for Mother. It's quite difficult to shout out 'Mother' a few times as 'Mother' is quite a mouthful, so I think that it may have been 'Mum'.

Dad is frantically clawing at his collar stud to release it and seems to be asking me to do it for him. I try. My hands shake as I fumble with the collar stud but I don't know what to do. He grabs my thin arm and groans again. There is no doubt now in my mind that he is dying. A doctor is needed. But how do I get one?

I remember that there is a red telephone box on King George Street near Ma Diff's place. It is about three minutes away. I decide to leave Dad and I run down the stairs, open up the main door to our flats and sprint up the road. There is no one in the telephone box. Thank God. I lift off the old fashioned black receiver and try to dial 999 on the chromium face dial. My sweaty fingers slip. I am on tip toes as I am too small to see the dial otherwise. I try to dial again and suddenly I am connected to the operator who asks me which emergency service I need: 'Fire, Police or Ambulance.?

How the hell do I know! All I know is that Dr Henry is our doctor so I want him to save my Dad. I say, 'Please get me Dr Henry quick as my Dad's dying.' So now the full adult questioning starts. 'Where are you? What is wrong? Who is Dr Henry?' All I want is help. I am unable to make the operator understand that Dr Henry is our potential saviour. Tears fill my eyes. I give up, torn between getting help and leaving Dad to die. I drop the phone and sprint back home, having achieved nothing. I open the unlocked outside door and run up the stairs, not knowing what I will see. The inside door is still open but Dad is gone

GONE. Nowhere to be seen. The undertakers have him already. God, that was quick. I stand in the hallway, a lost little boy crying. I feel utterly alone.

Suddenly, Aunty Molly materialises, almost like Scotty from Star Trek.[1] She emerges from the living room. She asks me what's wrong. Still emotional, I breathlessly babble out my story. She gives me a hug and says not to worry, Dad is just drunk and has now gone to bed. Not to worry...have a cup of tea...everything is all right ... *Well, no, it isn't, it isn't. it isn't.*

I will never forget the anguish, and the feeling of being powerless in the face of thinking my Dad was dying.

Even to this day, as I write, the feeling of helplessness is overwhelming. It transpired from intelligence later available that Dad had just returned from the annual police bash and had been brought home by kind, supportive – and supporting – friends who left him propped up against the front door. I believe that Dad's friends, fearing the fury of Mother on seeing Dad's condition, had fled the scene of the crime.

In the morning, after a pint of milk shaken up with five raw eggs and some Tabasco sauce, Dad seemed to be as right as rain. He was whistling and singing one of his favourite songs (he had a great Welsh singing voice) 'Wash me in the water where you washed your dirty daughter....' I don't think there were any other words to that one, or at least I never heard him sing them.

My parents married during the war.

They made a fine couple

Later, I look at the problems of growing up where we really get into some father-versus-son stuff but for now, know that Dad was a policeman who joined the RAF during the war. He was quite a gifted rugby player and cricketer. He attended the local grammar school and was an intelligent man.

He decided to leave Wales as soon as he was able to escape. His aim was to join the police in London. However, he was too short for the London Metropolitan Police. You had to be five feet ten inches tall and Dad's height was just under that at five feet nine inches. That minor detail did not deter him. Just before the physical examination, he asked his friend, Trevor James, to stretch him. He strapped himself to the wall bars in the gym, taking his own weight on his wrists, and Trevor attached weights to his legs. Dad dangled like this for nearly an hour and when it came to the height measurement, he was spot on. Now that is an example of a determined man.

During the war, Dad joined Bomber Command and was navigator with the rank of squadron leader. He survived in Bomber Command and was highly decorated. In fact, he gave the potential citation for the Victoria Cross, the highest decoration for gallantry in the country, to his gunner although Dad had dragged the pilot out of his plane which, on landing, was turning into a burning hulk. He told me that he couldn't be bothered with decorations. He therefore told his commanding officer that his gunner had saved the pilot and that he had simply helped him.

Such generosity was typical of the man. He was generous to a fault. Typically he would give away almost anything if you said that you liked it. This included a set of beautiful German handmade glasses taken from Hitler's club in Berlin. I still have one, slightly chipped now, together with a schnapps glass with a swastika on it. Funny, it doesn't look anything like the one I used to draw in class, on Howard Norman's leg.

One Saturday morning, a friend of Dad's turned up with a furniture van to be greeted by Mother at the door. 'Hello,' he said politely. 'Last night, Phil[2] said that you didn't want your Chippendale sideboard anymore, so I could have it.'

Have it! Mother nearly strangled Dad. The sideboard wasn't even ours. It belonged to Aunty Josie in Weston-super-Mare who had said that we could have it for a while as she had nowhere to put it. Aunty Josie tended to patronise Mother but, with Dad's wages being deposited regularly with the brewery, Mother had no reservations about seizing opportunities when she could in an effort to make the flat look respectable. Of course, when Dad woke up around noon on the day following his offer of the sideboard to his drinking companion, he couldn't even recall the conversation.

When I was little, I used to make a good deal of money if Dad brought his drunken police friends home after closing time. Dad seemed to be proud of the fact that he had taught me to stand on my own two feet. Well actually his feet. The trouble was, he was usually lying on his back with his feet aimed vertically at the ceiling!

Picture this. I stand on his hands, which are behind his head on the floor palms up. He slowly lifts me upwards. He straightens his arms so that I am now level with his legs which are in the air. He transfers me to his feet. I stand alone and unaided on the soles of his shoes. Dramatically I extend both arms outwards like a dancer. I wobble for a bit and then he puts out both hands, I step onto them and he slowly brings me back down to earth. How Billy Smart's Circus has overlooked me all these years is beyond me, but then so is splitting the atom. Where does the other bit go?.

Now all this was done after the pub closing time so it must have been about midnight or later. Mother would stand in the corner with her hands over her face waiting for me to topple but I never did. All Dad's friends would applaud and dig out pocket money for me. I was awash with silver, slightly bemused from lack of oxygen at that height and still half asleep. I wasn't scared as I never thought Dad would drop me but poor Mother must have been terrified, but too intimidated to interfere with the show.

After these performances, I had enough money to buy sweets for weeks. These days, the Social Services would have been called and, given their less than splendid record of placements, I may have ended up being fostered by Dracula or someone equally dubious.

I was, however, growing up and turning into a very inquisitive boy. Perhaps too inquisitive, some might say, as I next incurred the wrath of my brother, when unlocking the secrets of his watch. Later, when trying to unlock the secret called 'girls,' I met with similarly disastrous results.

NOTES FOR CHAPTER FIVE
1 – Scotty was the engineer in the TV series *Star Trek*. He was the miracle worker who devised solutions to insoluble problems and also controlled the equipment that allowed the crew to dematerialise and then materialise elsewhere.
2 – My Dad was also known as 'Phil' to some of his friends.

6

Puppy Love and Watch Springs

Sex. It's impossible to deny that there is an opposite sex. It's also impossible to deny that, after the initial part of growing up, most boys develop a fascination with girls. Not only are girls different, they can be very attractive. There is always a girl in the class that boys fantasise about and aspire to attract.

In our class at James Wolf Primary School, that girl was Christine Harris. I don't think that she was a stunner but she must have had something special as all the boys in our class fancied her. I never went out with her when we were at that school. Years later I discovered that she had a Saturday job in Greenwich Library. I asked her out and she agreed. She looked studious with her light brown hair and wearing glasses.

What she must have made of me at that time is difficult to imagine as I really only held her hand and chanced an odd kiss or two. Early on, I didn't get the hang of kissing. I had received no tuition in the subject. In my opinion you should learn the art of kissing as part of the school curriculum. It's a necessary skill for a significant amount of your life. Another failing in the school system. What exactly were a boy and girl supposed to do at lip level? I recall that we locked onto each other like a spaceship docking onto a space station. It couldn't have been much fun for Christine.

Kissing is a whole subject in itself and I didn't get the hang of it when I was young. In my experience your mother kissed you and you shuddered. You never kissed your dad. And whilst aunts demanded kisses, you could escape quickly after a quick peck on the cheek.

Often, the talk in the classroom was about the role of the tongue in the process of kissing. A boy would say something like, 'I put my tongue in her mouth.' For the life of me, I couldn't see the point of doing it. Perhaps the real aim of this diversionary tactic was to fondle a budding breast and this was where real bragging to your mates came into play. Anyone who confessed to more than a fondle was eyed with suspicion and a certain amount of envy. The employment of the tongue remained a mystery. Years later, when I was with Michelle in a club in Woolwich called *The Black Cat,* I spent the whole evening kissing her so hard that her lips almost fell off. I think that at one point I grafted my front teeth on to hers.

I don't think that Christine had a reputation for being free and easy but she did seem to have budding breasts and was therefore a challenge for the boys in the class. I think that they remained mountains unclimbed.

These days, children, with their exposure to all sorts of teaching, diagrams, and even soft porn on television, are practically as expert as gynaecologists unlike in my day when we barely saw a glimpse of anything at all thrilling and would have had no idea how to seize an opportunity should one have arisen. This is not strictly true of all boys as some were more mature than others, but the odds of my kissing progressing to greater physical contact were stacked against me: I had the ever-vigilant nuns on my back, Monsignor breathing fire and brimstone, and the general taboos about sex to contend with.

I once fondled Christine's bra strap and, even though she pushed my hand away, I got unimaginable excitement from that daring action.

Perhaps what I needed was that old remedy employed in 13th century China. Simply find a pair of red lizards whilst they are copulating and drown them in red wine. Leave them in the liquid for one year and then drink the potion in one swallow. I am unsure whether the man or the woman needs to drink it, or both. Apparently, it was guaranteed to get any woman hot enough to melt icebergs. Unfortunately for Christine and me, they didn't sell it in Greenwich market at the time I was going out with her.

I was fond of the idea of girls but ill-equipped to take that idea forward in any meaningful way. When I think about it now, sex and the rites of passage are so incredibly fraught with problems for both sexes that it is a wonder that meaningful relationships are ever forged.

As I was growing up, I had to share a bedroom with my brother, Mike. He was about seven years older than me and his mind was probably filled nightly with dreams of the fairer sex. I can't recall him having much to do with me on a daily basis: I suspect that he viewed his little brother with some disdain, and I can't remember him ever taking me out anywhere with him. To him, I was probably just a nuisance.

The conflict associated with sharing a room with a brother or sister is ageless. Mike used to smoke and had built a clever little ashtray attached to the underside of his bedroom cabinet that he could swing out of sight. He liked to read late and I suppose that I must have irritated him by asking him to put out the light and his generally having to humour an eight year old boy. He didn't seem too concerned about my hacking cough from his cigarette smoke. Passive smoking is a contradiction in terms.

He also was good at puzzles and quizzes, at least that was what he told me, and one summer at Weston-super-Mare he worked as an assistant at the fair which was located on the sands near the pier. It was there that he won the most wonderful Dan Dare[1] pocket watch.

The watch was an object of wonder. It was an old fashioned style of watch with a chain to attach it to your jacket. As well as Dan Dare, ray gun in hand, it displayed a fine red spaceship which moved across the face of the watch as it crossed the star-studded sky in time with the ticking sound it made. It was fascinating and colourful to look at. Mike usually left the watch on the mantelpiece of the black marble fireplace that dominated our bedroom and which, in winter, let in blasts of cold air that froze your skin to your pyjamas.

Think of me lying in bed listening to that watch ticking: tick-tock, tick-tock, tick-tock and picturing that space rocket racing across the face of the watch.

I wonder how it works? How does the ship go across the face of the watch? I get out of bed and go into the cupboard at the end of the hall where Dad stores his tools – not that he ever used them much, although I do remember he did once break up the piano with a sledgehammer. I was relieved to see the back of it as for years I had been forced by Mother to attend piano lessons.

For my sins, every Wednesday, when my mates were playing football, I would go for my piano lesson with Mrs. Sheldon who had a flat near the Cutty Sark[2]. There were Smarties – little brightly coloured sugar sweets – at one end of the piano and a ruler at the other with which she would give you a rap on the knuckles if you hit the wrong notes. At the end of each lesson you got a Smartie as a reward, despite poor performance. Big deal! I used to go home dragging my knuckles like a gorilla and then, to add insult to injury, I was expected to practise the lesson on the piano!

As soon as I could, I dropped piano lessons and my mind immediately wiped out how to sight-read music. I regret this now as I love the piano but I am still a bit on the slow side when reading music. I just want to get on and play it without all that agonising about crochets and quavers, never mind semi- demi- ones.

Back to the watch. I open Dad's tool kit which was housed in an old blue and battered steel container. I take out those old friends of every handyman that has ever had to put together MFI[3] furniture – the hammer and chisel. The chisel is about an inch wide. I look at the watch. It gleams in the light. The big problem is how to get the back off. I use all my strength trying to open it by hand but my fingernails just can't do the job.

I have a brilliant brain wave. I put the watch in the vice, hold the chisel at an angle so that the edge catches under the tiny lip on the rear of the watch and gently tap the end with the hammer. I just know that this will do the trick and reveal the secret of how Dan Dare's rocket moves across the face of the watch.

The first few light blows are disappointing and I look in dismay as the watch springs out of the vice. I think that the casing needs a bit more grip, so I turn the vice handle as hard as I can, to hold it firmly. In the light of the box cupboard containing Dad's tools, I think that I can see a better space in the casing into which the end of the chisel would fit. I rather neatly angle the chisel edge into that space.

Taking a firm grip on the hammer, I gently tap the chisel which to my delight holds firm and bites into the metal. This is more like it. Another few blows and the back will be off. Another few and then another few. Ah, I can definitely see the edge of the back turning upwards. I am getting somewhere at last.

I think that a few more even harder blows will do the trick and I am absolutely spot on. The back leaps off just as I had hoped it would. I have to admit that I am slightly surprised when I find that the inside of the watch seems to have disintegrated. There are small wheels and cogs spilling out on to the floor at an alarming rate. I remove the watch from the vice and, with some effort (what a career I have in store as an engineer) I force the chisel under the edge that is holding the watch face. Here lies the secret of the spaceship movement. I just know it.

Success! The spaceship jumps out and drops to the floor.

I am able to pick it up and examine it in some detail. I see that it does still move if you push it with your finger but somehow Dan Dare and his ray gun have disappeared. I am somewhat deflated that no light bulb comes on in my head to tell me just how the whole thing works. I feel hugely disappointed with my exploration of the watch's inner workings and am now quite tired of it.

Then the realisation dawns that Mike might be annoyed at my attempts to discover the great secret. The more I think about it, the clearer this likelihood becomes. Frantically, I scoop up ratchets, springs and cogs, bits of screw and the top of Dan Dare's head. Ah, there is another part of his ray gun. Somehow the metal pieces have now acquired bits of saw dust on them – very odd. I place the almost empty watch case back on to the bench. I then try to stuff various parts of the watch back into it. It is frustrating to see how the mechanism just won't fit perfectly into the case as it had before.

But how do I secure the somewhat mangled back plate onto the casing? Genius. Use the Sellotape which is staring me in the face, next to Dad's glue. So binding the mess of cogs and springs together with tape and then binding the back plate on to the casing with even more tape, I succeed in at least containing the mess. Whilst it doesn't exactly look the same to me as before my exploration and there is no sound coming out of it, in a poor light it doesn't look too bad. If you switch off the box cupboard light it looks fine.

I gingerly place the watch back on the black marble mantelpiece. All in all, this adventure has taken about ten minutes. With a clear conscience, I drift off to sleep.

Imagine my surprise when I am hauled from my bed by a snarling and spitting demon who looks a bit like Mike. It is hard to understand what he is yelling and the spit coming from his mouth doesn't help. Wide eyed and terrified, dressed in my night attire, I am swinging in his hands until Mother comes on to the scene. Then Uncle Fran and Aunty

Molly appear. Fortunately Dad is not there to join the hanging party.

It's very difficult for a child to understand four people speaking at once, especially when one of them looks exactly like a demon. I think that in between the tears, I make a decent stab at explaining my position which was not one of malice, but one of extraordinary inquisitiveness. I suspect that my explanation lacks credibility. The adults and Mike seem hell bent on accusing me of a variety of crimes, many of these accusations fly over my head. Somehow my tears temper the worst of the outbursts and the shouting dies down.

I think that I was punished by having to go bed early the next night and having my pocket money stopped, not that I got much in the first place. It was all diverted to Mike as compensation. To compound my punishment, for the rest of the week, whenever he thought he could get away with it, Mike would give me a crafty clip around the ear.

I still recall being baffled by the whole event, which just demonstrates the innocence of children. There was no malice in my actions but the adults misinterpreted what I thought were perfectly reasonable actions at the time. I have to say that I have shied away from DIY since, now taking it to mean 'Don't Involve Yourself'. I put this down to being gravely misunderstood in those vital formative years.

As sex and engineering did not seem to be strong points, I wondered where life would lead me.

NOTES FOR CHAPTER SIX

1 – Dan Dare was a classic British science fiction comic hero created by illustrator Frank Hampson for the *Eagle* comic story, *Dan Dare, Pilot of the Future* in 1950.

2 – The *Cutty Sark* is a clipper ship. Built in 1869, she served as a merchant vessel – the last clipper to be built for that purpose – and then as a training ship until being put on public display in 1954. She is preserved in dry dock in Greenwich, London

.3 – MFI a company that specialised in self-assembly furniture.

7

The Curious Incident of the Ironing Board in the Car

Of course no one knows the path that leads to the future, but youth advanced at its own pace and before I even knew it the 'eleven-plus' came zooming right in at me.

This examination determined if you went to grammar school. Selection marked your path for life in so many ways. It was grossly unfair. How on earth could some of my friends who came from rough homes ever hope to get through an exam that, in my opinion, seemed designed to weed out the lower classes? For some, the family situation meant that intelligence was shown in the daily lesson on survival skills rather than academic subjects.

I had no idea what I wrote in the actual exam, as it was all Greek to me, but I was an avid reader when young, as I am now, and did have quite a good command of the English language. At least a vocabulary that went beyond advising to have sex and travel.

I also had a brother already at the Roan Grammar School for Boys which was situated in Blackheath, about two miles from our house. I think having my brother in the school tipped the balance in the selection procedure when they reviewed the exam results, and I was chosen to go there. The alternative was the local secondary school. Nearly all my mates went to the latter. How would life have turned out for me if I had taken that path? Well at least I would have had Leslie Difford to look out for me, as long as he forgot that I had taken his mum's sweets that time – perhaps I could have bribed him? This was a significant crossroads in my life and a different eleven-plus result would have affected the whole course of my life.

Our school had a collection of children from nearly every background, and many of them came from lower-income families. If my family was middle-income then God help the rest, as we didn't seem to have two pennies to rub together. We did once try to have a holiday in Cornwall until Dad's car blew up en route and he had to get a new engine. We came home by train.

The case of the ironing board. Allow me to jump back a little way in time. Dad used to have a car which I think was an Austin A30. On another failed holiday, we were supposed to set off to stay with my Aunt Josie and Uncle Roy in Weston-super-Mare. It would have been a long journey, some 140 miles, as there was no motorway in those days and the roads at that time went through the middle of towns, leading to numerous hold ups. I believe that the plan was to leave early in the afternoon in order to arrive when it was still light.

Regardless of the plan, Dad popped into the pub for a lunchtime drink and returned home at about seven that evening. He seemed to be drunk but was in a holiday mood, laughing and singing. This change of plan wrong-footed Mother but she valiantly came up with a stream of excuses about why we shouldn't travel at that time of night. I don't recall her torrent of excuses but being drunk and driving with your wife and small child in the car must have been one of them. It's no coincidence that the Highway Code does not advise motorists to plan for a long journey by consuming pints of the foaming ale.

However she did come up with a good excuse for staying at home. She said that I couldn't travel by car at night as there was nowhere for me to sleep so we would have to wait until morning. The perfect excuse. Undeniable. There was no bed in the car.

But Dad's ingenuity knew no bounds and he remained undeterred. He disappeared out of the front room where I sat blearily with Mother. We listened to banging and crashing coming from the kitchen area and then, silence. The door to our flat opened and we heard footsteps going down the stairs and some clanging. Next, we heard the outside door opening and, again, silence. We looked at each other and Mother repeatedly turned a white handkerchief in her hands. I sensed that she was very worried.

An Austin A30 like Dad's.

I later bought a similar car for £15.

(image courtesy www.Free-Images.org.uk.)

After what seemed to be an eternity, Dad re-entered the room in a very good mood, his face beaming. He said that he had solved the problem of the bed and invited us to join him to see the solution. We followed him down to the car which was parked outside the flat with the back door opening on to the pavement. It was dark, and the light of the street lamp up the road didn't cast much light on the car. The interior light barely glowed.

Mother looked into the back of the car and gasped. She hardly expected to see her ironing board there.

Dad had put it on the floor parallel to the rear seat. Not only that, but he had thoughtfully placed a sheet and pillow on top of it. I was holding Mother's hand and peering into the back of the car as well. I saw a loose hanging belt lying across the top of the ironing board. Dad patiently explained his great plan.

'Gung' as he sometimes called my brother, or me, after Gunga Din[1], would sleep on the board, comfortably strapped on top, safe and sound.

Yes, the plan was for me to sleep, and I repeat it in case you might be incredulous; yes, sleep on the ironing board. This wonderful plan certainly did not meet with the approval of Mother and Dad, with a lot of clanging and oaths, was persuaded to remove the ironing board and return it to the kitchen. But Dad was not to be so easily beaten. Somehow, he persuaded Mother to get into the car and I was put on the back seat with the pillow, sheets and blankets all around me.

I remember that it had started to rain. Dad was wearing an overcoat and his hat in the car. Mother was sitting tight-lipped beside him. What luggage we had, was in the tiny boot. We were now all set for holiday. Dad started the car. We set off driving through Greenwich, turning up towards New Cross on the way out of London and then westward ho!

We actually only reached New Cross which was about three miles away from our flat. We stopped. To be more accurate, Dad was forced to stop when he ran into the back of another car which had come to a halt at a zebra crossing. The collision seemed to surprise Dad as, at the time, he was demonstrating to me that he could drive without his hands on the wheel. And indeed he could. It was such a pity the car wasn't fitted with the twenty-first century braking system that detects an object in front of it and then automatically applies the brakes. That really would have been most helpful. A slight altercation between Dad and the driver of the car in front ensued I believe.

I think that, by this time, Mother was about ready to murder him anyway and we came home and unloaded the car. I was sent to bed. The last thing I heard was Dad shouting. Suddenly he left the flat, banging the door as he did so. Mother came back and tucked me up in bed. She looked tearful. I drifted off to sleep in safety, at least for the time being. It must have been just awful for her. She must have been worried sick that there would be an accident, but perhaps just going along with Dad's plan had been the best way to keep the peace. I have never heard of anyone being quite so creative with an ironing board before. Incidentally, exactly how did he think that one leather belt wrapped around my body and binding me to the board, was going to keep me in place, let alone allow me to sleep? It's funny how creative the mind can be after a pint or two.

I did have holidays. Mother used to pack me off to Ireland nearly every summer. Mother had a bad back and so she often had to take to her bed and lie down for long periods to ease the pain. This might be one reason why I was sent away. She also had a friend called Maisie who, like her, was a staff nurse. They seemed to have in common a love of travel and this might have been the real reason for my trips to Ireland. They gave Mother the freedom to visit places in Europe with Maisie without me to restrict her.

Maisie had an Irish husband whose Irish name 'Padraig' sounded like 'Porrick'. She also had the loudest voice and most critical manner of any woman that you could ever encounter. On meeting you, she would look you up and down disdainfully as if assessing some sort of scientific specimen. Padraig was like a mouse to her twenty odd stone elephant. I imagined him inside her pocket while she walked around with him peering out of the top. Dad detested, loathed, despised and hated Maisie so much that he would often walk out of our flat when she walked in.

I remember hearing Mother discussing with Aunty Molly an incident that had happened in Lewisham. Somehow

Mother had convinced Dad to drive Mother, Maisie and Padraig on a shopping trip to Lewisham, about five miles from where we lived.

Picture Dad driving the Austin A30 down Lewisham High Street on a Saturday lunchtime. Cars are whizzing about everywhere in the one-way system. The plan is to drop off Mother, Maisie and Padraig at a safe place near the market. Maisie, who did not drive herself, is telling Dad how to drive and has been doing so ever since they left Greenwich. Her strident voice grates on his ears. She tells him to slow down or to avoid cars in her usual directive manner. She is used to battering poor Padraig when he drives. She is now wedged in the back of Dad's car with Padraig nestling under her enormous armpit. The discomfort apparently has no effect on the torrent of advice that gushes from her ample mouth.

Suddenly, a wonderful event occurred: an event which many a male reader will enjoy. The trigger for such an event occurs when a woman is banging on about a man not driving so fast, telling him to watch out for this car and stop for that pedestrian. He is a robot under her control. Women somehow don't seem to understand that when they are in a car their job is to shut up and look pretty. Anything else is just superfluous. Indeed, my own experience with Michelle has shown me that I would have to tear her tongue out to stop her making a comment about some aspect of my driving.

Dad listens to Maisie's last criticism. He has been smouldering slowly like a volcano but has stoically tolerated her motor mouth and caustic comments. They are in the middle of the high street. He calmly pulls the car to a halt at the side of a no-stopping area, turns off the engine, and gets out. He leans in through the window and then tells Maisie that, as she knows so much about driving, she can drive the car herself. His words may have been more colourful than that. His suggestion is unhelpful as Maisie doesn't drive. In response, Maisie, now screams at Padraig to dislodge himself from his position under her gargantuan armpit and get into the driving seat. Cars are hooting and honking all around them. It is absolute chaos and, of course, dangerous.

Dad simply walked off to the nearest pub. I have no idea what Mother said to him later but somehow they all got home with Padraig driving the car. I recall that Uncle Fran nearly killed himself laughing when he heard the tale and what a story it was. Despite this fine example of how to handle a bossy, interfering passenger, I still haven't had the guts to follow Dad's example, Maybe one day. But, of course I am exaggerating about what Michelle is like as a passenger in the car.

When Mother was either lying down with her bad back or off touring Europe with the crazy gang, Maisie and Padraig, I headed for my Aunt Beck's bungalow in Belleek, County Fermanagh. I loved to fish in the River Erne that ran at the end of our garden at the bungalow. Beck was married to Vincent, a lovely man, who was a manager in the Belleek Pottery factory which is still famous for its craftsmanship, creativity and expertise. They had one son, Harry, who later became a priest and died in the most unusual and tragic circumstances which need further investigation, in my opinion.

Why would a priest drive to a seaside town called Bundoran, some seven miles away from his home and then walk to a secluded bay? Why would he then leave his clothing in a neat pile near the cliff edge and put his car keys on top of his clothes? Why would he tie his own legs together with his belt? Why would he jump off the cliff? The inquest revealed that skull fractures indicated that Harry had jumped head first from the thirty-metre high cliffs causing fatal injuries.

Why would he leave his mother, whom he adored, when she was due to have her ninetieth birthday and he had been planning for the celebrations? Nothing adds up to explain the reason for Harry's death. There is so much to uncover that it would take a super sleuth to get at the truth, if 'they' let you. But who are 'they'?

This is a summary of what the local paper reported about his death:

'A PRIEST was found dead on a beach yesterday morning.

The naked body of Father Harry Bannigan, 58, was discovered lying face down in the sand in the popular Donegal resort town of Bundoran.

A couple out walking found him shortly after 9.30am and called gardai [police]. Officers sealed off the scene and removed the body to Sligo General Hospital, where a post-mortem was carried out.'

Father Bannigan, from Belleek, Co Fermanagh, was working as a chaplain to the circuses. He was also studying at a college in Navan.

His mother Becky told *The Irish Mirror* yesterday: "I can't believe he is gone. I wish someone could explain it to me. He was so good to me. He rang me every day. He was to stay with me for his mid-term break from college. He was such a good lad. He had been working in Sruleen in Clondalkin (West Dublin) for four and a half years and then he left in September to do a course in the college. He was always happy and they gave him a great send-off when he left Clondalkin. I didn't even know he was in Donegal. The gardai came to tell us about the body and I just couldn't believe it. He wasn't depressed or anything, he was a great son."'

Harry was a member of a close religious order, He joined it when leaving school. Initially, he denied all worldly goods which meant that after his death his estate, which comprised of his mother's bungalow, her assets and his own savings, would pass to the order.

He changed his will before his death. I do not know exactly when, but it meant that the order would not inherit the estate. He specified other beneficiaries.

I have no way of knowing if my cousin died in suspicious circumstances but, with my investigative background, I simply don't like it. The police didn't seem to pursue the case with any vigour and the verdict of suicide was not returned at the inquest at the Coroner's Court. Remarkable, don't you think, in the circumstances?

What I do know, is that both Michelle and I didn't take to the priests who attended the family home for my cousin's funeral and, in particular, those that came to the bungalow where Harry was lying in his coffin in the usual Irish tradition of an overnight vigil. The Bishop was a huge bloated individual in purple robes with a red nose. His corpulent body reeked of excess. He made Michelle shudder. These priests might have been saints for all we know but, instinctively, we didn't like them.

This is one story that will have to rest for a while but I keep being drawn back to it. I can find nothing to show me that Father Harry was anything other than a good priest.

Back to boyhood. I would spend hours fishing in the River Erne for perch, pike, trout or anything I could catch and I caught more fish then than I do now on that same river. But rivers can be dangerous and the River Erne can be more treacherous than most.

Ballyshannon[2] is about five miles from Belleek and is a strong Irish nationalist town. We had relatives living there and I used to stay with them from time to time. I do seem to have been passed around from relative to relative but I don't think that I was a troublesome child. Guess what I wanted to do? – Fish.

Down at the Mall, there was a quay from which steamers used to depart for America in the bad old days of the famine. It is a beautiful place that looks out on the estuary where my Uncle Jack, a great fisherman, died fishing in his boat. Is there any better way for an angler to go?

The river was particularly dangerous near the quay side and I had been warned by my Aunt Sadie never to fish there. The dam is about a quarter of a mile upstream from the quay and holds back the waters of Loch Erne, a huge thirty-nine mile long lake that stretches to the north beyond Enniskillen.

The hydroelectric power station was built there in the 1950s. The sluices of the dam are opened to generate electricity, powering the enormous turbines. Sometimes, if

Ballyshannon Quay.

Thank God for those watchful ladies.

there is heavy rainfall, they are opened to allow water to gush down to the sea and therefore prevent flooding upstream. When the sluice gates are opened, tons of water flood down. In less than a few minutes, the river can become a torrent. It can cover the rocks and cut you off from the land if you are standing on them to fish.

I stood on a rock some fifteen feet from the bank on a

sunny day, fishing for trout with my spinning rod. The water was low around the rocks. Three old ladies were sitting on a bench perched up on a ledge of grass behind me, idly chatting. After a while, I looked down and noticed that the water was almost up to my ankles. Being a bright English boy I politely brought this to the attention of the three ladies and asked if they could help me get off the rocks. I was quite calm as I had no real understanding of the danger I faced.

I was not prepared for the shrieks and cries that ensued which included, 'Jesus, the boy's gonna drown'. This cry was not exactly guaranteed to lift my mood. One of the ladies hopped up the grassy bank, shouting and yelling to the men in the factory close by. Whilst all this was going on, believe it or not, I still thought I might have a chance of a fish and continued to throw my spinner out into the torrent. The spinner seemed to be moving at about fifty miles an hour, judging from the way it swept passed me. The water was creeping up my ankles but I don't recall being the least worried although, with the benefit of hindsight, if I had fallen into that water I would have been swept out to sea and drowned.

Then there was action. Men came storming down the grassy knoll with sticks and poles and formed a human chain. At the end of the chain was a man with a walking stick who was encouraging me to jump and grab it. The men were being swept down river and it was difficult for them to hold their ground. But what about my fishing rod and spinners? I had paid all my pocket money for them. You may be thinking, what a cool head in a crisis. Alternatively, you may be asking, was this boy a lunatic? I threw the rod and spinners as far as I could towards the men and some-one grabbed them. They were shouting furiously at me by this time. I jumped off the rock and then grabbed the walking stick held by a very brave man. At first, I was swept downstream but the man who held the stick had an iron grip on it, and I too clung on. The human chain held and they pulled me in. I was wet. Very wet, and cold.

By now the three ladies were hysterical and saying their Hail Marys and Novenas: prayers of all sorts were being offered up to the good Lord at a furious rate. I mumbled some boy-like thanks to the men, grabbed my fishing gear and hot-footed it back up to the house which was about ten minutes away. The real challenge I faced was how to get in to the house and change my clothes without being spotted.

Hopping over the back fence, I crept into the house through the open back door. I dodged their only child, Paul, who constantly tormented me by asking me to play with him, and went up to my room. My priorities were a quick bath, fresh clothes and drying the wet clothes in the airing cupboard. No one noticed me and so I thought that I had got away with the whole thing.

Imagine my surprise when Aunt Sadie entered my room the following morning brandishing the *Ballyshannon Times,* or whatever the local newspaper was called. The two-page write-up showed the factory men saving an English boy from drowning. There were photographs. I hadn't bargained for that. No amount of negotiation would convince Aunt Sadie that it was just a storm in a teacup and so, at the first opportunity, I was sent back to Aunt Becks's place. I was actually delighted to get away from there as Aunt Sadie was too strict for my liking anyway.

As a postscript to this incident, shortly after I had met him at a funeral gathering, Paul died of a heart attack in 2009, aged fifty. He was overweight and had told me that he had to start taking more exercise. Too late I am afraid.

I never really wanted to stay on the family farm in Lisahully which is located between Belleek and Ballyshannon. My mother grew up there. It is idyllically situated. The mountains can be seen from the front of the cottage and they change colour as the light of the day fades. The cloud formations curling above them are sometimes breathtaking. If you walk up to the top of the hill behind the family cottage, there is a wonderful view sweeping down towards Ballyshannon and the estuary. It is a beautiful and tranquil place.

My work ethic, however, wasn't up to the farmer, Uncle Harry's remorseless expectations. Anyone who was in the house had to work. He would kill you with work and then my aunt Una would reward you by encouraging you to eat huge mounds of potatoes, cabbage and meat piled about three feet high. My appetite was small and I faced daily comments about not growing up to be big and strong unless I ate my vegetables. Even today, I hate cabbage and hope that I have passed that loathing for cabbage and Brussels sprouts to our three sons. I can die happy if I have achieved that much.

Incidentally, how on earth do some Irishmen have such enormous hands? Many of them had hands bigger than my head and they just oozed crushing power. My own hands are small and spade-like, maybe made for clawing coal out of crevices rather than lifting huge hay bales or digging the Suez canal. It often struck me as strange. Even when I worked later on in life with the police in Dublin, I noticed large hands were prevalent and I worked with highly intelligent men. I don't know if intelligence is linked to large hands, but if it is, then the population of Ireland must have a higher average intelligence than any other country on earth.

I grew up with many experiences and accepted a life that swung between England and Ireland. I have so many warm memories of my times in Ireland. I didn't have many friends of my own age there, but it didn't seem to matter. I had love, laughter and music a-plenty and I am sure that part of my personality was shaped in the Emerald Isle.

The foundation of my life was now established. Time to move on to the second part of the journey and what excitement I had to look forward to in my teenage years:

girls; top groups like the Beatles, the Stones, the Faces, and the Yardbirds; great guitarists like Hendrix and Clapton; spots on my face and the good doctor's burning cure for them; more girls but one special one; drinking and laughable experiments with drugs; poor school results; long hair and fights with Dad; nightshifts with Jesus at Broomfields Bakery; Mods and Rockers; scooters, a bubble car and near death; judo and a bit more; running with the bad boys. The crazy world of the 1960s and more.

But before I start to expand my experience, I first have to settle into life at the Roan Grammar School for Boys and, it is during my time at the new school that I do encounter my first really dead man, not just my Dad inadvertently playing the part.

Notes for Chapter Seven

1 – Gunga Din is a poem told by a British soldier about the heroism of an Indian water carrier, Gunga Din, who rescued wounded soldiers on the battlefield. The poem is typically Rudyard Kipling: full of the most appalling, and by today's standards, racist, attitudes towards Indians.

2 – Ballyshannon, which means 'The Mouth of Seannach's Ford' after a fifth century warrior Seannach, who was slain there. It lies at the mouth of the river Erne. Archeological sites have been found that date back to 4000–2500BC. Rory Gallagher, 'The World's Greatest Guitarist', was born there.

8

EDUCATION AND DEAD MAN

I went out of our front door, crossed over Crooms Hill Road and, accompanied by my friend, Ken Bowen, walked into Greenwich Park, on the two mile walk to the Roan School for Boys. Compared to some of the boys, I was mentally ill-equipped for dealing with the first days at a new school. I found it slightly odd that we were called the 'Turds' by the elder boys and, when Mother asked me the name of my year, she seemed just as surprised by my answer. No one told me that we were, in fact, the 'Thirds'. I was too naive to recognise the insult. At our school we tended to call a spade a spade. I don't think that at that time I knew what a turd was.

There was a succession of teachers involved in my education, many of whom were bizarre to say the least. 'Snozz' was one of the geography masters and he used to pick his nose and then wipe the contents on the side of his trousers or, worse, simply put it in his pocket. Perhaps he was hoarding it to use as a form of currency. We were baffled by this revolting habit.

Hank was also a geography master and a former rugby player – it was rumoured that he had played for England once. He was an enormous, fat, jolly fellow who used to liven up lessons by spontaneously bursting into song.

Maths was taught by an alien with a shock of curly hair and a wispy beard and the only useful thing I learned from him was that it made more sense to scoop your tea up with the spoon again and again rather than stirring it.

Apparently he had worked out the basis of dissolving solids in liquids and deigned to share it with us. Whilst I was red hot at my times tables up to twelve – Mr. Ford used to hit us if we made a mistake so who says violence doesn't get results? – I had no idea what calculus was nor what on earth a logarithm was used for.

I recall frantically flicking from page to page in a blue book filled up with pages and pages of numbers to find the answer to something that I didn't really understand anyway. I would have been better off going to the bookies with Howard Norman's dad and asking him to teach me how to work out betting odds. It's interesting that at school now there is some support for teaching children in this way. It makes real sense to me as it would bring maths to life.

French was interesting as it exercised neck muscles. A huge bearded man known as 'Cornie' used to write on the board while we made stupid French noises. He would suddenly turn and, with uncanny accuracy, fling the board wiper – a chunk of solid wood – straight at a target pupil. You had to be like a spitfire pilot on the look-out for the enemy if you didn't want to lose your teeth.

Why did we want to speak to the French anyway, unless of course it was to see the petite mademoiselle who took us for conversation? I used to memorise French passages just so she would be impressed with my fluency, which would give me more time to study her fine form: this began slightly below her neck for me. What could I glimpse through her crisp white blouse? Ah, the dreams of youth. Of course she thought I was rubbish and wondered what on earth I was babbling on about, but I couldn't care less. If you want to learn a language, sleep with the dictionary, I say. Unfortunately, I slept alone.

English was taken by a splendid man called Alfie Knott. He was never perturbed by anything. He made classes interesting and had eyebrows that flared up in a devilish way. When I was reading Dennis Wheatley books such as

'*The Haunting of Toby Jug*', Alfie seemed exactly the sort of man who, like the characters in the novel, might be involved in secret ceremonies and carrying out demonic practices.

I once asked Mr. Knott if he was a Satanist and he nearly fell over laughing – I suspect that he was covering it up. It was Mr. Knott who once said that I had the makings of a poet after I wrote some maudlin nonsense called '*Oh Rose That Art Sick*' which was basically about the destruction of the planet. Oddly, he was later mistaken for an IRA informer and shot when he answered his door. Luckily he survived and I believe is still alive to this day.

I was an avid reader and liked a variety of novels, particularly anything that had a bit of sex in it. When I was younger I loved the 'Biggles', 'Just William', Worzel Gummidge' and 'Billy Bunter' books and would often read a book under the bedclothes by torchlight after 'lights out' had sounded.

As I grew older and was exposed to more demanding reading, I was drawn to the French novelist, Zola whom I expected to be stuffy but proved to be anything but. If you want an earthy view of what life offers, then Zola's your man! I also took a liking to the poet Milton and liked the way his words just seemed to ooze richness and variety. I often wondered how on earth he had written in such a richly worded way. I couldn't really understand what he meant most of the time, apart from his hating women, but his poetry intrigued me nevertheless.

Most eight year olds have a useable vocabulary of about three thousand words and use about one thousand to get through life. Some linguists have a vocabulary of two hundred thousand to a quarter of a million words but, judging from the script of '*Eastenders*', all you really need is about ten words if you supplement them with expletives, grunts and gestures.

I liked English literature but my favourite book of all

time is *'The Master and Margarita'* by the Russian novelist Mikhail Bulgakov. It is just a splendid read on all levels: intellectual; sheer fun and frolics and pathos aplenty and all set in the most fascinating period of time in Russian history, juxtaposed with events in the Holy Land at the time of the crucifixion. I must have read that book ten times and still I am astonished by Bulgakov's ability to conjure images so powerful that they leap off the page at you. I think that reading defines you as a person and the more well read you are the more you are likely to be open-minded and receptive to new ideas and influences and that, in my opinion, has to be a good thing. I used to devour books.

Chemistry was a fascinating subject and, probably like every small boy, I had a love of fire and explosions. Our lessons were taken by a man who was so enthusiastic that he often blew up the laboratory himself. Unfortunately, he jumped out of the chemistry block window one night and committed suicide. What a sad end to an exciting life.

Physics was taken by an urbane sort of a fellow who really inspired me in the subject and, although I was not much good at formal maths, paradoxically, I was good at physics. If something made sense to me then I could work through its logic. I liked practical experiments that reflected the world around us such as investigating how a light bulb worked.

Add to this cocktail of learning the sports coach called 'Bill' who encouraged us to play football, tennis, basketball and cross-country running, and you have a school that sought to balance the mental with the physical – it was a pity that most of us were mental.

Greenwich Park was the link between home and school as we walked through it on a daily basis. It was in the park that I first saw a dead man. Ken Bowen and I used to walk our dogs together after school. Ken had more brains than you could shake a stick at, so was a good man to ask about the mysteries of my daily life at school – I think that I was in the 'slow but sure development' stream while Ken was in the 'likely to succeed' stream.

One evening, at about five o'clock, we were sauntering down the hill close to Crooms Hill Road, walking our dogs towards a path, when we spied a man slouched on the bench. He was tall and was wearing a gabardine coat. I recall that he was also wearing a flat cap. The two dogs bounded down the hill and seemed intent on licking up something on the ground beside him. Ken and I, full of curiosity, began to approach the bench just as another man ran across the grass shouting 'Get away!' or words to that effect.

The wretched man on the bench held a revolver, a big old-fashioned type of gun, loosely in his hand. He had a hole in the side of his head and blood was oozing from it. It was about this time we thought that the dogs should go on the lead rather than continue to consume what was left of his blood pooled on the floor. Ken and I exchanged some dialogue, unflustered by the sight, while the other man, now in front of us, was waving his arms about and shouting at us.

It was our first dead body, but we showed only a purely academic interest in it. Of course, we had no way of knowing the tragedy behind the bullet, but I recall that when I told my parents, my dad asked me if I was upset. I replied that I wasn't but later wondered if I should have been. I certainly didn't lose any sleep over it, and neither did Ken, which just shows how resilient children are despite all our parents' worries for us.

I think that a report in the paper later stated that the man had been a civil servant. Even today I can still picture his long pale drawn face and his body slumped in the corner of the park bench, a limp hand dangling over the side of the metal gun.

The teachers at the Roan School were struggling to bring out the best in me academically but, like so many other youngsters, I was mainly concerned with fashion, how to chat up birds and get to first base as quickly as possible with them, and how to be tough, or at least seem tough, to avoid being a victim myself.

I used to hang around with a gang which consisted of Roger Taylor, his brother and various 'hard nuts' from primary school. The difference was that now I was at grammar school and they were all at secondary schools, mostly at Creek Road Secondary which was about as rough as you could get in our area.

I was readily accepted by the gang members as I had a quick wit and was always ready to 'have a go' at something, especially if I was dared. The others were always knocking lumps out of each other and seemed to have a fairly free and easy approach to girls and sex. The girls seemed to be shared around the group but I have to say I didn't much fancy any of them even though the lure of a close encounter increased my blood pressure significantly.

One of the girls, Ann, took a shine to me when I was about fourteen or fifteen years old. She was the sister of Johnny Mead who was a real head case. We went out a few times together and had a snog: she was definitely up for the whole hog but I suddenly realised that this might not be the best idea when she confided in me that her brother regularly visited her during the night and had his way with her.

She said that this had been going on for years and she was quite used to it. No, her parents didn't know, or she thought that they didn't and he always used a 'johnny' so she couldn't get pregnant.

You can imagine that this piece of intelligence sent me reeling, especially because of the casual manner in which she dropped it into the conversation. I asked her why she didn't tell her parents about it and she said that her dad would kill Johnny if he found out so she just put up with it. The thought of following in Johnny's 'footsteps' was daunting to say the least and I thought that it could all go horribly wrong, even though 'the dinner was on the plate'.

I told her that I was afraid of what would happen to me if Johnny knew I was going out with her, so I would have to decline her offer. She said that if I did that she would tell Johnny that I tried to touch her up! I was placed in an impossible dilemma. What would you have done in my place?

I told her that I would have a think about it, gave her a quick kiss and fled back through the tunnel to Greenwich. This was where a lone traveller could often be confronted by gangs eager to question your football allegiance, 'Hoy mate, oo dew support?' with no clue as to what might be the right answer: Millwall, Charlton, Tottenham or Arsenal. Almost never Chelsea.

My general approach was to walk up to the leader showing as much aggression as I could and offer the retort, 'What's it to you ****?' and then run past as quickly as I could, usually hotly pursued by three or four of the gang but fear lights a fire under your feet and I was quick in those days. I would run like the wind. I hated that damn tunnel and would try to avoid it like the plague.

How did I resolve my dilemma with Ann? The next time I saw Johnny, I said to him, 'Here, your sister fancies me and wants me to go out with her.' I accurately second guessed his reaction which was on the lines of, 'If you **** lay a hand on her, I'll **** well kick your **** head so far down your **** throat that you'll wish you hadn't been born. Awright ****?'.

This was an excellent response. I thought that even if she did lie about me at least I might have planted a seed of doubt as to her real intentions: hopefully she eventually stopped him planting any seed whatsoever. On reflection, what an awful life she was living, having to cope with her own brother's unwelcome and illegal advances. Just this glimpse into her life left me feeling that I knew nothing about that sort of darkness and I wanted no further insights either! She didn't keep to her threat though but, as a precaution for a few weeks I steered well clear of Johnny and particularly clear of her.

Our gang, if you could call it that, used to meet down at a café called 'The Captain's Table', not far from Greenwich Town Hall. It was the usual dive of a café where dirty deals were often done and the customers were a mixture of older and more criminal lads and us fourteen to seventen year olds. Drugs, in the forms of amphetamines changed hands there and various sorties and raids were planned. Someone was always up for beating up another gang in Greenwich Park and often we would set off mob-handed to seek out other gangs on a Sunday afternoon. All of this went on even though my dad was a policeman who might have had more than a passing interest in our forays.

During one planning session of our intrepid group, one of the gang who had a car parked outside our meeting place, suggested that we all troop out to have a look at the 'tools' he had gathered for the next encounter in the park. So, out we went. I was slightly taken aback to see a range of weapons in the form of axes, knives, baseball bats and a sawn off shotgun menacingly lying there.

It was at about this time that I realised that being a member of the gang, despite my fine wit and repartee, intellectual insight and strategy, might land me in jail. This is where most members of my gang probably did end up.

For example, take the story of Harry Smith. Harry was a local boy who lived on King George Street. Resembling a gypsy boy, Harry was good looking in his own way. He fell out of school around about the sixteen year old mark when his teachers noticed that he was not the Oxbridge candidate they had hoped, and he seemed to have taken to petty crime.

His big heist had been planned for months. He obtained the tools of his trade, including a sawn-off shot gun.

He carried out detailed surveillance on the betting shop in East Greenwich that was to be his target. Intelligence of the highest quality led him to believe that money aplenty was available there on Saturday afternoons.

He reviewed his getaway transport and driver, not settling for the professional and traditional quick getaway in the stolen Cortina, but, staggeringly clever, decided that he would arrive by bus and get off outside the shop. This worked like a charm. Hopping off the bus with the shotgun in a shopping bag, he sauntered into the betting shop heavily disguised with a piece of cloth around his mouth. Pointing his gun, he demanded the takings from the till. All went perfectly to plan and he left the shop with wealth beyond his wildest dreams. He jumped on the bus back to New Cross Bus Station.

At home in King George Street, safe and sound in his bedroom that same afternoon, luxuriating in the feeling of a job well done and counting the spoils, he was a trifle irritated by the police arresting him having followed his complex and convoluted trail.

A master criminal at work. I could have learned so much from him!

One of the clubs that we used to frequent in Woolwich was 'The Black Cat' which was near the market and has now been turned into a public toilet – what a creative idea. You went down some stairs to the entrance where you got a stamp on the back of your hand that was supposed to resemble a cat but, if it did, the cat must have been called Smudge.

You entered the gloom. At first you thought that your eyes would adjust to the dark but they never really did until the band came on and you then you could see. The club was well known for drug dealing and fights used to break out regularly, mostly just the locals having fun. I recall one night when I was out with the 'boys,' sitting talking to a girl when the word went out that a fight was brewing. I stood up quickly to join the others just as one of our gang's finest, Ronnie Wicks, walked past and with, admirable reactions and quick thinking, he misguidedly thought that I was the opposition and nutted me!

I sat down again thinking that this was definitely the time to sever links with this lot. My decision was reconfirmed a little later, after midnight when we stood around admiring the black leather coat in Harry Fenton's clothes shop. One of the Taylors decided that he liked it as well.

For some unknown reason, he decided not to save up his pennies like the rest of the population but put his boot through the window and, amongst showers of glass that fell on all of us, grabbed the dummy and tore the coat off it.

The alarm bell and lights flashing were fairly stern reminders that shopkeepers didn't normally do business this way and we legged it down to the station with with smart Mr. Taylor now wearing the stolen goods. We all piled into the carriage of the train: there were about eight of us.

Even before the train was pulling out of the station, the light bulbs had been unscrewed, the seats had been thrown out of the window and one of the 'Ts' had hit another of the boys with a bottle and the victim was slumped on the floor with blood coming from his head. With the carriage in total darkness, what seemed to be a group fight ensued. I managed to find a corner and lashed out here and there making snarling noises.

Amongst all this mayhem, I thought that if I ever did make it away from the train in one piece, and out of Greenwich Station alive and not under arrest, my days of running with wild dogs were over.

Nearly over, as there was a commitment to join the 'boys' the following Saturday, in October 1965 to go to a disco at the Catholic Club in Woolwich. Not for any other reason than someone had heard that the bouncer thought he was ''ard' and therefore he was a legitimate target for a beating up. I knew that this would be my last expedition with the gang and that with any luck, there might be some 'salts' there, as we affectionately called the young ladies those days.

Also, I had arranged to meet a friend of mine from the grammar school, John Regan, who possessed a fine brain but a completely barking mad dad who sold flowers on street pavements and regularly threw his Sunday dinner at the rose wallpaper. John was a strange character himself but I liked him.

I once called at his council house in Charlton and was met at the door by a wizened woman he called Elsie but who was his mother. She greeted me with, 'What the **** do you want? That bastard is in the kitchen. He has dismantled his **** Landrover there so I can't make the tea. The old man will go **** spare when he gets 'ome.'

As I wandered into the kitchen I was assailed not by the rich smell of gravy but by the acrid smell of burnt oil and diesel. Sure enough, John had dismantled the gearbox of his Landrover on the kitchen working surfaces explaining that it was 'too **** cold' to work outside. It certainly made me appreciate my own home.

John's dad was arrested time and again for illegally selling flowers on the street and each time he went to court he begged the judge for a custodial sentence. He would usually shout out, 'Put me away, it's like a **** holiday camp in there and I haven't had a holiday for years,' according to John. Perversely, he was invariably given probation and a fine which somehow got paid.

I was about sixteen years old at this time and was cruising through the Catholic Club with John eyeing up the talent when we saw one blonde girl with long hair and another plumper, but attractive girl with shorter blonde hair. We tossed up for who got to chat to whom and I got Wendy whilst John went for Michelle.

As we danced the night away, talking a load of rubbish, as you do, all hell was breaking out at the main entrance where the 'boys' were now taking on the bouncer and half of the Catholic church by the sound of it. It was a wrong move as it happens as most of those helping out were sixteen stone Irishmen with hands like shovels and fists like buckets and spoiling for a decent bit of action after a few pints of Guinness. The boys made a hasty retreat.

I had now dissociated myself from the crew who left shouting insults. I was playing the part of a nice Catholic boy who wanted no trouble whatsoever. I told Wendy that I didn't know who the troublemakers were.

We walked the girls to the bus stop and talked about seeing them again. I really fancied Michelle who, with her long blonde hair and Swedish looks, was a bit of a stunner as far as I was concerned. John quite fancied Wendy as she had more up top to grab hold of and so, without any consultation with the girls, we simply swopped them over! It proved to be a fortuitous as Michelle ended up as my wife. Why did Michelle agree to go out with me? At that time I was very fashion-conscious and dressed a bit like one of the 'The Small Faces' group[1] with Elaine Doust cutting my hair in his style – not quite Rod Stewart. My face, however, was a bit of a trial to me as it would often resemble the craters of the moon as my young hormones raged and the curse of acne struck.

When you're interested in girls, at that age you want clear skin and not exploding pustules that might repel girls unless they are very short-sighted. I used to go to our local doctor who was called Dr. Brosnahan, Irish of course. I would explain my problem and ask him what I could do about my exploding skin.

Unfortunately, he couldn't see that I had a problem. His own face was terribly pockmarked and he had black heads as big as buttons dotted around his face with the odd eggy pustule suppurating down his nose. I refused to accept his 'looks all right to me son' nonsense and insisted that he do something medical.

He sent me to the outpatients' clinic at Greenwich Hospital to have my face burned with ultra violet rays! I had to wear goggles and, with my skin around my eyes peeled away, I was left looking a bit like a panda but at least the acne was burned off. God knows what damage it did to my skin, but Greenwich Hospital never stinted on the burning side. I tried to convince my mates at school that I had been skiing, but they were having none of it. Somehow, my ready wit and boyish charm wooed Michelle and we started to go out with each other. Maybe she liked Pandas.

NOTES FOR CHAPTER EIGHT

1 – The Small Faces were an English rock and roll band from East London, heavily influenced by American rhythm and blues. The group was founded in 1965 by members Steve Marriott, Ronnie Lane, Kenney Jones, and Jimmy Winston. The band is remembered as one of the most acclaimed and influential mod groups of the 1960s.

9

Mods, Music and Mayhem

Transport. The lack of my own transport worried me but a mate, Ray, who lived up the road in Luton Street, had a Vespa scooter and was selling it. I could buy it for £15. I didn't have that sort of money as my only income was from a paper round, lugging half a ton of the *Sunday Times* on my bike, cycling up Crooms Hill which was about a one in six climb.

Often I had to lean right over the other side of the cross bar in order to balance the papers bulging out of the grubby sack. The newsagent used to get complaints from upper class customers because the papers were torn. I had to hammer them through the small letter boxes in case the rain made them wet. I was trying to do them a favour but complaints still rolled in.

I worked for Betty who had the shop on the corner of Burney Street, next to the Rose and Crown pub. She was a lovely lady who always paid me five shillings after the paper round and told me to select some chocolate as a bonus. She never seemed to mind about the complaints. The only trouble was that the papers were getting heavier and heavier all the time and five shillings was not enough to fund my intended lifestyle. I just had to get transport. I had to get another job that paid more so I could run the transport, pay for clothes and support myself. I later found a solution to this problem that made a man out of me.

I asked Mother if I could borrow fifteen pounds from her to buy the scooter. At first she didn't want me to have a scooter and wanted to discuss the idea with Dad who I knew would say 'No!' I asked her again and to keep the loan a secret until I had the scooter. I would tell Dad that I had just bought it once it was safely in my possession.

She went along with this which is strange when I think about it, as usually she did share things with Dad but maybe this time she just wanted to support me. Mums are always scared about losing their sons and daughters in accidents. Probably they worry more than dads who, when they were young, had themselves pushed out the boundaries and survived.

The year would be 1965. With fifteen pounds burning in my hand, and full of excitement, I ran up to Ray's house and bought the scooter. I think that I had a licence at that time, but if I had, it would have been only a provisional one. I certainly had no insurance and what's more, had never driven a scooter before so I had no idea how it worked other than that you twisted the throttle and off you went.

Ray showed me how to start it up, and it made a great sound as it started first time. This was at about six o'clock at night, so it was getting dark. As Ray gave me a cheery wave and went back inside his house I was too proud to admit that I needed more instruction so I sat on the scooter wondering how to get going. Yes, the throttle revved the engine up and I knew that you had to twist the handle grip to get a gear, but what else? I twisted the grip and there was a satisfying clunk as it engaged and I wobbled down the hill towards the T-junction that led into my road.

I was concentrating so much on the gears that the junction approached all too quickly and by the time I had worked out how to stop the thing, I careered across the road and hit the wall opposite. This was built about three feet high in front a small semi-detached house. I remember thinking that if the scooter was damaged then I had just lost my fifteen pounds. Not good. I stopped the engine and pulled the scooter upright to look at the possible damage to the front wheel. I couldn't see any and breathed a sigh of relief.

I thought that what I needed was professional help. I walked back up the road to Ray's house and I asked him to teach me how to ride it. He seemed reasonably happy to help which was unexpected as he and his family were quite unpredictable and inclined to violence. I didn't want to upset him.

He sat on the back of the scooter. I had no 'L' plates, no licence that would permit me to carry a passenger and no insurance. It was odds-on that my Dad wouldn't have seen the funny side of it if I had been stopped by the police. Ray leaned forward and took the controls and I put my hands on his and felt what he was doing with them. He took me up the road that led on to Blackheath where we could practise even though there was a lot of traffic. By this time it was night so the scooter headlights were on. I drove the scooter for about an hour until I got the hang of it. Ray bellowed instructions in my ear, constantly repeating '****
idiot,' which I assume was directed at me.

We then went back to Ray's home and I dropped him off. I confidently roared off around the block, intending to end up outside our flat. Half way around the block in Gloucester Circus, I stalled the engine. I was furious. In vain I tried to kick start it but all to no avail. It was about eight o'clock by now and I had told Mother I would be about half an hour – she would probably be frantic and might even have told Dad before I could. It was all going horribly wrong. There was only one thing for it, I had to push the scooter home. I pushed it to the end of the road and then up Crooms Hill, finally turning into King George Street. It took about thirty minutes. By the time I arrived outside our flat, I was completely exhausted.

I was sweating and fearful about what might happen next but Mother was quite calm and said that she had been a bit worried about me and thought that maybe I had changed my mind about buying the scooter. She said that, on reflection, she would pick a suitable moment to tell 'Daddy' about the new addition to the family.

This did indeed happen a few days later and he was none too pleased and told me to sell it. I faced him and answered him back but the right hand slap across the face seemed to end any fruitful discussion. Funnily enough, he never mentioned it again to me. However, I think he blamed Mother and who knows what she had to put up with on my behalf?

We don't really appreciate what we have until it's too late and while my mother was no saint she was definitely the glue that held our family together.

At that time I was the only son living at home as Mike, my brother had moved out when he was about seventeen years old, taking the opportunity when my parents went on holiday. Mike and Dad clashed repeatedly so it was no surprise he chose to move in to a mate's flat. This really upset Mother and caused Dad to consider going around to the flat and flattening Mike and his mate, the flat owner. It was a rocky time and Mike, who had brains and could have stayed on at school to do 'A' levels and then go on to University, decided that he should look for work in the City. He has his own story to tell, but he rose to be a very successful stockbroker and made a reconciliation of sorts with Dad once he became his own man.

So now I had transport – Colin, another mate, who lived a couple of doors down our road and was a Rocker with his own motorbike, sorted out the scooter for me – a blonde girlfriend whose mum owned her own house, a reasonable lifestyle but still no income. I had little academic interest and paid scant attention to my studies, even though I told Mother that I was doing homework in my bedroom.

The truth was that I used to slip out of the back window, climb over the wall and meet my mates. We tried to get into pubs or just hung around together. I scraped by at school only really showing interest in languages which I love still. French Spanish and English were subjects which pleased me. My novel approach to passing my GCEs (General Certificate of Education) as they were then called, might have worked if I had been a gifted individual, but I was not. I took nine GCEs of which I managed to pass only one – English Literature.

Mother was very disappointed. Dad refused to talk to me. I took it all quite lightly as I didn't really care one way or the other. By this time my life was changing quite a bit as Michelle was such a stabilising influence. I wouldn't say that I had grown up, but I had matured considerably although I could still be quite aggressive orally and physically.

But now I had wheels and the world opened up. We were Mods. It's worthwhile spending some time here to describe this era as it was so important for many people and is still viewed with great interest, even today.

Mods were part of the Modernist Movement. The 60s had shaken off the post-war blues and people were pushing the boundaries and challenging society in every aspect: in film, fashion, music and culture.

Mods liked blues and jazz – Jimmy Smith, a keyboard player was one of our gods – and dressed as sharply as wages would allow. The sort of clothes that we wore were mohair suits with pressed shirts and smart shoes bought in a shop called Ravels. If you had a scooter then a US army surplus fishtail parka was worn to protect your clothes. I felt that I was really fashionable when I bought a full length green leather coat and dyed the collar black. I loved that coat. Of course you also had to customise your scooter with white wall tyres and extra mirrors if you wanted to look cool. I chose extra mirors as they were cheaper.

On one occasion there were four of us going to Carnaby Street in Soho, London, to buy shoes. Alan Baneham wanted to spend money on the latest fashion. We set off cheerfully on our scooters, riding in the rain. We had just arrived at New Cross and I was riding behind a white van which I think had *Advanced Laundry* written on the back of the door. Suddenly, the van braked hard in order to stop for an old lady crossing on a zebra crossing. I saw the van's brake lights come on and I braked hard too.

Unfortunately Vespas were not known for their balance under harsh braking conditions and the scooter slipped from under me. Like a cartoon character, I sailed through the air until I collided with the back of the van. I slid down it in slow motion. The scooter had gone under it and its engine was still revving. I heard voices shouting, 'He's dead. He's dead,' (there seems to be a theme here) as I lay on the ground, so I thought I had better open my eyes. There was quite a crowd around me and my mates had stopped and dragged the scooter from under the van.

It was a great
time to be a Mod.

I jumped up with no thought of any injury to me but far more concerned to see if the scooter was damaged. Someone was calling for an ambulance but one of my mates had restarted the scooter, bent the front brake back into some sort of shape and kicked away a couple of other bits of the scooter that lay smashed on the ground.

This mate told me to stop 'hanging about' and get back on, so I did. We drove off, completely unconcerned about the crowd behind us which included old ladies and a van driver concerned about my life. I think that there was an ambulance on the way. The resilience of youth – you just can't beat it.

Arriving at Carnaby Street, the shopping Mecca of Mods, we parked and went window shopping. Being a Mod was as much about showing off what you wore as what you were wearing and how you handled yourself so Carnaby Street was a great place to be seen. We left Al in a shoe shop and sauntered off, intending to catch up with him later.

When we did catch up with him, he told us that he had found the shoes he liked but had said to the shop assistant that they were too tight on his toes. The assistant told him not to worry as the shop had a special machine which eased shoe leather and made the fit better so, if Al really liked the shoes, the assistant would put them on the machine and stretch them slightly. Al agreed to this course of action and the assistant disappeared to do the stretching. After waiting for about five minutes, Al decided to tell the assistant that he would be back in a second as he wanted to find his mates so he went downstairs.

He was surprised to see the assistant hanging on to the heel of one of his shoes and pulling it downwards onto the 'machine' which, in fact, was the end of a broomstick. Conversation: 'What are you doing to me shoes, mate?' Answer: 'The machine's broken, sir, so we are having to make do.' Reply: 'You can keep the **** things....' Exit Al with no shoes. I wonder how many other customers were taken in by the 'stretching machine'?

I sold the Vespa for ten pounds and replaced it with a Lambretta scooter known as an LI 150 which I customised with a back rack, an aerial with a furry tail hanging from the top and front crash bars with chrome mirrors. I painted it a dark blue as I liked the contrast of the chrome with the blue. Michelle and I went everywhere on that scooter and it rarely let us down. We had no helmets to protect our heads if we came off and no real weatherproof clothing. We must often have been cold and wet but youth overlooks discomfort when fashion is involved and the last thing we wanted to do was look like Rockers with their greasy lifestyle and motorbikes.

We loved the music that was emerging from that era and there was so much talent around at that time that it felt like Christmas Day every day when we tuned into the radio. One of my favourite off-the-wall bands was the Bonzo Dog Doo-Dah Band with Vivian Stanshall leading it. We used to watch this group, whacky, talented and alternative to the straight blues and rock that was filling the airways, in the Iron Bridge Tavern which was across the water from Greenwich.

In no particular order, I loved to listen to:
Long John Baldry; The Beatles; Chuck Berry; John Mayall and the Bluebreakers (one of my particular favourites) Cream; The Rolling Stones; The Searchers; The Yardbirds; Marvin Gaye; Aretha Franklin; Bob Dylan; The Beach Boys; The Temptations; The Kinks; Jimmy Hendrix; Led Zeppelin; James Brown; The Who (my favourite-ever band) Otis Redding; The Animals; The Supremes; Simon and Garfunkel; Jefferson Airplane; Booker T and the MGs; Ben E. King; The Strawbs; Roy Orbison; Elvis; The Pretty Things.

So many great songs came out of that era and amongst my favourites were:
Satisfaction (The Rolling Stones); *Respect* (Aretha Franklin); *Like a Rolling Stone* (Bob Dylan); *Good Vibrations; Get Around; God Only Knows ; Wouldn't it be Nice* – our special Michelle & Roger song (The Beach Boys)[1]

I still get a tingle in my spine that takes me back to that era whenever I hear any of these and so many other songs. It was an age of fantastic and vibrant talent. We were truly spoilt but didn't realise it at the time.

We used to see quite a few groups in their early days playing at the Lewisham Odeon; Chislehurst Caves; the Black Cat; Mr Ts at Catford; Eltham Baths; and many others. I recall seeing The Who playing in a church hall one Sunday afternoon in St Mary Cray near Sidcup, Kent. We went on the scooter to see them and there must have been about two hundred of us packed into a tiny church hall on a hot summer afternoon. It was so hot that rust was dripping on us from the steel girders above. The Who played at full volume, and they weren't too good either but we didn't care as, at the end of the set, Pete Townsend smashed his guitar into the amplifier, sending smoke billowing. Keith Moon kicked over some of his drum kit. These days, the Health and Safety Gestapo would never allow any such gig to go ahead. Indeed, such destructive behaviour was dangerous, but the energy from the band and the crowd was an explosive and heady mixture.

When we finally got outside, we gulped down the air just to get oxygen inside us and we flopped on the grass to cool down but what an afternoon it had been. The Who might just about have made enough to cover their wrecked equipment but what a following they were building up. Keith Moon seemed to be absolutely crazy. Daltrey and Townsend are true survivors and, in my opinion, Townsend was one of the best songwriters of that era.

My roots were also in Irish music as I listened to my Uncle Fran play many a jig and reel as I was growing up. Has anybody ever heard of *The Man that Fought the Monkey in the Dustbin* which he said was a favourite of his? I also grew up listening to my brother's record collection. He was really into traditional jazz so I listened to Chris Barber and Acker Bilk. I loved the way Ottilie Patterson[2] sang and can still sing the words to *Sister Kate*. Mike liked Lonnie Donnegan so I have a whole history of his songs in my head including, *Does Your Chewing Gum Lose its Flavour on the Bedpost Overnight?* which is a real brain teaser.

Mike sold me my first guitar, a Spanish guitar which had strings so high off the fret board that I had to use my right hand to hold down the fingers of my left hand in order to engage a note, then make my fingers leap back down the neck of the guitar in order to strum it! My fingers were bleeding most of the time and it wasn't until Michelle bought me a Framus cello acoustic guitar for my birthday – and I still have it – that I was really able to practise properly, without needing a blood transfusion.

The blues were my real love and I used to visit a record shop in the New Cross Road which had great blues imports. I spent every spare penny I had on buying obscure blues records, including chain gang recordings made in the Deep South of the United States. I must have had over one hundred LPs, most of them obscure, and I would have just loved to have kept them. Why did they have to go? To raise money, is the answer.

The Lambretta engine eventually blew up and I just had to have wheels. Being without transport was simply not an option. I took all the LPs back to the shop and sold them. I can't remember how much I got but it was enough to pay for the engine to be replaced. Although this gave me temporary pleasure I lost the long term pleasure I would have had from listening to those prized LPs. How many times have we all done that in our lives – never being able to see beyond the horizon because of pressing, but not important needs?

I still love to listen to blues players such as Muddy Waters, Sonny Terry and Brownie McGhee, the craziness of Clarence 'Frogman' Henry and John Lee Hooker. My all time blues hero is Howling Wolf who, at three hundred pounds weight and six feet three inches high, had the best blues voice ever and people seldom argued that fact with him face to chest. He is still alive.

You can almost see the drift of hazy blue cigar smoke late at night in a shebeen – an illicit bar – when he sings.

He developed musically after Sonny Boy Williamson married into his family and he still remains a giant in all ways on the blues scene. *Smokestack Lightning* remains one of my favourite songs. Listen to him as he hammers the words of the song into your mind.

Blind Willie McTell's recordings form the base of many blues players' bottom drawer and his mastery of the twelve string acoustic guitar was unique. Even today it is inspiring to listen to old recordings, his extraordinary range of styles varying from ragtime to hillbilly slide and his nasal voice which he used with such variety.

I still love to play guitar and keyboard for my own pleasure and sometimes jam with friends. I never joined a group as such at the time but dearly wish I had given it a go. Mind you, most of the rock and blues stars of that era have to ask members of their fan clubs to tell them what happened during that time. A heady combination of drink, drugs, fame, wealth and no limits to excess seem to almost invariably have led to the loss of a considerable number of brain cells.

It is a remarkable tribute to the Maker of the human body that some of the rock giants like Eric Clapton, are as eloquent as they are today, as I am sure that the sort of life they led would have left lesser mortals, like me, permanently wrecked.

As Mods, we listened to great music and looked for our natural enemies, who were Rockers. Rockers were scruffy and looked 'hard', spending money on their bikes and racing up and down the old London A2 road running from Johnston's café – a key meeting point, up to near Catford. My friend, Colin, who lived a few houses up the road from me, used to lend me a leather jacket and helmet, rough me up a bit and stick me on the back of his bike which could do about a ton (100 m.p.h.) and we would speed down to the café with the bike pegs scoring the road as we screamed around bends, sparks flying behind us. It was really exhilarating and I loved it, especially after driving the sedate scooter. If you leaned the scooter steeply into a corner then you would fall off.

Colin and I got on fine but on bank holidays in 1965 it was war between the groups. We would ride down to Southend, Clacton, Margate, Bournemouth or Brighton and there would be thousands of Mods on scooters. An army of Mods on scooters with furry things hanging off our aerials and birds in short skirts clinging on behind. Once there, if we got past the police road blocks, we would park the scooters and get on to the beach. Some Mods without scooters arrived by train and were met by the police who would be at the station to confiscate any 'bother' boots. The police then let the Mods proceed, walking in their socks. This was the police strategy to prevent fights from breaking out. Of course the Rockers had the same idea about fighting as we did and the papers would be full of reports of clashes between us. In reality, there would just be a bit of name calling, and an odd skirmish or two and then everyone would just get on with life. From the Press reports, you would have thought that Armageddon was imminent. Michelle and I often went on these weekends and never experienced trouble ourselves although we were in the middle of hundreds of other Mods. It was time of energy, constructive and destructive energy. We all felt it and it separated us from our parents' generation.

For many of us, that era was summed up in the words of *My Generation* by The Who when Roger Daltrey sings, 'hope I die before I get old.' We thought it just couldn't get better,

But the Beatles really nailed down what I needed at that time: 'The best things in life are free. But you can keep 'em for the birds and bees. Now'give me money, (that's what I want) that's what I want.'

NOTES FOR CHAPTER NINE

1 – Favourite songs that evoke the 60s for me: *Light my Fire* (The Doors); *My Girl* (The Temptations); *Hey Jude; Imagine; She Loves You* and *Back in the USSR* (The Beatles/John Lennon); *You Really Got Me; All Day and All of the Night; Waterloo Sunset* (The Kinks); *Sunshine of your love* and *Layla* (Cream/Eric Clapton); *All Along the Watchtower* and *Purple Haze* (Hendrix); *My Generation, Can't Explain, Pinball Wizard* (my favourite of favourites) *I Can See for Miles; Mr Tambourine Man* (The Byrds); *Whole Lotta Love* (Led Zeppelin); *Green Onions* (Booker T and the MGs); *Hi Hi Hazel* (Geno Washington and the Ram Jam Band); *Whiter Shade of Pale* (Procol Harum); *I Shot the Sheriff* (Bob Marley); *House of the Rising Sun* (The Animals); *Sound of Silence* (Simon and Garfunkel); *Born to be Wild* (Steppenwolf); *Pretty Woman* (Roy Orbison); *Gloria* (Them); *In the Cannons of your Mind* (The Bonzo Dog Doo-Dah Band) and *The Wonder of You* (Elvis).

2 – Anna-Ottilie Patterson, blues singer, born 31 January 1932; died 20 June 2011. A demure white woman from Northern Ireland who replicated the classic African-American blues style. She sang with a lusty clarity and an innate grasp of the idiom. A fellow blues enthusiast, the vocalist and commentator George Melly, likened her to Bessie Smith,

10

CREAM CAKES, JESUS AND BUBBLE CARS

'Give me money, that's what I want'. The Beatles said it for me in their song. Yes, I definitely needed more money than the paper round paid if I was to lead the lifestyle I wanted. However, Michelle insists to this day that I was careful with money at that time as she remembers that we often shared the cost of tickets when we went to the cinema. In truth, after paying the running costs of the scooter and trying to keep up with the fashion of the day, I had no spare cash.

Michelle has never forgiven me for selling her, rather than giving her, a purple mohair jumper that I no longer wanted – I think she gave me about five shillings for it. Although my selling it to her was meant as a joke, her mum took exception when she found that Michelle had actually bought it from me. I suppose that I was not the image of the protector she wanted for her daughter and it certainly cast me in a poor light.

My mate, John Regan, told me that he had Friday night work in a local bakery, 'Broomfields', which was situated near Deptford. The wages for Friday night were nearly five pounds. This represented a fortune to me so I put my name down on the Friday night waiting list. In order to get work, you had to arrive at the gates of the factory at 6.30 pm and if there was a big food order that night, you might be offered work.

I was about sixteen years old and it was hard work. The night shift was run by a big Scot called Mr. Ross and you didn't want him on your back. He never smiled, just swore at you. He never asked you to do anything but told you to '**** get on with it' and he meant now.

The staff in the early part of the evening, until about 8.00 p.m., was made up of a mixture of men and women. Quite a few of the men were of West Indian origin. As the evening wore on, the women left the factory, leaving only the men working.

My first job of the shift was working on a machine that sliced sponge cakes in half at the start of a conveyor belt. I put the sponges through the machine. The sponges fell in two halves on to the belt. A grizzly, wizened, thin goblin of a man, Bill, who looked about ninety years old to me, stood next to a large vat of strawberry jam. Using his hand, which was filthy dirty and had black fingernails, he scooped up jam and smeared it on to the sponge. The sponge then moved down the belt towards the next person who was ready for the next stage.

Behind the conveyor belt was a big sign fixed to the wall telling employees that hygiene mattered and advising them to wash their hands before working with food. I couldn't believe that the goblin could use his hands in this way and asked him to explain why he didn't use the ladle provided. He told me that his way was the most effective method of applying jam to the sponges and then he told me to, '****-off you ****'. I took this to mean that no further enquiry about the jam process would be welcome.

The jam-smeared sponge then smoothly arrived in front of the next person in the process who was usually a woman. She was supposed to use a hand-held bag, which she would fill with cream, to facilitate squeezing a circle of cream on to the sponge. This seemed quite straightforward. A scoop was provided to fill the bag but it was almost impossible to scoop stiff cream into a floppy bag and then apply the cream to the sponges which were travelling at the speed of the computer game, Space Invaders. You had to be quick or the sponges would just pile up one on top of the other.

The woman operator simply dispensed with the scoop and used her hand to scoop up the cream and put it into the bag. As a result, there were three lots of hands touching every part of the sponge in some way before it arrived at the end of the belt. The bacteria must have been building up nicely. At the end of the belt, another woman would, again with her hands, place the cut sponge top over the one with jam and cream and then sugar the top and put the finished item into a box for sale to the public.

I once saw Bill, with the ever-present fag hanging out of the corner of his mouth, visit the toilet and then, without washing his hands which now had jam and piss on them, march straight back to work on the conveyor belt. I never ate another sponge after working in that factory and even today, I am wary of eating any shop-bought pastries or cakes with a cream filling.

How the bakery could proudly display hygiene awards on its walls was beyond me. Everyone knew what was going on. The women used to tease me mercilessly with sexual innuendoes but I didn't mind them at all: they were good fun and livened up the evening.

'Hey, Chinaman!' the West Indians would shout at me. Why did they call me 'Chinaman?' They reasoned that because my eyes became slits when I laughed then I must have some Chinese background. This was despite my telling them that I had been born and bred in Greenwich and was of Irish and Welsh parents. They refused to call me by my name, Roger. However, they were a great crew and because I was a sixteen-year-old lad they were constantly ragging me about how much 'pussy' I was getting and wanting explicit details. To keep them quiet, I would tell them any old thing so my sex life must have seemed on the up, as it were, when in fact I was very much still trying to get it going.

One Jamaican, 'Jesus' was paranoid about leaving his wife alone at night. He left traps to see if his wife was cheating on him and nearly drove himself crazy thinking about it. Of course, all his mates would fuel his paranoia as much as they could by saying that she surely must be cheating on him and they would also think up traps to set for her. He tried to catch her out one evening when he left the factory during his break. He drove like a lunatic to get to Lewisham, about six miles away, and burst in through the bedroom door at about midnight only to find her asleep in bed. When he told us about this, he seemed actually disappointed not to have found her in her lover's arms.

Jesus was accident prone and one night he came into work with plasters on the back and the palm of his right hand. I asked him what had happened He explained that it had happened in a car wash. He had been waiting in his Ford Cortina for the car in front of him to finish its wash and move away. He was just putting his car into gear so that he could pull into the car wash when he heard a shout telling him that his aerial was still up. Clearly, if he left it up it would be bent by the car wash brushes. He leaped out of the car and using the flat of his hand as a hammer, swatted the aerial down in one strong motion. The trouble was that he had lost the cone-shaped tip at the top of the aerial so there was no protection against his hand being penetrated by the sharp metal. The aerial just went straight through his palm and came out of the back of his hand, leaving his hand jammed on it and about a foot down its length.

The only way he could get his hand free was to ask two men who had been watching the incident, to grab his hand and force it back up the aerial. His pain must have been excruciating but he laughed it off saying that he was just stupid.

He didn't laugh after losing his forefinger two weeks later when he fell asleep on the job near the doughnut jam injector. His finger was sliced off when, on waking suddenly, he saw that the doughnuts were being forced together under the injector as one of them was stuck. In that event, you had to reach across with a stick and clear the jam. However, Jesus didn't bother using the stick, instead he used his hand in the middle of the jammy mess in order to clear it. The injector came down relentlessly and sliced off his finger.

Matters worsened when the injector forced the finger into a doughnut which then went on down the line and was fried in hot oil. It was finally tipped into a large turning sieve that sprinkled the doughnuts with sugar before coming to rest with thousands of other doughnuts.

Mr. Ross sent him to hospital and then ordered the rest of us to find the dismembered finger by opening the doughnuts. One by one, we opened the doughnuts, looking for his finger. Of course nobody actually wanted to find it. Mr. Ross' intention was not just to find the finger to send it to the hospital so that it could be sewn back on, but to try to save as many doughnuts as possible from being wasted. He didn't want the company to face legal action from a customer who, on biting into a delicious jammy doughnut, had bitten into a severed finger. Understandable.

We did find the finger which was sent to join Jesus at the hospital but Mr. Ross was ruthless and more concerned with keeping the production line going than with the welfare of his workers

I worked at the bakery every Friday night and became a regular. Of course I missed going out with my mates especially as Michelle would go out then with her mates and I was jealous of what she might be getting up to. She assured me that her activities were innocent. I must have caught the paranoia bug from Jesus.

In time, Mr. Ross became quite friendly towards me and usually would give the awful jobs to newcomers rather than to me. However, he knew my weak point was working on the ovens so he would always give me a spell on them. I think that he was toughening me up, in his own way.

The ovens. They were about one hundred feet long and heat rolled off them. The bread was put in as dough on iron trays at one end and rolled out as a baked product at the other. The heat was intense, fierce and sapping.

At the end of the oven, two workers would wear thick oven gloves and heave the iron trays, containing about ten loaves in tins, up on to the metal mobile stacks which, once filled, were pushed away. At the same time as pushing the full stacker away, an empty stacker had to be brought to the front of the oven, ready for the next trays.

It was remorseless work and timing was everything. If you got the rhythm wrong for picking up the trays then the bread in tins would just fall on the floor. All hell and chaos would break loose as the next trays would simply fall on to the floor until someone stopped the oven. If the oven was stopped it was a major hanging offence which meant Mr. Ross shouting unintelligible things at you about an inch away from your face. You really didn't want that to happen. I hated that job. It was heavy work for a slightly built sixteen-year-old and although I worked there for only an hour at a time, in order to relieve the regulars who were big burly Jamaicans, I could easily lose one or two pounds of body weight in water loss. Sweat just poured out of me and in the heat of the summer I sometimes felt that I would pass out. I thought that if I could survive working on the ovens, then I could survive anything that life might throw at me. My mind would be numb with fatigue. My limbs would tremble with effort.

At first, I was hopeless at this task and the Jamaicans with whom I worked cursed me so much that I thought that they would kill me, but slowly I got into the rhythm of it. It was a formidable muscular effort to lift an iron tray containing ten tins of bread to stack as your first placement on the top of a six-foot mobile trolley.

As I staggered with the tray, my mentor showed me how

to spread the weight by working with my legs, as we use the 'Horse- Riding Stance' in karate – a wide legged stance with the weight distributed evenly on each leg forming a pyramid with your head at the top. I would then lift the trays up using a powerful thrust from the legs.

After a while, it became effortless and although I still sweated profusely, I could keep up with the regular workers who gave me back-handed compliments about my work always linked to 'pussy', of course, such as, 'Hey Chinaman, yuh getting strong, soon yuh be able to lif' yer dick off the floor, hah hah hah.'

This Friday night job meant that I had money and transport of a sort, but I was still too young to drive a car. I hit on the idea of buying a 'bubble car.' In October 1956, the Isetta Moto Coupe De Luxe, known as the 'bubble car', was introduced – also known as Sargwagen in Germany or 'coffin on wheels'. The maximum speed on a good day was about fifty m.p.h. but it had the advantage of needing only a scooter licence to drive. You didn't have to pass a full driving test for a car. It took about thirty seconds to get up to thirty m.p.h. and seated two of you in comfort as you

Michelle and I with the Bubble Car: lucky to be alive.

sat on the bench seat, staring through a Perspex bubble window. The bench seat was also very good for courting, although some gymnastics were needed to capitalise on the opportunity.

My mate, John Regan, had bought a bubble car and I was resolved to buy one myself. I found one in *Exchange & Mart*, a trading magazine, and it was being sold by a man who lived just outside Lewisham. On a filthy night in winter, with the rain lashing down, I went over to see it. John drove me over in his own mobile coffin.

We parked outside a semi-detached council house and were met by the owner, dressed liked a Teddy Boy[1] with a big quiff in his hair, a drape coat and winklepickers, smoking the ubiquitous fag.

We inspected the car and asked him to start the engine. He said that the battery was flat so we would have to push it. It started at a push and the engine made lots of noise. There was smoke coming out of every corner, including inside the car, but John said that it sounded fine to him. I paid twenty pounds for it. No papers changed hands that I can remember and of course I had never driven a bubble car before but John had said that they were easy to drive.

The rain was lashing down with a vengeance. I closed the car door. I was dripping wet. As a precaution, we had left the engine running after starting it. There was no heater and I had to open the side window for ventilation. I would have been choked to death by the fumes if I hadn't done so. The manual gearbox gave four forward gears and one reverse and John had shown me how to put the clutch in and engage a gear so I set off after him, bumping and careering across the road following his rear lights. I could hardly see out of the windscreen as the wiper blade was useless and it was raining too hard to make a difference. How I got home is quite a mystery to me – it must have been really dangerous – but I arrived home, the proud owner of my first car. Well, almost a car.

The house opposite our flat, on the other side of the road, was owned by the Gearing family and behind it was a yard where there was a small garage. The garage was run by an interesting character called Mr. Snell. Mr. Snell had been an RSM (Regimental Sergeant Major) in the Second World War and was a master mechanic. He could fix anything but specialised in fixing lorries.

He was about 5 foot 5 inches tall and was one of the most aggressive men I have ever met. If you owed him money he would pursue you relentlessly, usually with a monkey wrench, and he took on big companies that wouldn't pay their bills by taking a lorry down to their parking spaces and blocking their entrance. He would just sit and swear at all and sundry until someone came down with a cheque or cash to settle his account. He was definitely not a man to mess with and he told me once that he had lost count of the people he had killed. I didn't want to think about it. I believed him.

He swore constantly, chain-smoked but was still full of energy. He seemed to like me as I took an interest in mechanics and asked him lots of questions. Sometimes he would give me work, doing minor repairs on cars. I was also careful to sympathise with him over his constant battle to get companies to pay him. He could go from calm to enraged in an instant and it was quite disconcerting to be near him when this happened.

Early the next morning, after buying the bubble car, I pushed it across the road to the top of Mr. Snell's driveway and let the car roll down to the garage. I asked Mr. Snell if he could charge the battery. He laughed so hard when he saw the car that I thought his red face would burst a blood vessel and of course he knew all about it mechanically. I was a bit downcast when he said that it was a 'F**** heap of junk' but he agreed to look at it for me.

After school, I went over to see him and the car was in the corner of the garage but I couldn't see any battery wires sticking from the charger leading into it. I assumed that the battery was now fully charged. I saw Mr. Snell in his office and he gave me a pitying look. He asked me if the man who sold it to me had push started it and I said that he had and that he had explained that the battery was flat.

Mr. Snell snorted contemptuously, 'Flat,' he said, 'There's pieces missing, mate.' He told me what was missing but I have forgotten how. I recall feeling a complete idiot to have been caught out in this way

Fortunately, his soft spot for me eased the situation and he said that he had found missing pieces for it and put the 'f**** things' into this 'f**** heap of ****' as well as servicing it, sorting out a gear that didn't work, replacing a wiper blade and welding the exhaust that would have killed me from the leaking fumes. He then started it and I was as pleased as punch to hear the car burst into life.

He wouldn't accept any money from me, simply shaking his head continually as if in total disbelief at my foolish behaviour. I can tell you that I had a grin on my face as I drove the car up from the yard and parked it outside our flat. I proudly showed my mother my purchase and I think that she thought that at least it was safer than the scooter and as such it was a good buy. Michelle viewed it with some suspicion but I suspect that she realised that at least she would be drier inside the car than on the back of the scooter. We were finally moving up the transport ladder.

We did quite a bit of running around in that death trap as well as a bit more courting in it up at Abbey Wood, near Plumstead, where there was a nice secluded parking area. Not that we went the whole way although, believe me, I tried, but Michelle was a 'nice' girl and the brakes were often applied to my ardour.

One fateful night the gods definitely were watching over us. We were coming down Shooters Hill after a cuddle session in the love nest, and I was just approaching the traffic lights opposite the police station on the corner.

The lights were green but about to change and I wanted to turn right towards Woolwich so I changed down a gear and pushed hard on the accelerator. We started to accelerate and might just have made the right turn had not the driver of a van, coming from the other direction, also decided to try to beat the lights. He hit us, full contact on the side of the car, just as we were turning. Bang! Blackness.

The car door burst open and Michelle and I were thrown out on to the road. The van continued to push the car in front of it until it hit the wall opposite. The van almost completely crushed the car. It was a miracle that we survived. Someone surely must have been looking after us. We should have died in that accident.

Fortunately, there was an ambulance almost directly behind us. We were quickly driven to the nearby hospital. We ended up with cuts and bruises and Michelle had a head injury but, fortunately, it wasn't serious.

I later saw the remains of the bubble car in the scrap yard where they had taken it and it was just a cube of metal. It was hard to believe that it had been a car. It was shocking. My parents and Michelle's mum and step-father were really shaken up. If we had not been thrown out then we would have been crushed. We recovered quickly because of our youth and truthfully, after about a week, I thought no more about it. I think that Michelle took longer to get over it.

Disaster. I now had no transport. I didn't want to go back to using a scooter so I thought that it was time to take a full driving test and get a real car which would provide more protection.

After a few driving lessons with an instructor who lived up our street, Dad decided to take me out in his big old Wolseley car – I think that it was Wolseley 63, Series 3 – which had column-change gears. The engine was so quiet that, when waiting for the traffic lights to change, I often thought that it had stopped and went to start it again just to have the starter motor engage to the sound of an almighty clashing of cogs. This was normally accompanied by Dad confirming what Mr. Snell thought of me.

I took my driving-test at Lewisham. It had a testing start, you might say. I had parked the car outside the test centre and had left plenty of room to pull out. However, when I returned with the examiner, I was hemmed in by a car on either side. The examiner took a look at the situation and asked if I was confident enough to edge up to the car in front and nudge it forward to create space.

I didn't expect him to say this but nudged the car forwards about three feet. This allowed me to pull out from the parking space. I suppose that it was a good example of car control but I thought that perhaps this was the first part of my examination. Should I do this in the first place? He passed me. Oh, the joy of passing your test first time! When I told Dad that I had passed, he said that his mate, Ernie, a jeweller, was selling an Austin 35 car. It was old but reliable.

The car was grey. The fact that Ernie let me buy it for ten pounds gives a clue about its condition. The car pulled violently to the right when you applied the brakes and the only way to stop in a straight line was to apply opposite lock on the steering wheel, and use the handbrake. As you accelerated, it jumped out of third gear so you had to hold the gear in with your left hand while accelerating and then jump it into fourth gear. We did a good amount of travelling in that little car before I sold it to a man who, despite my listing its faults, said that he wanted it to teach his wife to drive! I asked him if he was trying to kill her but he bought it anyway.

On reflection, it's interesting how each mode of transport seems to recall different stages of our development and we can all relate to that special car, bike or scooter linked with an important event of our life. My other cars include a Triumph Herald – bought and sold by me twice – a Mini with a highly-tuned engine and a Sunbeam Alpine coupé that was really my first sports car, even though it was classed as a roadster. I loved all those cars, especially the Sunbeam Alpine which had white paintwork and a blue detachable top. It made me feel that I was really moving up in life.

Back at school, I had knuckled down to study and was benefiting from a steady relationship with Michelle. I finally started to show academic promise, retaking and passing all of my GCEs, apart from Maths which I never really understood. I loved Physics and Chemistry which included many mathematical principles. I just couldn't relate to the abstract. In Chemistry, there always seemed to me to be a beginning, middle and end. For example, if you put an explosive device on a bench and triggered it, the bench blew up. Simple.

After passing my exams, I moved up into the 'A'level stream in the sixth form, and studied French, Spanish and English Literature, all of which I really enjoyed. I found that I had a talent for languages, not so much on the written side, but more the spoken word. I thought it was fun to be able to communicate in another language. Respectability was conferred on me when I was made a school prefect. Prefects had their own common room to share with other prefects in free lessons.

School life was now comfortable and even enjoyable. I didn't have to go into the morning assembly for hymns as I had worked out some time before that all you had to say was that you were a Jew, atheist or Catholic and you didn't have to attend, except for the notices at the end of the service. I just played the Catholic card, although I wasn't going to church at the time, and I lounged about with a couple of others, swapping jokes until it was time to join the rest. Nobody bothered us – it was great.

Life had now settled into a stable pattern for me but it was still an exciting time. So much good music to listen to, parties to go to and my brain seemed to be finally emerging, which was a bonus.

All was not calm at home though, and I clashed with my Dad in what was to be a key moment in my life and one that I will never forget.

Notes for Chapter Ten
1 – The Teddy Boy youth culture first emerged in Britain during the early 1950s, and was strongly associated with American rock and roll music of the period. It was typified by male youths wearing a modified style of Edwardian clothes. In Britain the name Edward is commonly (though less so these days) shortened to 'Ted.'

11
The Sleeper

I have always enjoyed fighting – except when I was getting beaten up – and so I decided that I would join the Judo class at the night school in Deptford. I was about fifteen years old and most of the others at the club were men or youths.

The instructor was a bull-like man with no neck. He was a brown belt, one grade below a black belt, and had been so for many years. Every time he went to a grading examination he was disqualified for being too aggressive. His specialty was strangles and chokes and he used to lie on the mat and tell a student to try to choke him out. If the student didn't do it, then he would simply choke him so it was a great incentive to try your best. There was many a delirious time I spent watching stars spinning in front of my eyes as I emerged from another bout of unconsciousness but, even today, I can put you to sleep very fast if I have to, thanks to his unusual approach.

He also taught us to execute judo throws left handed. This gave you an advantage over your opponent, most of whom were right handed. When I entered competitions, I would often win, not because I was a better player but because of the element of surprise as my opponent would usually be expecting a conventional attack.

The promotion examinations were held at the Budokwai, Gilston Road, Chelsea and I recall travelling up there in the winter. The *dojo* (training hall) would be freezing and long lines of candidates would sit on the floor until their names were called. We seemed to have to wait for an eternity. Then suddenly it was your turn to fight. There was no time to warm up your body. You were expected to spring up and fight your opponent in order to gain the next grade. You were expected to beat him. If you lost, then you didn't get a promotion. I liked the simple honesty of it. The fighting was fierce as no candidate wanted to repeat the experience. I fought my way up to green belt which was about half way up the totem pole to black belt. Our instructor didn't bother putting us forward for many gradings so we were probably more advanced for our grade than the others and our small group nearly always succeeded in the examinations.

I loved the close-in fighting that judo exposed you to and if you want to test your fitness then try judo as it is truly exhausting when you try to move heavier competitors around the mat or are thrown and used as a mat yourself. In my view judo and boxing are the two bedrocks of martial arts and anyone interested in giving their children a firm foundation to protect themselves, could do no better than to introduce them to these disciplines. I say this even though karate has been a part of my life for so long. Whilst I got many injuries fighting, including a time when my hip almost came out of its socket, no lasting harm was done to my body but I have the greatest respect for the dedication of Judo players.

Our small club broke up as the instructor became increasingly unreliable. At one time I was the one doing the instructing which wasn't what I wanted at all. I drifted around to other clubs in our area but I was unsettled. I decided that I would stop training until I could find one that suited me. Can you believe that later my Dad and his Buffaloes showed me the way forward?

The atmosphere at home was fairly calm now. I had a regular job on Friday nights at the bakery and a steady girlfriend that even Dad liked – he called Michelle 'a little cracker'. I felt quite mature. Dad was still drinking quite heavily and every so often Mother would have to put up with him being unreasonable. He would more or less ignore me except for the usual comments about my long hair but we did have another major confrontation which unsettled me. He was drunk and I think from her demeanor that he had slapped Mother. I decided that enough was enough.

As he stood in hall to our flat I called him every name that I could think of including many that I thought would be hurtful. I told him that if he wanted to fight then he could fight me. I think that it was about 7.00 pm. I remember him standing down the hall with the front door at his back. I picked up the chair that I was going to hit him with. I was so angry I was almost tearful.

I recall him calmly taking off his jacket, unbuttoning his shirt collar, taking off his tie, taking his cufflinks out of his shirt sleeves and slowly and deliberately rolling up first one sleeve and then the other. Now all the time I was holding a heavy chair at shoulder height but the weight of it was bringing it down nearer and nearer to the ground.

Dad must have faced countless violent criminals in his life in the police. He had worked in one of the toughest parts of London, Chinatown, when he was barely a man. He had lived with violence all his life. He knew it. He could smell it and he could smell the fear that went with it. He knew that I was angry with adrenaline pumping through me at turbo-like speed causing my limbs to shake.

He knew that my heart rate was raised and that I was breathing harder than he was even though he was drunk but now had suddenly become stone cold sober. To him I was a bit of a wild kid who had never really been tested in the field of serious combat where a razor across the face could finish you in an instant or a lead cosh could bring on a darkness you never knew existed. Experience of dealing with fear is what counts. Of course you never lose fear but countless fights let you master it for the briefest of times before it seeks to dominate you again.

That is why you might be a better fighter than the man in front of you but if he has mastered the blackness in himself and can read you like a road map, you have lost already. There is no such thing as a fair fight: there is only a winner and a loser and make no mistake, losing hurts like hell and stays with you for your whole life. You never forget the humiliation of a kicking and will dream of revenge all your life unless you can find ways of moving on.

Dad watched me like a wolf watching a lamb. He never even spoke as I reigned down insults on him until finally, when he knew and I knew that he had beaten me without even throwing a punch, he said with low menace, 'When you're ready boy'.

He had the dead flat eyes of man who has seen darkness and survived and he had seen darkness. He had seen his pals burnt alive; gunned to death in the screaming darkness of a howling bomber returning shot up from a mission in Germany. He has seen the flash of a knife held in the hand of drunken Swede as he tried to skewer him near the docks. He had gagged as he fished half rotten bodies out of the Thames with slimy limbs falling off the boat hook. All this and much more in his life had formed his background which I learned about much later. No wonder he was not worried by my anger. His own anger was probably much worse and only brought under control by heavy drinking. He spoke little about the horrors of war but once had become enraged at me when I had been flippant about war. I dropped the chair. The only way out was to back off into my bedroom and shut the door. I tried to hold back burning tears of humiliation. I had failed to stand up for Mother and of course for me. I knew it. My small dream of playing the hero and rescuing Mother was ground to dust. I waited for my bedroom door to turn. I heard the front door slam instead and sat on my bed dejected.

No mention was made of the confrontation the next day by any of us and life went on. It wasn't however, until about six months later that I finally gained my self respect, but at what cost? It was one Sunday lunchtime and Dad had just had dinner after returning from the pub. Conversation focused on the subject of judo and he asked about how my judo was progressing. His question had an aggressive edge to it and he dismissed judo as being a waste of time in a real situation.

He then personalised it by saying that it would be impossible for me to strangle him if he was ready for me. Mother tried to laugh it all off but now this had become serious. He had thrown out another challenge. I asked him if he was sure he wanted to test me and he laughed. I stood up from the table and so did he. We were opposite each other. This time, however, I felt confident in my abilities and feinted to his left with a jab watching him turn to avoid it. I then dropped my right shoulder and cut a 45 degree angle to my right on his blind side. I span around on my left foot and was now behind him.

I got what is known as a sleeper hold on him or a Japanese strangle. I placed my left arm around his neck, with my forearm bone bearing on his Adam's apple. I then put the back of my right arm, above the elbow, on his right shoulder and clasped my right bicep with my own left hand. I placed my right hand on the back of his head and pulled him backwards with my left forearm and pressed his head forward with my right hand. He tried to kick his heel back at my shins, he tried to butt me with the back of his head, he tried to bite my arm but I maintained pressure. I could feel him losing consciousness and he suddenly slipped to the ground. I let go.

This is a very dangerous hold and you can easily kill your opponent with it. If you know the right way, you can dislocate his neck. Worse, once the carotid arteries are compressed, there is a chance of them not opening up in the same way which can result in a stroke even if you take the pressure off the hold.

Part of me was exhilarated by my action. Mother had her hands thrown to her face and asked me in a trembling voice what I had done. I quickly dropped down to the floor in a panic but Dad thankfully was already starting to come round. I helped him to his feet and the reality of the situation flooded in to me. I tried to hug him as I held him up but he pushed me away and sat down at the table. He mumbled something about not being ready but I knew that at that instant, the balance of power had changed. I knew I would never let him slap Mother again. Part of me was elated but most of me just felt sick. I grabbed my coat and left the flat for the park.

I felt so sad. I also felt ashamed of what I had done. I thought how could I possibly have hurt him? I felt nothing but a feeling of emptiness and regret for a relationship that might have been. Later, when Dad was suffering from cancer, I thought that we felt closer to each other as I understood him more, but this was a bad time for me.

I love all our three sons and hope that the lessons I learned from my own relationship with my father have helped us build for the future. Some lessons are about not being afraid to show your true feelings, trying to speak honestly about things that matter to each other, having the courage of your convictions and trying to do the right thing even though it will cost you. All these things take a lifetime to learn and sometimes we only see what is broken when it is too late to repair the damage.

12

SHIPBROKING AND HEARTBREAK

Michelle was a bright light for me. Even though I had successfully attained three A-levels, I decided not to go to university fearing that it would break up our relationship. Instead, at the age of nineteen, I accepted a job with Stephenson Clarke Shipping Ltd, as a trainee shipbroker. I had little real idea of what was expected of me except that once a week I had to study shipping law at Holborn College. Can you think of anything duller?

Meeting Derek Beadle, who was my immediate boss, was the one saving grace of this job. Derek has the most mellifluous voice which I am sure could still charm women into bed over the telephone even though he is now in his eighties. Derek, a poet and patron of the arts, was my mentor. I still keep in touch with him and his charming Irish wife, Yvonne. I soon learned that I didn't have to worry about studying at Holborn College. I was enlightened by an older trainee: none of them bothered attending. You just signed in, or got someone else to do it for you, and then went to the pub. That was more like it.

However, my first job did give me an insight into the dreary nature of office life. The daily journey from Greenwich to London Bridge convinced me that whatever the future might hold, I was not going to be an office worker for the rest of my life. The journey itself was soul destroying. We fought for a seat on the overcrowded train or stood swaying and holding on to a chrome pole trying to read a paper through bleary eyes. I rubbed shoulders with ghostly, cold-eyed, silent pin-stripe types who haunted the carriage. You could have heard a pin drop on most days. This was not going to be my future.

Michelle and I spent all our spare time together, and I grew to know her and her family. We exchanged thoughts, aspirations and secrets. She had experienced much tragedy in her life already as she had lost her father, a petty officer in the US Navy, in a bizarre accident.

Michelle's parents,
Eve and Art,
were very much
in love,

Her father had an interesting history. He was the rebel in a very large Lutheran family in North Dakota. At the age of fifteen he had won a car in a lottery when gambling was seen by his family as the Devil's work. He ran away from home at a young age to join the navy. He was descended from Swedish immigrant farmers but seemed to love the bright lights more than the land and was a gambler with an eye for a good time. Michelle recalls his winning a flat in Mayfair and a Rolls Royce when playing poker in London.

He courted Michelle's mum, Eve, and they were a good-looking couple. Eve's was a classic beauty with fine chiselled features, almost Asiatic in bone structure. Michelle's parents were very much in love. They had two children, Michelle, and her younger brother, Peter. They lived in Italy for a while and Michelle remembers speaking Italian with the children there when she was about four years old.

Theirs was an ideal loving family until one night in Naples when the lights went out for them all. Michelle's Dad, known as 'Red' because of his red hair, apparently stood up from his desk, stepped back and fell down an open trap door located behind him. He was six foot two inches tall and falling down on to the floor below killed him. That was the official version. He was only twenty nine years old.

It is hard to imagine the impact of this accident on the family. Michelle's poor mother was devastated. The children were too young to understand what had happened but not too young to feel the loss.

There are so many questions about the incident that remain unanswered. Red was a well known gambler and had told Eve in a letter that all was not well. Did he owe money to the wrong people? Naples has a reputation for crime. Was Red mixing with dangerous people?

Michelle would dearly like to know the truth. She has never seen the official records but they will almost certainly contain the ambiguous statements on the lines of 'death by misadventure.' The trail is now so cold that it would be very difficult to pursue an investigation although we are inclined at least to obtain the official records.

Eve, Michelle and Peter flew back to cold England in a Dakota aircraft. Michelle remembers seeing the American flag draped across her Dad's coffin. She was sick on the flight. A fear of flying stayed with her for a long time, spilling into her adult life as she linked travel by aircraft to the powerfully bad memories surrounding her father's death. Thankfully, she has now mastered her fear of flying, having rationalized how those high definition images of her Dad's coffin had affected her.

Aged twenty four, Eve was now a widow with two young

children to support. She had a pension from the US govern-ment and was able to buy a modest semi-detached house in Plumstead but her children were fatherless and she ached daily for the loss of her beloved husband. She was never the same person after his death.

Eve's mother, known to me as 'Nan', lived in Teddington but she provided no emotional support for her daughter Her own husband had died of cancer at forty-nine, and she wallowed in self-pity. She could be great fun to be with but longed to be looked after herself and rejected any kind of personal responsibility for others. Eve had a sister, Shirley, who had also married an American serviceman as had their other sister, Grace. They both lived in the USA Shirley was an alcoholic although she would never admit it. They were not a close family, so Eve was isolated.

At the time I was introduced to Eve and Peter by Michelle, Eve was having a relationship with Bob, who lived in their home. Those of you who have seen the television programme *Only Fools and Horses* would recognise Bob as Del Boy, the main character; shifty yet likeable in his own way. Bob was a small time entrepreneur and distributor of goods, some of which were stolen. He worked in a local factory. He was short and stocky, going bald, and always dressed immaculately when he went out. He was a great man for cricket and captained his local team.

What Eve saw in him still baffles Michelle. Even though he had a kind heart, there was a very selfish streak in him and he could be very argumentative although he was never violent. He was constantly doing dodgy deals. For example, he once brought home some coats that had the label of a well-known fashion designer sewn into the lining. Michelle was trying on one of these coats and pretending to be on the catwalk when a picture of the very coat that she was modelling suddenly appeared on the TV. It was on the programme *Police 5* which sought help from the public to solve the crimes shown.

The coats had been stolen the previous week and Michelle was horrified when she discovered that she was actually wearing a stolen coat. Bob also brought home whisky and cigarettes which he stored in the shed. He often had to bribe the local police to turn a blind eye when their enquiries led to his door. He had a dry sense of humour and was never stumped for an answer. His phrase for all situations was, 'You've got to 'ave a laugh'. That phrase drove Michelle mad right up until Bob's death many years later: it covered up just about any inappropriate action.

Peter was rudderless. He had no role model for a father and Bob provided no emotional support for him. Aged fifteen, Peter had dyed his blond hair black and it hung down to his shoulders giving him a funereal look. I acted like a big brother to him and encouraged his interest in music. I gave him my old guitar and taught him basic guitar chords. He seemed talented and was keen to get a band going with his friends.

Peter was quiet but very bright. He suffered from a lack of hearing in one ear: he had been whacked so hard by a teacher that the ear had bled and the eardrum had almost burst. This in turn affected his academic performance and he started to play truant more and more regularly. He had no guidelines to keep him focused and he was drifting through life. He was angry but with no outlet for that anger.

Eve had a sad life with Bob. Michelle saw things happen to her Mum that a young girl should never have been exposed to. I liked Michelle's mum a lot. She could be funny, but smoked and drank too much for her own good. She ate like a sparrow.

Eve and Bob would row constantly. The rows usually caused by Bob's womanising for he fancied himself as a ladies' man. He had gold in his backyard and still had to mine for more, but mostly ended up with tin.

On occasion, Eve's mum had taken an overdose of pills, basically as a cry for help. However, she had always pulled through as she had a robust constitution. Eve despaired of Bob's infidelity and was driven to follow her Mum's example. She took an overdose of pills. Michelle is sure that she never intended to kill herself but just wanted Bob to see how his behaviour had become unbearable.

Eve did not have a robust constitution. She suffered from jaundice. She was rushed to hospital. I was taking part in a cricket match for Stephenson Clarke Shipping Limited. Michelle was there supporting me. No one had told us how serious Eve's condition was and we arrived at the hospital expecting to see her poorly, but alive.

We were in the waiting-room when the nursing sister came up and said in a cold voice that Eve had died. This seemed impossible to us. Michelle and Peter were devastated. Their mother was dead. She was only thirty seven years old. It was impossible, just impossible.

We were all in shock. Bob was useless to Michelle and Peter. He was dealing with his own demons. Michelle said she thought that no god would be so cruel as to take more of her family away from her after her Dad had died. She couldn't understand how Fate could be so merciless.

We were aged only seventeen and nineteen when this happened. We had no-one to help us and we made all the funeral arrangements and dealt with the endless details that death demands. Michelle displayed a maturity beyond her years. I took charge of the administration. Peter was too young to play a part and was a lost soul. Bob was... Bob.

For Michelle and Peter, Nan was now their only surviving relative in the UK but, as she wallowed in self-pity, she never gave her grandchildren any comfort.

Of course Michelle had me with whom to share her feelings, which helped, but Peter had no-one and just drifted away from home. Bob was true to form. It is hard to believe just how insensitive his actions were. About one week after Eve's death he invited another woman into the house for drinks. Michelle has never forgiven him for this.

One bright event did emerge when Red's family in the USA reacted to the tragedy by sending Michelle's uncle and paternal aunt, Len and Blanche, over to the UK. They came to see the situation for themselves and to make an assessment of the future needs of Red's children.

Their paternal family in the US had made contingency plans to care for Michelle and Peter and to take them back to the US with them to continue their education there. Blanche and Len were professional people. They reviewed the situation. Bob had applied for guardianship of Michelle and Peter. He held the house in trust for them and continued to pay the mortgage. Michelle had recently started a job as a secretary with an American company, Varityper, and her boss had been very kind to her during this difficult period. Peter was still at school, but he lacked commitment. Neither Michelle nor Peter wanted to move to the USA, despite the family offer of support, so Len and Blanche decided to let things be and returned to the USA. They were still determined to keep a close eye on how Michelle and Peter were coping with the aftermath of this latest tragedy.

Michelle is very appreciative of how Len and Blanche quickly sought to look after her and Peter and while they didn't have an immediate impact on the family, they would play an important future role in shaping Peter's life.

At the time, Michelle had settled down into her new job as a personal assistant to the sales manager at Varityper. The sales environment was lively and took her mind off problems at home. Bob was still womanising and Peter had gone completely off the tracks and had no job. He often slept rough and we suspected that he was doing a fair amount of substance abuse.

Life continued as it does, indifferent to tragedy or happiness. Michelle and I both worked in London and met for lunch almost daily. I spent some of my lunchtime before meeting Michelle going through the *Daily Telegraph* job section sitting on the top of the roof of the Stephenson and

Clarke's building looking at the splendid view of the river. I used to apply for any job that caught me eye, just for the hell of it, and became really confident at interviews. Mostly, I didn't care if I got the job or not.

At one interview, I was asked to fill in a profile test that finished by asking for a description of my personality in one hundred words. I wrote, *'Concise'*. I didn't get the job.

I remember another occasion when I was idly flicking through the *Daily Telegraph* on a bright Wednesday lunchtime while looking at the great views of London from Tower Bridge to Vauxhall Bridge, when I saw an advert which mentioned brothels. Sex. That caught my eye. It must be worth a read. The advert said that if brothels closed down in one part of the world then the impact of that closure could be a problem for the UK. Why not join the Immigration Service and help resolve it? I had no idea what the Immigration Service was, and couldn't have cared less, but the advert did go on to say that candidates should have at least one foreign language and I had two.

Something happened at this time which confirmed my opinion that it was definitely time to get out of my current job. One of my tasks was to manage the arrival of ships discharging coal at the power stations on the Thames. If you were on duty, you had to get into the office for 7.00 am. You might get a call from a ship's agent to confirm that the destination to unload coal was as previously stated and that there had been no change of circumstances. Together with the Central Electricity Generating Board, Head Office was pivotal in deciding where the ships would discharge their cargoes. If Head Office told the ship's captain to unload coal at Blackwall Point then he would head there.

I had a note to say that a Stephenson & Clarke vessel was to proceed to Blackwall Point, below the bridges and unload its coal. I confirmed this in a subsequent telephone call from the ship. Some hours later a furious captain, spitting feathers, contacted our office manager and cursed me for all he was worth. Apparently, it had been impossible for the ship to get on to the berth at Blackwall Point because it was being dredged. Therefore, 3,000 tons of coal were not unloaded on schedule. Which idiot had told him to unload there?

The director, Mr Pipe-smoking, Tweed-jacketed, boring Dallimore, confirmed to me that I was the idiot who had lost the company a substantial amount of money by sending the ship to the wrong place. Great morning! There was much merriment in the office and most of it was directed my way. My management did not take part in the merriment. Derek Beadle was thoughtful, Mr Creelman, head of the section, strangely, avoided my eye.

I knew that shipbroking was not what I was cut out for. Most people treated me as an idiot that day but I still could not, for the life of me, find the note. Had it existed before the decision was made or had I made a mistake? Was an office scapegoat needed? Of course readers who already know of my previous mishaps and failings will come to the conclusion that it was obviously my fault but it still remains a mystery to me until this day. What do you make of my fellow worker Bruce's comment to me during the coffee break? – 'I told you to watch your back here.' It was true, he had in fact told me to watch my back. This was easier said than done.

Just as I felt that the bottom was dropping out of my current job, a lifeline opened up for me. I had forgotten all about my application to join the Civil Service until I received an appointment for an interview four months afterwards. It was to be held on a Wednesday. I took the day off. I can't remember where the interview took place but it was in a grand old building with lofty ceilings, not far from Whitehall. The chairman of the interview board put me at ease asking me about my background and interests.

One of the board members then asked me to imagine working on a ship as an immigration officer. He gave me this scenario: I am required to examine the passport of an American national who is drunk. He is belligerent and refuses to show me his passport. What do I do? I explained that I would humour the American. I had had experience of dealing with drunk people, including my own father. Generally most drunks respond well to humour. The aim is to see if he is a potential problem and, if not, get him back up to the bar and out of the way.

I was sure that I could get the drunk to show me the document without having to threaten him with the law. The interview panel seemed to like my answer and then another board member asked me if I would like to join HM Customs & Excise. I told him I wouldn't mind but did not have a great knowledge of their work. I had very little knowledge about what an immigration officer did either. I told the board that if I was accepted then my job placement would be best decided by their judgment. I thanked them for the interview.

One month later, I received a letter congratulating me on being selected to join HM Immigration Service. I was ordered to report to State House near Holborn for a three-week training course. Funny how I had just escaped from one side of Holborn and now was going back there to start a new adventure. After the course, I was to be posted to Dover. Dover, the gateway to England. My future.

13

DOVER – GATEWAY TO A NEW LIFE

Michelle and I got engaged. My proposal of marriage was made in the most romantic of places. We were in Normandy at the time, touring in a beaten-up old Mini. Its rear suspension needed fixing and as a consequence the exhaust pipe banged onto the road surface when we went over bumps, leaving showers of sparks in our wake. I didn't have enough money both to fix the car and go on holiday.

We had been together for nearly four years and had shared difficult times. I loved her and saw our future together. One evening, I arranged for us to have dinner in a restaurant situated in an old chateau. There were suits of armour standing silently watchful in the corners of the dining-room and pennants flying proudly from the rafters. The tablecloths were starched white and there was an elegance about the dining room that was slightly intimidating. The menu was in French and therefore incomprehensible – all French menus in four-star and above restaurants are meant to intimidate, even if your knowledge of the language is reasonable.

I stumbled my way through the menu and dealt with the numerous questions from Michelle concerning content, in a disingenuous manner. I ordered oysters to start with. I had never eaten oysters before. An unwise move.

As I slipped the first one down my throat, all traces of sophistication were lost. I choked on the seawater left in the shell. My spluttering certainly attracted attention from the other diners and the waiters looked on contemptuously.

We soldiered on in true British fashion and, once I had regained my composure, we attacked the main course. We drank sparkling wine from Normandy vineyards in crystal clear glasses. At the right moment, I asked Michelle to marry me. She said, 'Yes', and we toasted our love. We were just children in so many ways and yet in others worldly wise beyond our years.

When we returned from our holiday, my parents, Michelle's mum and her step-father, Bob, were all happy with our news. Our friends were delighted. Dad threw an engagement party for us in the Rose and Crown pub in Greenwich and we celebrated with family and friends.

We were now formally engaged to be married. In hindsight, neither of us had set out with this intention and the realisation that we were making a commitment for the future had us both worried. Michelle had been through so much that taking such a decision must have been difficult. The keystone, however, was that we cared for each other enough to see a future together, even if that future was unclear.

Dover was to play a big part in our future. We needed to visit the port in order to find out what we were letting ourselves in for. One grey rainy day in winter, we left London, driving in my white Sunbeam Alpine with the blue hardtop. I had bought the car as I had wanted a sports car and this was the nearest affordable substitute. It was actually classed as a coupé and so it cost less to insure than a sports car – a prime consideration. We travelled on the old A2 Canterbury-Dover road. Canterbury is an interesting historical city and you can see the cathedral and enjoy the sight of the old city walls as you drive through it. Otherwise, the road to Dover at that time was straight and uninteresting. The closer we got to Dover, the greyer the skies became.

We parked on the sea front. The horizontal rain was heavy and you could just about make out ships anchored in the gloom within the harbour. Giant waves smashed against the harbour walls. All seemed grey. It was dispiriting. We both sat in the car thinking about our future. It didn't feel like a happy occasion. We drove nearer to the town centre and thought that a plate of fish and chips might cheer us up If your spirits are low, a piece of battered cod can make all the difference. After two hours, we left Dover and returned to London. I don't think that we spoke much during the journey. I was thinking about the sort of life we would have in this dull, grey place. I think that Michelle must also have been wondering about her future.

The dice were cast. Shortly after our return, I had to move to Dover by myself until I could find a place for us. I left Michelle in London, living with Bob. I moved into a flat with two immigration officers, Ian Osborn and Gavin Littlejohn whom I had met on my immigration foundation course in London. The address was 10 Park Avenue, Dover. Ian was from Stow-on-the-Wold and had an easy-going manner, a good sense of humour and a complete disregard for fashion. He was an accomplished artist with a real eye for detail and was very good company.

Gavin was from Scotland. He had lived in Kirkintillock, a 'dry' town which meant that no alcohol was sold there on any day, and he was unworldly. Everything was new to him. He was spindly thin and suffered from horrible nightmares. He would wake up in the middle of the night screaming. It was always the same dream. He would be running down an alley pursued closely by a man with a knife who was getting nearer and nearer. He could hear his pursuer's breathing. He could feel the cut of the knife as it struck his back. He would wake up just as the knife was sinking deeper into his flesh. It was a terrible dream for him.

However, Ian and I soon became sick of the screaming and we would tell him to shut up and let us get some sleep. We were kind and caring companions. Many years later, Gavin took his own life. The demons that pursued him during the time he lived with us eventually killed him.

The house we rented was large. I had the bedroom on the top floor. The bed had an ancient mattress that folded when you got into bed. It felt like you were actually sleeping on the floor, and that in fact may have been more comfortable.

I missed Michelle and encouraged her to join me in the flat at weekends. I wanted to test out what marriage was like before we took the final step. She came, she saw, she was not impressed. Her first act was to wash the kitchen floor and find that the grey tiles were in fact yellow. Michelle was used to looking after a household and she quickly established what needed to be done with ours in order to make the flat at least habitable. She organised us.

Michelle was a fine-looking young woman with long blond hair cascading down on to her shoulders. I think that Gavin fell in love with her almost immediately. I would often see him giving her sideways glances that spoke of his undeclared love. I didn't mind. Michelle was not the kind of woman to flirt and I didn't either, although I have always had an eye for a pretty woman.

We began to assess Dover. It was a strange place. There was no real centre. The port generated income from passengers, cars and freight traffic arriving and leaving on the cross-channel ferries. A high proportion of the people who lived in Dover worked on the boats, or represented the immigration and customs authorities or the police. There were many estate agents selling property at the lower end of the market. The locals had a pronounced Kentish accent and the town centre often seemed to be filled up with men, women and children with grim faces, wearing anoraks and facing hopeless futures, locked in an area of high unemployment. The once thriving mining community had failed, leaving large numbers unemployed. There was a welfare culture here and that was evident from looking at the shops which catered for the lower end of the market.

Dover once had a magnificent sweep of houses on its sea front. However, probably after money changed hands, the council pulled down the Victorian houses of character in order to put up the Gateway flats which were originally council houses and are now private flats.

The flats retained the original curve of the sea front, following the line of the promenade but were an example of the bleak, unimaginative architecture of the 1960s. In spite of this, the sea front still provided an excellent promenade with interesting views of the castle and bustling harbour.

That harbour was big and boiled with boats during the busy summer period. It was interesting. However, looking back into town from the sea front presented a poor vista: a tired high street and a range of dreary pubs that had a weary down-trodden look about them.

Nevertheless, the magnificent mediaeval castle built in the 12th century dominated the hill to the east. Dover Castle has a historic past and of course experienced French domination. It has been described as the 'Key to England'. It is magnificent. It has a complex of tunnels built in the 1800s which could accommodate nearly two thousand soldiers. In the Second World War, these tunnels played a vital role when they were used as the HQ for planning and executing the withdrawal of our forces from Dunkirk.

Oddly, Dover was growing on me. We had so much fun in the flat in Park Avenue and at times it was bedlam. An old lady, the mother of the owner, lived downstairs and we would often take it in turns to go down and chat to her to keep her company. She probably had early-stage Alzheimer's but we just thought that she was a bit batty. She regularly left the chip pan on which meant the smoke would billow up into our lounge, choking us until we ran downstairs to put out the fire. We were indifferent cooks ourselves. Our most memorable meal was one that Ian and I prepared. We had invited twelve guests to join us for dinner to celebrate New Year's Eve. The provision of drink was not a problem as we obtained it when travelling on the cross-channel ferries during our work as immigration officers. We paid duty-free prices and we had endless supplies of liquor. We thought about the meal. I based our strategy on the *Art of War* by Sun Tzu. The first principle was:

> An attack may lack ingenuity, but it must be delivered with supernatural speed.

We definitely lacked ingenuity but we thought that we could handle the speed requirement in a manner that was both super and natural. We needed food fast but not fast food. We had planned the whole meal while drinking one lunchtime in The Park Inn in Dover. We launched ourselves into the butcher's in Dover High Street and bought the largest turkey we could find. We also bought vegetables and potatoes at the nearby greengrocers. So far, so good.

We lugged the enormous turkey home and at 3.00 p.m., we threw it on to the kitchen table. Neither of us had ever cooked a turkey, but how hard could it be? I jabbed it with my finger only to find that it nearly broke the digit – hmmm. We agreed that it needed defrosting and explored various ways of doing so.

We hit on the idea of filling the bath with very hot water and immersing the frozen fowl in it. We also poured a couple of kettles of hot water over the turkey to make sure that it defrosted. We decided that two hours of immersion would do the trick. This left ample time for us to prepare the vegetables and spuds while drinking red wine. Our guests were due to arrive at 6.00 p.m. All was going to plan. All we needed was patience. Sun Tzu advised us on this:

> If a general is unable to control his impatience and orders his troops to swarm up the wall like ants, one-third of them will be killed without taking the city.

Therefore, with this in mind, we resisted the urge to check the temperature of the bird too early as clearly it needed to thaw at its own pace. At 5.30 p.m., I sauntered into the bathroom and gave the bird a light poke. The result was nearly another broken finger. An urgent discussion with my co-chef ensued. We had a brainwave, again based on Sun Tzu:

If the enemy is strong and I am weak, I temporarily withdraw and do not engage.

This bird was definitely strong. My finger was weak. Time to withdraw.

There are suitable times and appropriate days on which to raise fires.

Excellent advice from the sage. We would borrow the blow lamp from our neighbour. We would not fight the bird until it was significantly weakened. This was a brilliant idea and Ian went on a mission, returning in double quick time with the blow lamp.

We took the turkey down to the garden and put it on a piece of cardboard. We decided that it would be best if we removed the cellophane wrapper – a key joint decision. I lit the blow lamp and Ian waved it about, rather recklessly in my view, perhaps as a result of that last large glass of red wine. A fierce discussion ensued between us about the correct distance from which to torch the bird and there was some alarm when a wing start to blacken as Ian experimented with this distance. The smell of paraffin from the blow lamp assailed our nostrils. This was not the mouth-watering aroma that we had been anticipating.

There seemed to be no point in standing over the bird with a flame and so the blow lamp was positioned three feet away. Its flame made a rather pleasing heat haze as it warmed up the turkey. We decided to go back upstairs for a refill of red wine and let our strategy play out. After all, we could still see the damn thing from the upstairs kitchen window while we sat and chatted.

Our leisure was short-lived. There were signs of burning. We decided that putting the bird back in hot water in the bath was better than burning it so we extinguished the blow lamp and carried the turkey back upstairs, inhaling a mixture of paraffin fumes at the same time. We added more hot water to the bath and supplemented it with boiling kettles. We were resolute.

> One defends when his strength is inadequate; he attacks when it is abundant.

We thought that it was time to defend, as time itself was marching on and we had forgotten about the guests who were due to arrive at 6.00 p.m. We heard knocking on the door and the sound of guests singing merrily. Doubtless they were eager for food and drink. We needed to reverse that order.

We exchanged determined glances and welcomed them in. Michelle kissed me heartily and asked how our preparations were going. I dealt deftly with her enquiry about this and the food and dining arrangements. The key thing was to get them all drinking, and to do it fast.

Time crept on and occasionally we prodded the turkey until, eventually, we found that the skin actually gave way a little under pressure. We had a feeling of success. We decided simply to ignore the burnt parts of the bird from the blow lamp episode. Our oven had been on for some time and so we agreed that now was the time to cook the bird.

We doused it liberally with cooking oil, sprinkled the skin with some herbs from an ancient jar that we had found in the kitchen and then put the bird in the oven. Now we really could get the party started.

Someone noticed that the table had not been set so we

delegated that task to the guests and drank more red wine. We even had Christmas crackers to pull as well as serviettes to wipe the mouth-watering gravy from diner's lips. It was all going wonderfully well.

In spite of the tribulations we had faced over the day, Ian and I had not exchanged one cross word between us. Some of you men might find that a bit of a puzzle. It is not unusual to be only five minutes in the kitchen with your partner and feel that you are in the middle of a war zone, battered by advice, some well-meaning and some downright hurtful. But it shows that by sticking to the advice found in ancient Chinese philosophy, harmony can be achieved.

It was now 10.30 p.m. and the guests were nearly all as pissed as parrots, ravenous and would probably have eaten a chair leg if one were to be put in front of them.

Delicious smells were coming from the oven – mixed, it has to be said, with a faint whiff of paraffin – and Ian sank a fork into the bird's leg. The fork went partially in and some juice ran out of the flesh, mixed with a bit of blood. Ian had now taken over the role of Master Chef and so he declared that in precisely one hour we would be ready to eat. There were drunken cheers at this announcement.

But then, in genuine alarm, he took me aside and said that we had forgotten the pudding. It was true. We had to have a pudding. What did Sun Tze have to say about this?

All warfare is based on deception.

After a hurried discussion, we assessed what ingredients we had in the kitchen cupboard that might be suitable. There were two bunches of bananas and a jar of strawberry jam. A dessert formed in our minds which focused on chopped bananas with a dribble of jam – *la nouvelle cuisine.* I chopped the bananas and Ian dribbled the jam on to twelve plates.

We were ready.

The table looked wonderful in the candlelight even though there were not enough crackers for everyone. We noticed that a couple of guests seemed to have passed out but we woke them up and announced that we had deliberately kept dinner back to 11.00 p.m. so that we would be finished eating by midnight, in time for the New Year celebrations.

Nobody cared by then. I have to say that I was feeling a bit wobbly but I was in great spirits. The evening was reaching a climax.

The guests were now seated at the table in the lounge. We carried the turkey from the oven to the kitchen table and carved it. We didn't really want the guests to be worried about uncooked or burnt bits. Truthfully, it still smelled slightly of paraffin but we decided that this could be masked by the great gravy that Ian had whisked up, adding to it a substantial slug of whisky. The potatoes and other vegetables were heaped and ready to serve.

By this time, our guests were completely beyond caring about food and a few could not actually be encouraged to wake up, but we sat down, raised our glasses to toast humanity and saw in the New Year, replete, intoxicated with alcoholic liquor to the point of impairment of physical and mental faculties, in danger of food poisoning, but still merry.

With the praise for the triumph of the banana surprise still ringing in our ears, with crackers exploding and noisy kissing, we finished the evening. Despite all our efforts, no-one ended up in hospital. We sank gratefully into oblivion and left Gavin to do the washing-up, telling him that it would be better if he stayed up all night in order to avoid his recurring nightmare. Helpful to the last.

Of course Sun Tzu summarized our entire success in these wise words:

When the wind blows during the day, it will die down at night.

There was wind from the turkey gases and that night we definitely all died down, or passed out. I recall waking up the next day with a brain full of cotton wool, little Swiss gnomes wielding hammers in my skill and thinking that I might leave next year's New Year's Eve dinner party to someone else.

My immigration career began at Western Docks. This part of the port is formed by the western arm of the harbour, Admiralty Pier, and its associated port facilities. It was initially used as a terminal for the 'Golden Arrow' and other cross-channel train services. It had its own railway station – Dover Marine, later renamed Dover Western Docks. The railway station closed in 1994.

Originally, this was where all passengers seeking to enter the UK at Dover arrived. The train from London used to arrive in the station and passengers then walked along the platform to immigration controls under an immense glass roof. The whole place had a pre-war air about it. You expected to see khaki-clad soldiers with tin helmets, smoking Players cigarettes and chatting to nurses as they got off the train. In reality all you saw were heavily laden tourists, trailed by disgruntled children, grimly determined to head for the Continent.

My initial immigration course at State House in Holborn had prepared me for work at the Western Docks control. It was on that course I learned how to consume enormous amounts of bitter at lunchtime and how to hold my bladder most of the afternoon until the coffee break came. It was a vital skill that had to be mastered if you were to survive the course, as you didn't want to interrupt a speaker by leaving the room. It was considered bad form.

What little knowledge I acquired for safeguarding the realm from 'Johnny Foreigner' was drilled into me on the course. I also met some great characters, many of whom became lifelong friends. These included Dave Woodward and his French wife, Nelly.

Dave contributed significantly to Nelly's ability to speak English and so she spoke Cockney-English with a French accent: a delightful combination. She was also celebrated for producing bottles of her uncle's home-made hooch. This was a deadly concoction. We spent many an evening in digs in Dover during our early days sharing this killer potion and feeling like death the next day.

Once we had finished the training course at State House, we were fully-fledged immigration officers and expected to be fully functional immediately. It was a vain hope.

My job was to interview incoming passengers from Belgium and France to see if they qualified for entry into the UK. If they didn't meet the requirements of the immigration rules, we would arrange for them to be returned to their point of departure. Just imagine the variety of people who were seeking entry. Some were bizarre and others plain nasty. They included Iranian tractor salesmen, gaming-machine operators, Japanese chicken sexers, (yes it's true) Italian waiters, Algerian thugs and ex-Nazis posing as happy tourists. It was an amazingly multifarious list.

It was my job to spot the fraudster amongst the genuine applicants. We had an astonishing group of linguists among us to facilitate communication. In fact, the only way to get a pay rise in the immigration service, apart from promotion, was to learn another language. I spoke French, Spanish, Portuguese and Serbo-Croat to a reasonable level and managed some German, Dutch, Italian and Japanese. Later on in life, when I worked on the car booths at Eastern Docks, I could say to the car driver, 'Switch off your engine' in thirteen different languages before I started on my interview. This was a practical necessity as it stopped me being choked to death by fumes.

The Home Office paid us extra for reading and speaking two 'easy' languages, generally Latin-based European languages, and then up to two 'hard' languages, for example, Arabic, Chinese or Slavonic languages.

I was selected to go on to a six-month Serbo-Croat course in Holborn. This is the third time Holborn has featured in this story. I hadn't realised until writing this chapter that it had played such a notable part in my life. The course was paid for by the Home Office. My reason for selecting such an esoteric language was that there were hardly any Serbo-Croat speakers working at the port despite having many problems caused by the arrival of Yugoslavs seeking entry. With fluency in Serbo-Croat, I could spend my time interpreting for officers rather than working behind a desk interviewing passengers. This proved to be a fine strategy, if only for a short time.

You were expected to pass an examination in order to be paid the language allowance and a Home Office language exam was the equivalent of the Foreign Office's lower diplomatic level exam. The exams themselves were often unintentionally hilarious.

You were required to take a written paper and translate passages from your chosen language into English. After the written paper came an oral examination which lasted about twenty minutes. The aim was to test your understanding in a wide-ranging interview. If your exam was in the afternoon, you would meet up in a pub close to the examination centre. More often than not, you would have far too much to drink in order to relax inhibitions and loosen your tongue. One colleague, taking his German exam, went in, wrote his name to confirm who he was and then was unable to utter a word as he was too drunk to do so. The examiner was unimpressed and an official complaint ensued.

I also recall going in to take a French oral exam with a pipe-smoking examiner who wore a tweed jacket and, fuelled by alcohol, I chose to start the conversation by telling him two filthy French jokes, the second of which made his pipe drop out of his mouth. I passed the exam. God alone knows how.

A friend of mine from Cornwall was on the Serbo-Croat course with me and we had a drink in the pub before the exam. He was also thinking of impressing the examiner with a saucy story. He told me about an experience he had had with a French girl. He had given the girl her first orgasm. He said that she had been so impressed with his technique that she had told her friend what a great lover he was and had invited her to hide under the bed in advance of their next session in order to confirm her assessment. The friend had hidden but she could hardly bear the moaning and groaning anymore and jumped up, tore off her clothes and hopped into bed. This was much to the alarm of my friend who nearly fell from the mounted position and on to the bedroom floor.

He said that the girls had giggled and he had been invited to perform his wonders on the new guest. The original girlfriend had then given him helpful hints so that her friend could also achieve an orgasm herself. That story fired my imagination and, understandably, he remembered it as the highlight of his life. On reflection, and after many pints, he decided that his vocabulary in Serbo-Croat would not be up to the challenge. Worse, the examiner might not have a sense of humour. The drink left him in high spirits and we laughed about his exploits and tried to translate parts of them in to Serbo-Croat.

He wasn't in quite such high spirits later that afternoon, however, when, on taking his oral Serb-Croat exam with an examiner called Mr Jovanovic from the BBC Foreign Languages Department, he couldn't recall any words of the language. He suffered a complete mental block. The examiner told him that he was useless – in English – and suggested that he practise more and try again next year.

Saving what was left of his dignity, he stood up, did an about turn (he had had a drink or two) and marched swiftly and confidently towards the hotel door – exams took place in London hotels then – only to find that he was staring at the broom cupboard! He said that he could still hear Mr Jovanovic's laughter as he finally left the room the right way.

Serbo-Croat is a difficult language. In fact it is two languages, Serbian and Croatian, so it was challenging to learn. My own experience with Mr Jovanovic was just as amusing. He asked me to describe what steps I would have to take in order to cast a vote in the British elections. Now this seems a straightforward enough task but, in a foreign language, with a limited vocabulary, it is much more demanding.

The key thing is to keep it simple. I told him that I would leave my house, get into my car and drive down to my local village. On arrival at the village hall, I would be given a piece of paper with the names of the candidates written on it. I would then write a cross against the name of the candidate whom I had selected. I only got as far as that because he had started laughing.

In English, he said, 'No you wouldn't, my friend. You just told me that you pissed on the candidate.'

Metaphorically, I might have done, but not practically. I left without securing a pass in the oral that day but succeeded the next year with an outstanding mark in both the written and oral exam: 90%. I thought that they must have confused my paper with someone else's.

As immigration officers (IOs), we regularly used to cross the Channel on the ferries. The destinations were Ostend, Zeebrugge, Dunkerque, Boulogne or Calais. Some crossings, such as those to Ostend, were done at night-time.

This is how a typical night crossing took place. On arrival for night duty at Western Docks, you would meet the other IO who was to cross on the boat and work with you. You would go to the immigration office located upstairs at the end of the platform to prepare and update your 'Suspect Index' which recorded the names of persons of interest to the enforcement agencies. You would acquaint yourself with what was happening in the immigration world and then you would go to the pub, the Cinque Ports, at the entrance to the dock to discuss the night ahead. There might be other IOs in there who had just finished their shift.

Four to six pints later, and now full of local knowledge, you would collect your immigration case and march on to the ship together with the other crossing officer. You would deposit your official cases in the secure storage and your bags in the cabin allocated to you. You would stroll to the bar to converse with the purser and others while drinking your preferred drink of beer, whisky or wine. By this time, the ship would have left the dock and been at sea. In the winter months, the ship would be rolling badly and the passengers would be starting to be sick. Time for dinner. The best place to be when passengers are being sick is in the bar or the restaurant as only those with strong stomachs are there.

Usually, you would drink a small aperitif before dinner before tucking into a splendid steak – if it was a Belgian boat, the steak would be horse meat – and chips. This fine meal would normally be accompanied by a bottle of wine. By midnight, you would have already consumed far too much alcohol. The ship would arrive in the port of Ostend at 1.00 a.m and it was time to see your police counterparts and discuss any matters of mutual interest with them.

We would always take an offering of some sort, usually a bottle of whisky, and would be offered refreshment in return, usually in the form of Pernod. After an hour or so of small talk, we would know that the ship had been loaded with passengers. We would bid farewell to the police and board the ship. This is where our work would begin. We now would drink only coffee as clearly we were on duty.

There were often endless lines of people to deal with and we had to examine them and determine if they qualified for entry. We were always highly professional and we would never appear worse for wear. Anything less was considered to be the height of bad form by fellow officers.

We would arrive at Dover at 6.00 a.m. when we would hand over our detainees to the day shift. The detainees would be applicants whom we considered did not meet the criteria for entry and needed further examination on arrival in the UK. We would visit the office in order to complete our paperwork and it would be routine to have completed the shift by 8.30 a.m.

At that time, our thoughts should have turned to going home, however, this was not always the case. There was much to discuss concerning events during the crossing and so we would sometimes go down to the bar on the station for an early morning drink. We would have breakfast at a greasy spoon café at the end of the platform if we had not already had breakfast on board in which case, it might well have started with a gin and tonic at the bar. Whatever the level of alcohol in your blood, you drove your car home.

Michelle had usually gone to work by the time I returned. Blearily, I would fall into bed only to repeat the sequence the following night. I was once awoken by my elderly next door neighbour who was enquiring why I had parked our car in the middle of our lawn and left the doors open and the lights on. Time to reconsider my lifestyle.

In retrospect, it seems amazing that we managed to consume that amount of booze and live. How did we do a credible job at the same time as drinking so heavily? Why were we allowed to drink on duty? How did we avoid hitting anything or driving off a cliff on the way home?

Of course not all IOs were drinkers but I have to say that most of my friends were. The situation couldn't go on, and after a few incidents such as an IO falling off a bridge in Calais and drowning, the noose on loose behaviour was tightened and the drinking culture rightfully started to be brought under control.

It was just as well, as livers are costly to replace. Still, the camaraderie within the immigration service was great and I made many good friends, some of whom I still keep in touch with today.

Western Docks started to run down in the early 1970s, and Eastern Docks, situated at the other end of the Dover promenade, became the main focus for cross-channel traffic. It was also a freight terminal with a huge capacity for dealing with high numbers of arrivals onshore. This meant that the system of having immigration and customs officers crossing on ships was no longer effective. I volunteered to transfer from Western Docks to the new controls at Eastern Docks as I could see that was there that the future lay for immigration control at the ports. Western Docks were dying. I left behind the old lags who were mostly pipe-smokers with only a few years left before retirement or death.

The early wild days of immigration lay behind me. Having survived them, I can look back and view them as great fun while they lasted.

14

Marriage, Lobster and Fine Cognac

Michelle and I were married on 20 June 1970 after a one year engagement. We wanted to get married at our local Catholic church, Our Lady Star of the Sea, which was near my home. It was our family church. However, the priest was not prepared to make our pathway towards marriage a smooth one.

To have the wedding we wanted, Michelle would have to promise that we would bring up all our children as Catholics. It was blackmail. I was not happy about entering into this agreement but Michelle was unconcerned. There was pressure from my family to have a Catholic wedding and my mother had asked my cousin, Father Harry Bannigan, if he would come over from Ireland in order to officiate. It would be an honour if he accepted but we felt that we were losing control of how we wanted the wedding to be arranged. But we were young and, in the end, we just went with the flow.

Michelle didn't like the start of her wedding day. In fact she didn't like her wedding dress either. Having lost her Mum, she lacked the support she needed to make a choice of dress that she really liked and she accepted a dress that looked good on her but was not stunning in the way a bride would want it to be.

On the day of the wedding she was alone in the house. Bob went off to work with the intention of returning at midday. Peter was not around and her Aunt Shirley, who had come over especially from the USA for the wedding,

137

chose not to be with her at the start of the day. Michelle recalls cleaning the doorstep before she changed into her dress. She was sad that she had no family support. I didn't realise that she would be so alone. I just assumed that Bob and Shirley would be with her. It was not very caring of me.

Our Wedding Day.

After an unfortunate start, the wedding day went smoothly and Mother and Dad were really proud of us. Dad especially loved Michelle and Mother was also very fond of her. We arrived at the church in a vehicle that looked like a mafia staff car driven by a huge fat man in a chauffeur's outfit that was bursting at the seams – because of his bulk. Bob had paid for the car. He always confused quantity and quality. Hence the size of the car.

Many relatives came to the wedding from England, Ireland, Wales and the USA. It was a big wedding party and our guests seemed really happy for us. We went to Woolwich for the reception. Our timing was uncoordinated and we arrived early at the Shakespeare Hotel in the mafia car. It was apparent that the staff were not ready for us and so we had to wait outside in the car for ten minutes before being asked in. Guests then arrived in large numbers and the party began to swing. The band that Bob had booked for the evening was a small three piece combo which lacked fire. Big Ken, father of our old friends Elaine and small Ken, decided to take over and front the show that evening. Ken was a born entertainer and loved the lime-light. His flow of jokes and general good-natured banter helped the evening on its way and the band seemed to appreciate his showmanship. All our guests enjoyed themselves and the evening passed in a blur for us, in the midst of all the excitement.

Michelle and I spent our wedding night at the Westmoreland Hotel in Blackheath, which later became the Chinese Embassy. It's good to have a connection with the Chinese in this day and age when they are poised to take over the world! I don't think that our first married night together was memorable for romantic reasons. Michelle struggled to get the thousand pins out of her hair and the ones that escaped during this complicated procedure made it dangerous to walk on the bathroom floor. We were both exhausted when we eventually fell into bed. That night, sleep was more important than romance.

The following day we awoke to sunlight streaming in through the bedroom window. A new day was born. We were now married. We set off for a honeymoon in Jersey. When I had planned the journey I had been conscious of one consideration in particular – money. I was almost broke. As an immigration officer, I could benefit from a concession on rail travel, and this included travel to Jersey, therefore I bought two cut-price tickets. I remember our departure day well as it coincided with the day of the World Cup quarter final between Brazil and England. You might think that I should have taken this event into consideration during the planning phase. The train took us to the ship. I hadn't thought it would be necessary to pre-book seats onboard. It never occurred to me that seating would be a problem. Imagine my surprise, and Michelle's comments, when we found that the ship was packed and that all the seats were occupied. It was only a nine-hour crossing! Apparently, at this time of the year, it was not unusual for the boat to be full. Michelle still recalls, with some venom, this uncomfortable start to our honeymoon.

I had chosen the hotel from a brochure and price had dictated my choice. It not exactly in the budget category, but no-one staying there, except us, seemed to be under the age of sixty. After our first night, as we entered the breakfast room, the guests actually clapped us in, much to our embarrassment. Michelle was unimpressed with our room, having found an old sock under the bed. I thought that it served her right for looking under hotel beds. In retrospect, my poor selection of the hotel didn't set the right tone for the rest of our lives and Michelle must have been thinking that she had made a big mistake in marrying me. But I had to face reality. We had spent our money on the wedding and there was very little left in reserve. We wandered about Jersey thumbing lifts to various coves, sunbathing and saving our money for a blow-out last night feast in a posh restaurant. We actually had a good time there in our own way but on reflection it was a poor choice of honeymoon location by me. On the last night we dined on lobster and wine and it was the highlight of the week. We haven't been back to Jersey since then but, if we ever do go, then have no doubt that I will pre-book seats on the boat, find a great hotel in which to stay and make up for the poor show that I made of the honeymoon all those years ago.

We returned to Dover broke but married. We could hardly get into our bedroom at Park Avenue for wedding presents. We started married life folded together at night in our single bed. Our bedroom was literally in the attic. It was spooky and Michelle never felt safe when I was on night duty and she was left alone. Once the presents were unwrapped, she had nothing to do but could hardly live the existence of a princess for long, so she started to look for work. She was offered a job as a dental receptionist in a practice just a few minutes walk away. He was a foul, pipe-smoking old lecher who was constantly leering at her. He was also incompetent. He extracted one of her teeth just because she said it was aching. He convinced patients to pay privately for their treatment with him but Michelle said that he gave them exactly the same treatment as they would have been given under the NHS dental scheme. She detested him and left this employment as soon as she could. She then applied for a job with Halpins, a transport company.

Coincidentally, my Dad knew some of the owners of Halpins from his police days and he thought that they were rogues, but all the management were very good to Michelle. How did she get the job? The local Dover manager had advertised for an office worker for their Halpins office located within Eastern Docks. There were many applicants. When Michelle went for the interview, she was wearing a short red dress and had long blonde hair. That seemed to be enough for him as she rocketed to the top of the list with barely a question being asked. He offered her the job there and then. He also offered her a lot more later, even though he was married with children, but she warned him off. Apparently, he was a known womaniser with a track record but, despite having to fend off her boss, Michelle enjoyed working there and the office had a lively atmosphere.

With my salary supplemented by Michelle's, as well as income derived from my sideline of teaching karate, we were able to save a deposit for a house. We were innocents in our dealings with the housing market and had little idea about what we really wanted. We jumped at the first bungalow that was on offer to us in our price range, a small two-bedroom property that was located in Castle Drive, Whitfield, just three miles outside Dover. It was a mistake as it needed money to be spent on it in order to modernise the kitchen and the lounge. Fortunately, the deal fell through. We then bought the bungalow opposite.

We loved our first house which was bright and cheerful. It was situated in a quiet road surrounded by similar houses. It had a kitchen which looked on to a small garden with a concrete path running down the middle. There were no flowers. The lounge was spacious and we put our dining table and chairs at the garden end so that we had a pleasant view when we were eating. We had two bedrooms and a small bathroom, and it was cosy. The detached garage provided room to store our rubbish and park the car. The house had a family feel to it and we were happy there. It was our first real home and that made it special.

We lived next to an old man, Jack, who was in his eighties and had been a gunner in the First World War. He was a fascinating character. He had started smoking at the age of fourteen and smoked until the day he died. His desperate coughing sounded like someone starting up an old diesel engine in the morning and it was unpleasant to hear but he was a lovely old wizened man. He had spent a part of his early life as a gilder of gold leaf, a specialised job and he was a highly skilled craftsman. He spoke with fondness about his early days working with gold leaf in the restoration of ornate ceilings in mansion houses. He loved Michelle who always made a point of speaking to him every day. We came to generally look out for him.

Jack was not the only interesting member of his family. His brother, Bob, had led a life which would have provided a fascinating base for a novel or a film He was in his seventies and had a pleasant face with a pencil moustache that was neatly trimmed under a nose which was starting to show blue veins. He liked his red wine. He dressed like a gentleman and paid close attention to his appearance. The handkerchief in his top pocket was carefully folded, just so. He oozed elegance and charm and shortly after we first met him, he sent Michelle a dozen red roses. I once bought her some daffodils. Bob had been maitre d'hotel at the Savoy Hotel in London and he took us out to the best restaurant in Dover, not a great claim, and he charmed the entire staff by paying attention to them and saying just the right thing to raise a smile. His tactic was to identify the head waiter on arrival and a bank note would pass between them. He would then slip the waitress another note with a smile and an aside that he was 'in the business' and would give a promise of more to come if we were well cared for. It worked like a charm. It was embarrassing as other diners were desperately trying to attract the staff's attention which was inevitably centred on our table.

At another restaurant in Deal, about five miles from Dover, Bob taught the pompous owner a lesson in a classic way. At the end of the meal, the owner asked me if I would like a really good cognac. Now I didn't know much about cognac so I deferred to Bob who asked the obsequious owner for two large glasses of his best cognac. The owner returned with two balloon brandy glasses which he produced with a flourish. He said that the cognac was a five star 1943 and that we could be assured that it was excellent. Clearly it was expensive. Bob took a good sniff, rolled the dark golden liquid around the glass and held it up to the candle. He looked at it thoughtfully. He then took a sip and said that while it was indeed a good cognac it most certainly was not the five star 1943. He smiled pleasantly. His tone was matter-of-fact and not at all patronising. The owner reacted indignantly and pointed out that he had worked all over the world in the catering business including the Savoy. There could be no doubt that the cognac was a

1943 vintage and he was quite prepared to bring the bottle to the table. Most of the diners in the restaurant were now fully engaged in this exchange of views. Bob, as calm as a lake at midnight, responded that he didn't want to make a fuss but as he himself had been maitre d' at the Savoy from 19— to 19—, he would be most interested to learn when Maurice, the restaurant owner, had worked there: in what department and in what capacity. All said with the most pleasant of smiles.

The bold Maurice was now not quite so bold as he realised that he was in checkmate and accordingly swiftly switched tactics. He deferred to Bob and offered the drinks on the house hoping that he had enjoyed his meal. It was a wonderful moment of drama and Bob didn't bat an eyelid but said that he really appreciated this kind gesture. This incident served as a warning: be careful what you claim as you never know when you might be called upon to prove it.

One year later I met Bob again at his home on the Isle of Wight. I was on a survival course run by ex-SAS officer and survival expert, Eddie McGee. After his training, we spent five days living off the land in a dense forest near the sea. We were positioned there at dawn with just what we were wearing and a survival knife. We had no matches or food. It rained incessantly and, on the first night, two of the group were taken to hospital suffering from hypothermia. I will never forget the misery of trying to start a fire using just a flint to make a spark with the rain lashing down through the trees. I eventually lit a fire and never allowed it to go out after that. I washed in water from pine branches, caught fish and crabs in traps, rabbits in a snare and rolled my own cigars made from briar leaves which proved to be slightly hallucinogenic. Hmmmn. I built a shelter that kept me warm and dry. I burnt my boots when I left them to dry too near the fire and fell asleep. Only the soles survived. I have never felt so alive in my life as I did during that week when the whole day from dawn to dusk was devoted to water and food. It was a wonderful experience that has stayed with me to this day. Eddie McGee was an exceptional instructor with a wealth of experience. He had survived in the most dangerous of places and he passed on his knowledge willingly and expertly.

At the end of the course I decided to drop in on Bob who owned a house not too far from the Isle of Wight ferry. Bob cultivated vines. Within the garden of his charming house he had established a small cottage industry, making red wine as dark as blood. He left the skins of the grapes in the wine in order to increase the strength. It was delicious and, as I shared a bottle with him, he began to reminisce.

He said that he had left his job at the Savoy in the thirties and travelled to New York to seek adventure. He quickly established himself within the restaurant business using his wit, good looks and expertise. Soon he owned his own restaurant but this was at a time of prohibition in the USA – the legal act of forbidding the manufacture, transport and sale of alcohol. There were severe penalties for those who broke the law, but there were fortunes to be made if you walked on the wild side. Indeed, Bob made a fortune selling illicit alcohol. He told me that he became a millionaire and lived like one. He was later caught by the police and imprisoned. I believe that he was incarcerated in the notorious Alcatraz Prison, Al Capone's residence until he died. Bob said that as long as you had money, you could live like a king in prison but the aim of the authorities was to bleed you dry financially. Once his fortune had gone, he was deported back to the UK where he picked himself up and started again in the catering business. Over a bottle of red wine, he had given me a glimpse of his fascinating life. The wine was indeed potent. Three hours after arriving, and somewhat the worse for wear, I left Bob's house to catch the ferry.

My primary reason for going on the survival course was to hone my skills which included unarmed combat as well as karate. I felt that I needed to test myself if I was to achieve a latent ambition to start up a successful karate club and ensure that I could handle the tough characters that I would surely encounter as my club grew in reputation.

It proved to be a sound decision.

15

KARA-TE EMPTY HANDS

Karate is an unarmed method of combat in which specific parts of the anatomy are used to punch, strike, kick or block. Karate originated in Okinawa, one of the Ryuku Islands with allegiance to Japan. It was introduced there by visiting Chinese monks and government officials. The islanders were forbidden by their Japanese rulers to carry weapons so they developed self-defence techniques which they practised in secret and which were based on Chinese martial arts. These became known as Okinawa-te or the hand techniques of Okinawa.

In 1722, Master Sakugawa, who had studied martial arts in China, systemised and developed the indigenous techniques to a point where they became known as *Karate-no-Sakugawa* or 'Chinese hands of Sakugawa.' This is the first known use of the word 'karate.' In 1879, the Okinawa Islands were annexed by Japan but in 1916 a group of Okinawan karate masters, led by the renowned Gichin Funakoshi, were invited to give the first official demonstration of karate in Kyoto, Japan. Master Funakoshi, a philosopher and artist, subtly changed the meaning of the character for Kara from one meaning 'Chinese' to one which meant 'empty.' This interpretation was significant as it not only reflected his deep feeling and wider appreciation of the art but also allowed the nationalistic Japanese to embrace and develop it.

I have a scroll hanging in my studio that was given to me by my karate master, Kaicho Nakamura, which says that the

Karate and Zen are inseparable. The development of Zen philosophy starts in the fifth century with the foundation of Buddhism in India by Shakyamuni Buddha, also known as Gautama Buddha. Bodhidarma, whom the Japanese call Daruma, was an Indian patriarch who left India for China in 520 AD. Martial arts were born in China out of his spirited search for enlightenment. The monks spreading Buddhism arrived in Japan in the middle of the sixth century and it developed into the Zen practice that we know today as part of a search for spiritual perfection.

The simplicity of Zen appealed both to the warrior and the religious classes and it quickly became established in Japan as early as the thirteenth century. Among many features, it stressed a unity with nature and led to a wonderful period of Japanese landscape painting. The samurai class imbued Zen with its stoic attitude and this fusion allowed Zen to flourish and become a major influence in the development of martial arts.

Karate, as we know it today, was developed in Japan and then exported abroad by Japanese instructors representing the main styles of Karate: Shotocan, Wado Ryu, Shito Ryu, Goju Ryu and Kyokushin. The UK and the USA were particularly fertile grounds in which to plant eastern seeds and they embraced karate with great enthusiasm. With my background in judo I had developed a fascination for eastern fighting arts and read avidly about them.

I first started training in karate in 1972. My Dad was instrumental in this change of direction from judo. He used to be part of a group called The Royal Antediluvian Order of Buffaloes. This was a social and benevolent fraternal organisation open only to men. Its aim was to aid members in need, and their families, and the families of deceased members as well as to support other charitable groups. His group used to meet in the upstairs room of a pub in Hither Green.

His group was not Masonic. Dad disliked the Masons and

the Masonic Order with a passion. He said that the police and courts were riddled with Masons and if you were not a member of their society then they would block your progress at every turn. He detested their secrecy and the way they protected their own interests. He had seen how quick they were to use influence and nepotism to advance their own causes despite their public charitable face.

Dad told me that a new karate club had opened up above the pub. It was called The Za Zen Karate Club and he thought that I might like to have a look at it. The relationship between me and my father had improved to a point where we could at least talk to each other civilly but he surprised me when he told me about the club and encouraged me to review it. It was 1972, and we were back up in London as I was studying Serbo-Croat for six months on a language course in High Holborn. We were living with Bob at Michelle's family house in Plumstead.

At that time karate was not popular in the way it is now and it had a dark reputation. I thought that only the toughest characters who wanted to rip each other apart with their bare hands would train together. I was nervous about going to train with the club. Nevertheless, I felt a powerful attraction to see for myself what would happen during a training session.

I recall climbing the pub stairs on a Monday night and seeing a pleasant young woman sitting on a chair outside a small room. She was taking money from students who were dressed in white karate suits as they bowed and entered the sparsely furnished room. It had a stretched canvas covering the wooden floor. Standing next to her was a man in his early thirties. He was short and stocky with a pock-marked face and intense eyes. He introduced himself in a friendly manner as Jon Alexander, the instructor. The woman on the door was his wife, Jenny.

His group was called The Za-Zen Karate Association which he had founded in 1971. At that time it was just getting established and there were only twelve students at the training session. I told Jon, who was known as Sensei Jon, *sensei* being Japanese for teacher, that I would like to watch the session. I had brought my judo suit with me even though I didn't intend to train that night. I am not sure why. However, Sensei Jon encouraged me to train with the group. I was very nervous but thought that I would give it a try. I paid a small fee and changed into my practice suit, known as a *gi* in Japanese.

Mike Knight and I in the Za-Zen Karate days.

Sensei Jon took the class through a warm-up session. He then demonstrated punches, blocks and kicks. I tried my best to copy the others but felt uncoordinated. Everyone was encouraged to shout as the techniques reached their full power. We didn't do this in our judo practice and so it seemed strange to me. I felt exhilarated as energy generated by the shouts flowed through the room. We then did push-ups on the canvas floor on our knuckles. It was painful. The other students all looked tough to me and were sweating and concentrating hard. After half an hour, Sensei Jon told us all to line up. He then allocated a partner to each student.

He said that we would fight each other, using only karate techniques. We had little in the way of protective or safety equipment, although some students wore light hand mitts. We bowed to each other and he told us to begin. My opponent wore a yellow belt which indicated to me that he must have some experience. He was moving around me in a fluid manner and then suddenly he would whack me in the chest with his fist or kick me in the side of the head with his foot. I just couldn't work out the mechanics of how he was kicking me.

I did know that I felt exasperated at my inability to counter his moves and also that I was experiencing pain. While I didn't know what I had to do to defend myself using karate techniques, I did know how to use my judo skills. The next time he moved towards me and launched a kick, I quickly moved inside its arc, grabbed his karate suit with one hand at the lapel and my other hand at his neck and executed a throw called *uchi mata*, or inner-thigh throw. This is executed by spinning around with your back to your opponent, pulling him powerfully towards you while lifting him a little, and then sweeping your leg between his, your thigh against his at groin level, and twisting your hips and your head in a frontal direction. To complete the throw, if you really want your opponent to stay down, you land heavily on top of him. I should not have really done this, but I was angry.

His body hit the canvas just before I fell on him. He tried to breathe but all that came out was a gurgling noise. I pushed myself up from him and stood up. I heard the instructor shouting and turned towards him, realising that he was shouting at me. He was saying that this was karate club and judo was not acceptable here. I asked him how I could defend myself from being kicked in the head if no-one showed me the proper way to act. I knew only judo. He calmed down. Everyone in the club was staring at me and I thought that I would be in for a beating. However, the next fighter was very considerate and explained how I should keep up my guard and how to move in fighting stance. All my following partners moved cautiously with me and much to my surprise they explained what I was supposed to do. It seemed that although I had made a mistake, my fighting spirit made me acceptable to the other students. Afterwards, we all went for drink in the pub downstairs and I was encouraged to join the club. Even the man I had thrown shook my hand and said that there were no hard feelings. He asked me what I had done to throw him so quickly. I was now hooked on karate and determined to join the club the following week.

Jon Alexander was a talented and innovative instructor and I am grateful for his support during the early days. His style was built around his personality. He promoted himself to sixth degree black belt outside the traditional Japanese karate structure. It was his own karate foundation and he could set his own limits. As his enthusiastic students, we didn't really care about the politics of karate. We wanted to fight and would enter competitions in order to gain experience. We would often be told by Sensei Jon to meet at a certain place on Saturday morning and then we would drive, to a distant venue such as Birmingham to compete. We didn't really care where we were going. I once won the All-England Weapons Championship, which was held in Bradford, with an exhibition of the six-foot wooden staff. On that day, I had had no idea even that I was going to Bradford in order to compete and no idea that I would be entering the weapons competition. It was crazy but we had fun and in fact I learned a lot about how to handle fear before the fighting begins.

Karate became a part of my life and while I was in London I trained nearly every day. I quickly rose through the ranks of the Za-Zen Karate Association. Seven months later, when we moved back to Dover, Sensei Jon encouraged me to open up a club there. I was a brown belt, one rank below black belt, and usually only black belts run clubs but this didn't seem to concern him. I had also advanced very quickly through the Za-Zen grading structure. Far too quickly in fact even though I was training daily but Sensei Jon didn't see this as a problem. If you had ability, then he promoted you. Normally, it would take at least three years in a traditional Japanese system, training intensely, to reach the rank of black belt. I didn't really deserve my rank but, judging my ability against other students from different clubs and certainly in the fighting arena, I was clearly able to hold my own.

Following our return to Dover, I put an advert in the local paper, *The Dover Express,* announcing that there would be a karate taster course at The Eagle pub on Monday night. I expected a low turnout, perhaps ten people, but the second floor room of the pub was full to bursting point. I received one amusing telephone call from a man before the taster night saying that he was interested in starting karate but thought that I should know something about him first. I asked what it was. He said that he was a Hell's Angel but that he wasn't really tough. I told him that I wasn't tough either and that I looked forward to meeting him. I noticed him later in the room as he was wearing a tee shirt with the name of a Hell's Angel group on it. I walked over to him and shook his hand, saying that I was glad he had made it. He did look tough and had a surly, humourless expression. He grunted at me but I noticed that his eyes looked away from mine. He might well become a good student as he recognised his own weakness and that was a good starting point.

On the night of the taster session I was very nervous. I wondered what I was letting myself in for. Kent has a hard history and its people are flinty. The villages around Dover were the homes of miners. A Kentish man would have a reputation to keep up. Perhaps I had bitten off more than I could chew. A noisy crowd of rough-looking people came up the stairs and filed into the room. I stood in front of them in my white karate suit. I asked them to take off their shoes and socks. There was a lot of laughter and joking at that. I arranged them in five lines of ten people. There was hardly room to breath and I opened the big window which looked on to the main road to let air into the room.

I knew that I had to grab the group's attention quickly. I showed them how to do a few simple punches and a knee kick. The space was so tight that I thought a fight would break out as the men were inevitably making contact with each other. I asked them all to sit down as I wished to explain how to use the power of karate to defend yourself. They all sat on the stained carpet and the room became silent. I had already identified a man in the room as the one I would ask to assist me. He was a big man, about six-foot plus with broad shoulders, shoulder length hair and a face that had seen many a punch. I asked him if he would help me and explained that even though I was lightly built, I would demonstrate how karate could be used to withstand his punches.

I swallowed hard and my mouth was dry. I felt butterflies in my stomach, more technically known as the vascular shunt when blood pools there from the extremities. I looked and sounded calm but inside I was fighting down my fear. I told him that he should not punch at my head but that he should punch as hard as he could at my chest or stomach area. He was only to stop punching if he wanted to. I would do nothing to him except block his punches. He looked at me in disbelief, approaching contempt.

You have to relax your body when you face such a test so you must centre yourself and focus on your breathing. I looked intently at his hands as if they were live bombs about to explode. He was strong and went into a boxer's crouch so I knew that he had been in a few scrapes. I saw that there was a sneer on his face. I could see that he would enjoy humiliating me. If I didn't make an impression on everyone there I knew that once I had opened my karate club, there would be a steady stream of men wanting to challenge me. It was make or break time.

The students waited expectantly. You could have heard a pin drop. I told my opponent to throw a punch when he was ready and he let go his right hand aiming straight for my chest. It was a big looping punch that had a lot of power behind it. I used a technique I call 'waterwheel' to deflect it downward. Your forward hand descends in front of you in a blur using the hard edge of the wrist at the base of little finger to strike downwards on to the attacking arm just as your rear hand moves into position above it ready for the next strike.

The key is to allow the punch to accelerate but not to reach its full power before you drop your body mass on to the pressure point of the arm located one hand span from the wrist towards the elbow crease between the radius and ulna bone. You must gauge the rhythm of the puncher in order for the technique to be effective. It won't work if you don't bring all the elements together. The power went out of his right arm and he withdrew it in order to punch again. I hit it with the next descending hand in exactly the same spot. I knew that it had weakened him by the way his arm dropped. It was time to talk to him. I told him that he had a really hard punch and asked him if his arm was tingling. He said that it was and I explained that the reason I had been able to deflect such a strong punch was that I had found his pressure point. I then asked him if he wanted to try again with his right hand and perhaps put all his power behind it. I looked at his eyes which looked confused but he shook his head quickly from side to side as if clearing his mind and said that he would try again. The atmosphere was still tense. I saw him flex and for a split second thought that he would go for my head or rush me and take me down using his body strength but he didn't do this. He threw the punch and as I blocked it again I could feel that the strength had gone out of it. I measured the block and hit the arm with a softer blow but again I bit into the pressure point, weakening not only the arm but his whole body. He was now at his most dangerous as his plan to humiliate me had failed. I reiterated that he was one of the strongest punchers I had ever seen but said that he could now hit me in the head if he wanted with either his right or left hand. I knew that I was taking a real chance in saying this, but I had felt his power waning and knew that I could cope with the punches.

I was watching his breathing and saw the inward breath that he took as a prelude to launching his right haymaker punch again but this time at head height. I simply stepped inside the arc of his punch and blocked it using my ulna bone, again aiming for the pressure point on the inside of the arm. As I took the punch, I launched my own punch which snapped right in front of his eyes, not once but three times in quick succession. He didn't even know that I had thrown it as he was so busy concentrating on his own attack. I had quick hands in those days.

It was most important that he didn't 'lose face' and, in all honesty, I think that with his huge size and weight, if he had attacked me full on I would have gone down, but fighting is all about outwitting your opponent and that can be done in many different ways. First with the head and then with the heart. I warmly thanked him and asked everyone to applaud him for coming forward and I again praised the strength of his punch. I asked if anyone else wanted to come forward.

This is always a dangerous time. Many fighters or would-be fighters might be waiting to see my technique before they committed themselves and now my problems might really start. I heaved a big sigh of relief when no-one came forward. I had survived. It was my lucky day. I then explained, in some detail, how I had been able to take the power out of the punches using karate techniques. I asked all the men to stand up and we did some more punching and a simple karate block. The hour was over. I'm sure my explanation was too technical for many of those there that night but they were impressed that I had matched the power of a man they respected as a fighter. That night I had nearly twenty men sign up for the new programme. It was beyond all my expectations.

There are so many good memories of those early crazy days. I was fearless and would try anything that improved my karate. For years, in order to toughen my feet, I ran in bare feet both in winter and summer on stones, tarmac and icy roads until one day I trod on a rusty nail and ended up in hospital for a week with blood poisoning. After that, I decided that wearing trainers might be a better option for me.

While it may sound daft to run in bare feet, only this year I read an excellent book on running, *Born to Run* by Christopher McDougall, which investigates the subject of extreme running. The book describes in detail how the major footwear companies have convinced us to buy their trainers when they are actually detrimental to the runner. The architecture of the foot is a marvel and the book describes in detail how the arch of the foot is the best weight-bearing design ever made and suggests that running in trainers is like putting your feet in plaster. You would hardly expect your feet to be effective. It tells us to work our feet hard as they respond very well to use. These days I run in thin-soled martial-art training shoes with little cushioning within them. I aim to keep the weight forward on the balls of my feet with my back straight, head steady, arms high and elbows driving forward. My foot touches down quickly on the forefoot and then kicks back and upwards towards my backside. I have no feet problems whatsoever and regularly run, mixing stamina work, where you keep going at the same speed, with speed work, where you run fast for a set distance and then drop back into your normal pace. Perhaps all those years of running barefoot did create a strong foot structure which now protects me from injury.

The karate training was hard. I used to link students together by tying them with the belts that denoted their rank and then we would run up Castle Hill in Dover, a steep and taxing run. You would drag the weight of the person behind you if they got tired and could not keep up. We would run along the beach, pounding our feet on the stones that moved under the arches of our feet causing us to run faster in order to lessen the pain.

We would do hundreds of kicks and punches and pump out press-ups and sits-ups. Many of my students were miners who loved to fight and loved the challenge of it all and I made many friends in the mining community. Of course I made some enemies as well as friends, but no-one really challenged me. When I was fighting, I could be dangerous and I had no fear no matter how big or strong the opponent. If someone hurt me then I would try to attack them even more aggressively. I think that I was working out demons in those days. My mind was focused on being tougher than my students in everything that we did.

One of our much-loved students was Chiu Kwok Keung, the man who ran the local Chinese restaurant. He loved to train and was only little more than five feet tall but he had a good physique and was stocky. He was a fearless fighter but he kept getting disqualified in competition. He would try to score a point by kicking his opponent in the stomach area but, because he was so low to the ground, he kept kicking them in the groin instead.

It was hard to stop our team from getting disqualified as no matter how many lectures I gave about control, in the heat of battle, one of them would knock out his opponent, break a rib or break an opponent's nose. Often the team match would be awarded to the other team because we had been disqualified. It could be embarrassing to see the winning opposition hobbling or stemming bleeding noses while our losing team didn't have a mark on them. At one time no one in the Za-Zen clubs would fight us such was our reputation. Those men were great company. They trained hard and drank hard if they chose to, which they often did.

It was at Dover that we met our friends Mike and Pat Knight. Mike started to train in karate with me when he was running a local garage. We quickly became great friends with him and his wife, Pat. Their children, Joanne, Kate and Toby were of similar ages to ours. Even to this day, after the many twists and turns in life's path, we remain firm friends and Mike is one of our most senior and respected karate instructors in the karate style to which I now belong, the World Seido Karate Organisation.

We had built a firm foundation in Dover and I now had both work and karate helping with our finances. Michelle and I had outgrown our bungalow and decided to move to a larger house three miles outside Dover in a small village called Martin Mill. The house was called High Rocks. Michelle was unhappy. Although she had the use of our car, she had no real friends in the village and the nearest shop was a mile away. She went through a bad period of feeling depressed and ended up in hospital for a short time, suffering from an undiagnosed illness. In hindsight, her form of depression was most likely brought on by a sudden feeling of being overwhelmed by life itself. She had lost her parents, had taken the role of mother in her family until she married me, and then she had taken on even more responsibility bringing up three children. We had a good life but she had no time for herself and no time to develop personally. Apart from a love of travel and the family, we didn't share many interests.

She wanted us to share a hobby and decided that we could go horse riding. She arranged lessons for us locally.

On the first day I was allocated a large horse and Michelle a smaller animal. She just didn't feel comfortable on her mount but in contrast, I loved being on the horse and was attracting favourable comments from the instructor. We returned from the lesson with me in high spirits and Michelle feeling discouraged. This was not the planned outcome. I could see that she was unhappy but didn't really know what to do about it.

Previously, I had experienced similar feelings, when we had been on holiday in Norfolk. I felt the responsibility for our family lay heavily on me and worried about our future. I was not good company at that time. We both sensed that we needed to change the direction of our lives, but we didn't know how best this could be achieved. The key question was: how could we do it? At this time it seemed that we were trapped in Dover forever.

16

HAPPINESS AND REGRETS

Children change you. It is inevitable. You have to think less about your own needs and more about theirs. In 1972 Michelle fell pregnant with our first son. He was conceived in Wales when we stayed with my Uncle Bryn, in the family house in Gorseinon, South Wales.

We were attending the wedding of old friends, Geoff and Maggie Kemble, and, as the family home was near the wedding venue, we decided to stay with Bryn. Bryn had inherited the family house called, 'Y Goeweig' (translated, 'of the forest') where my Dad had been born. My Aunt Josie, then living in Weston-super-Mare, didn't want us to stay with Bryn. She knew that Bryn would not keep the house clean and had odd habits. He was a miser. He would dress in old clothes, put on sun glasses and hold a white cane of the kind used by the blind. He pretended to be blind. He would go to charity shops and bargain for shoes and shirts playing on his disability in order to negotiate a lower price. Often, he was given clothing and shoes without payment. Josie was ashamed of his behaviour.

Although he was wealthy, in order to save money, Bryn would not put on the heating in the house and he lived a poor and miserable life. He ended up with diabetes and, ironically, went blind. He was an enigma. Each year he would dress smartly and visit London where he would stay at the Army and Navy Club. He would go to a casino daily and play roulette. He told me that he had a system that made him money but he never revealed its details. He was a talented man, a great dancer and also possessed the skill of a professional snooker player but his mind was unsound. Josie used to make an annual visit to clean the family house. On one visit, he was absent and she found him at the local hospital. His health was so poor that he had collapsed. Josie was still determined to clean the house and, on her return, found some fifty of his shirts discarded on the floor of the wardrobe in his bedroom. She ran a bath, put in two packets of washing powder and dumped all the shirts in the bath. She then pounded them with a broom handle to get them clean, and left them to soak.

She was astonished later to find that there were pieces of soggy banknotes floating on the surface of the grimy water It was evident that Bryn had hidden about five thousand pounds inside the shirts in case a burglar came to rob the house. He reasoned that no-one would look in old shirts left on the floor of a wardrobe and he was probably right. However, the money had now been reduced to pulp by the combination of washing powder and Josie's enthusiastic pounding. When she returned to visit Bryn in hospital, Josie admonished him for being so stupid and he in turn berated her for interfering with his security system. When Bryn went blind as a result of his diabetes caused by neglect of his health, he sold the family house and went to live with Josie and her husband, Roy. Bryn tried to make their lives a misery and Roy loathed him but Josie proved easily capable of managing him, and his health improved dramatically over his later years as a result of her care.

It was against this background that Michelle and I went to stay at Bryn's house. He made an effort to welcome us and had warmed up our bed with a hot water bottle and a bedpan. Unfortunately, these sources of heat only seemed to make the bugs more active. Poor Michelle was bitten to death after just one night there. Her arms were covered in angry red bites. For some reason, they ignored me. Perhaps they didn't like the taste of Brains bitter, a Welsh ale that redeveloped the drinker's brain. When Michelle opened the fridge to get some milk for our tea, she saw a large dead bluebottle lodged in the chip fat. An unusual snack. The faded blue cloth used for cleaning the sink was full of mice droppings. She dropped it instantly. I was starting to regret my decision to stay with Bryn. However, he took us out to his working-man's club that night and danced with Michelle, playing the part of a caring host. She confirmed that he was an excellent dancer. The next day, Bryn cooked Sunday dinner for us (we didn't like to think about the detail of the preparation) and did his best to make us feel at home. He was likeable in his own way, but still quite mad.

He regarded himself as a handyman and proudly told me that he had re-tiled the bathroom using attractive plastic tiles. He was quick to show me his handiwork explaining that he had had some difficulty making the tiles meet at right angles around the corner of the bathroom wall. He hit on the idea of using a blowtorch. He simply heated the plastic tiles until they started to melt and then bent them with pliers in order to achieve a right angle. An unusual approach which I have yet to see recommended in guidance manuals. When you looked at the corner of the bathroom you could see that all the edges of the tiles were black, burnt and misshapen but he seemed delighted with the outcome and gave me a detailed account of his achievement.

Bryn's favourite story was about the night during the war when he had been on watch on the cliffs near Dover docks. He had decided that he would go down to the rocks and fish as he watched for the enemy. He cast out his line. He was shaken when a submarine surfaced in front of him with his fishing line draped across it. It was a British submarine with engine trouble which had surfaced in order to carry out repairs. He loved to tell the tale about how he had expected to catch a sprat but had caught a whopper instead.

It would be hard to forget our first and only stay with Bryn. We enjoyed Geoff and Margaret's wedding where I bet Michelle a dress of her choice that she could not drink a pint of beer in one go. Michelle normally lingers over a drink so I thought that my bet was safe. Wrong. She took the glass in her hands, looked at it thoughtfully and then sank the pint in one gulp. She then claimed the money for the promised dress. Michelle is not a woman to be under estimated.

After Geoff and Maggie's wedding, we were delighted when we discovered that Michelle was pregnant, but she almost lost the baby early in her pregnancy. This was because she used to walk, carrying shopping from the shops in Dover to her job at Eastern Docks, a distance of about one mile. I didn't think about the possible consequences of her doing this until she started to complain of pains. Fortunately the doctor was able to treat Michelle and the pregnancy proceeded as normal. Gareth Philip Thyer-Jones arrived into the world on 8th May 1973. I thought the name Gareth was appropriate because of my Welsh connection, the place of his conception and also, at that time, I was a fan of Gareth Edwards, the Welsh rugby player.

Gareth was born at St. Francis Hospital, Plumstead, at a time when I was studying at Holborn College. We had been in London on the day of the birth and, when we returned home, Michelle thought that she needed to go into hospital as she felt unusual pains. She had previously been told by our neighbour in Whitfield, Dover, that childbirth was so excruciatingly painful that she could expect to almost faint with the pain. Once in hospital, Michelle was expecting horrific pain to hit her. Nevertheless, she felt hungry. She went to buy some crisps and, on her return, the midwife noticed that the baby was almost due to be born. Michelle had no idea that Gareth was so close to birth. Perhaps our neighbour, raising unnecessary alarm in a young wife with her lurid descriptions of childbirth, actually did Michelle a favour, as she didn't find the reality of childbirth too much to worry about.

I was present at the birth. Gareth was born a bouncy, healthy baby with an abundance of energy which he displays to this day. He tends to move about at warp speed. He was hyperactive before we knew the meaning of the word. He was like a wind-up toy: you could put him on the floor and off he would go at speed but not necessarily in the direction you expected or wanted!

But the joy of his birth was mixed with grief. My father had died just eight weeks before Gareth was born. He had cancer of the mouth and over a period of time underwent the most horrible treatment including the removal of his upper palate. He had hypodermic syringes filled with anti-cancer drugs inserted into his eyes, presumably because the condition of his mouth was so bad that there was no other option. He was reduced to a shell of his former self. In the end, the hospital could do nothing more for him. He was stoic and rarely complained about the pain he was in, although its crushing effect was evident when you looked into his eyes.

He was a determined man even when fighting cancer. I recall our going to see him in Lewisham Hospital one Saturday, the day after he had had a major operation. We went into the ward and spoke to the nursing sister, asking how he was. She said that he was very ill and was in bed in the ward. She warned us that we were not to be alarmed by the number of tubes that were feeding in and out of him. This was to be expected after a major operation. We were not to spend long with him as he would be tired and needed rest to recover. We were alarmed when we approached his bed only to find that there was no-one in it. We feared the worst.

We asked the man in the next bed if he knew where Dad was and he told us that he was down in the TV room watching the rugby! Wales were playing. Sure enough, we found him there sitting on a chair, with three stands containing bags of various kinds, and multiple tubes penetrating his body. He was calmly watching the rugby and smiled when he saw us. The sister was angry when she found out where he was, and ordered him to return to bed but he would not move until the rugby had finished. We sat with him and watched rugby.

When he was discharged from hospital, I went to pick him up by car to bring him home. He was very ill and I walked slowly with him to the kitchen where the electric fire was heating the room. He felt very cold. I tried to make conversation. I said that it was great to have him home and that this was a good place to start his recovery. You say stupid things at such times. He looked at me with a steady gaze and said that he had come home to die. He said that he had had a good life and had no regrets but that he would die in his own home and not in the arms of strangers.

I choked emotionally as I held him. I felt powerless in the face of his honesty. I felt useless and heartbroken at that moment, I was intensely sad. I was not seeing the man who had dominated our family for so long. I was seeing my Dad who was dying. I thought about all the good that he had in him. He had so much to offer but for years I had focused on the bad. He could be funny, had a great voice, and a talent for poetry. He had a real zest for life. He was always first to buy a round of drinks at the bar where he would spend whatever he had on others, without a thought for himself. I know that, in his own way, he loved Mother and I suspect that he was proud of my brother, Mike, and of me but he rarely showed it and, when he did, it was with a gruff acknowledgement. He rarely displayed emotion but was held in high esteem by his friends and ex-colleagues from the police. Clearly, there were many sides to his character.

If I had walked in his shoes then I might have seen his life differently. The trials of leaving home early and joining the police force in London had toughened him up.

The war tore at him as he would fly mission after mission in Bomber Command, bringing death and destruction to Germans and seeing his comrades wounded or dead from enemy fire.

He was shot down in the North Sea twice and survived in freezing conditions, precarious in a small life raft with his aircrew. He repeatedly went over the side of the raft and swam to untangle the sea anchor that was saving the small rubber dinghy from capsizing. He told me that swimming on the Gower coast in Wales as a youngster had prepared him for this trial and the task fell to him as none of his crew were competent swimmers. He survived and lived for months behind enemy lines and fought his way back to England. My brother, Mike, was born in Wales in Dad's absence when Mother was living with Dad's parents. She was told that Dad was 'missing in action' and this meant that he was presumed to be dead. It is hard to imagine how she felt, losing her husband and being left to bring up a newborn baby with in-laws. It is even harder to imagine how she felt when Dad knocked on the door and announced that he was far from dead. Mother gave Mike to him to hold and Mike was immediately sick on Dad's uniform. What a welcome home. He was home for only a few days was and then summoned to return to battle. It is small wonder that many of our forces found solace in drink both during and after the war. Drink to forget the demons that plague you.

After the war, Dad left the RAF and rejoined the police service. He became a detective. He fought his way up the promotion ladder to the rank of sergeant. He was known for his integrity and honesty. Once again, he highlighted the pervasive influence that those in the Masonic Order exercised within the police force and the judiciary. He said that his refusal to join the Order prevented his promotion for years and placed an invisible ceiling on progress up the ranks.

Knowing his background does not excuse his behaviour

which at times frightened me and I am sure frightened Mike and my mother. If he was drunk, especially on whisky, he could change mood alarmingly swiftly and was quick with his hands. But he was always affable the next day, trying to smooth everything over in his own way. His appeasement didn't work and, instead, resentment built in me during my teen years. I really wish that he had lived to see his first grandchild born and to see our other children grow. I am as sure as I can be that he would have made a loving granddad, as age mellowed and tempered his character.

When he retired from the police force, at the age of fifty, he took a job as a schools inspector with the responsibility of tracking down truants. He must have been a nightmare to manage especially as his boss was a woman. He was not receptive to taking instructions from women. Ironically, he was popular with troublesome parents as they respected his strength of character and his reluctance to shirk a challenge. Challenges occurred when he had to confront the parents of truants and had to threaten them with court action. He told me that he gained their trust once they knew he was serious and wasn't a pushover. 'Trouble is my middle name,' was one of his favourite sayings.

My mother nursed Dad at home during his last dying days. However, there was no peace in the house as my parents were being harassed by the landlord. The owner of the house wanted the tenants out so that he could restore the house, rebuild the flats to a higher standard and then break the existing rent agreements. One day, when my parents were out at the hospital, he ordered his men to bulldoze our garden in order to make a car park for the flats. This was done without any consultation. Even though Dad was ill, he still had some fight in him and enlisted the help of the local press as he sought to expose the landlord's unscrupulous methods. However, the landlord was wealthy and ruthless and easily deflected the adverse publicity.

The landlord wore down the other tenants until our flat was the only flat left to renovate. The workmen were banging, drilling, shouting and whistling while Dad was dying in my old bedroom, which previously had looked on to the garden. In fairness, on the day Dad died, the Italian workcrew refused to work as a mark of respect for him even though they were harassed and threatened by their boss to continue working. It was a sad time for Mother. She had nursed Dad through thick and thin. Those who have nursed a patient dying of cancer will know only too well what an enormous strain it is. Mother refused all help, except from Aunt Molly and stoically fulfilled Dad's wish to die in his own bed. At the time of his death, I was in Dover working with a friend, Pete Gibbons, putting up pine cladding in the lounge of our bungalow in Whitfield.

Michelle phoned me with the news of Dad's death. Mother had previously advised me to stay in Dover when I had spoken to her about how close Dad was to death, wanting to visit him. It was typical of her to spare my feelings and to take the burden of care on herself. Part of me felt guilty for not being there with her and part of me just wanted to remember Dad as the man he had been a forceful figure ready to take on the world at the drop of a hat. At his passing, I swept away all the antagonism of my youth and just concentrated on seeing the positive aspects of my life with Dad. I thought of the wasted years when we had been estranged. We were separated by an age gap that seemed unbridgeable but he had been far more open with me after my marriage and had treated me as an equal, sharing some of his life with me. Mother seemed to take Dad's death in her stride but I think that she was using valium to help her cope during those last months.

I had lost Dad, and Michelle had lost both her parents. The challenges of daily life preoccupied us and we moved on. We had Gareth to look after and I had work to cope with. Dad faded from my memory quite quickly at that time but now he comes back to me often and I feel at peace when thinking of him. This does not stop me from feeling sad over a relationship that might have been. While this feeling may be familiar to many, I find it hard to put into words.

Mother moved into a nearby flat in Blackheath which was comfortable and spacious. She started to rebuild her life without Dad, with the help of valium, Uncle Fran and Aunt Molly. She would often come to visit us in Dover and, of course, she loved her grandson, Gareth.

We were still stuck in Dover with little prospect of moving but now our family had expanded. Alex Roger was born on 3 May 1976 and Andrew Michael was born on 8 February 1980. All the boys were highly individual even from birth. Gareth was loud and energetic; Alex contented and placid; Andrew demanding and competitive. All had one thing in common: they were fine looking boys. After the birth of Andrew, I told Michelle that I had made the decision to have a vasectomy. I felt that I had to take care of my family as best I could and that three sons was my limit. Michelle would probably have chosen to have another baby but I was resolute. I had the snip. I had decided that we would have no more children. Michelle wasn't very happy living in Martin Mill. We were out in a small village and she was often lonely. But an unexpected opportunity in life suddenly materialised.

17

PASSPORT TO PARADISE

I took a decision that was to have a profound effect on our lives and I took it without consulting Michelle. Each year the Immigration Service invites officers to work abroad as entry clearance officers (ECO) or visa officers. The distinction is that ECOS work in Commonwealth countries in the British High Commission. In general, the posts without immigration problems are allocated to Foreign Office staff. The main ECO posts for immigration staff therefore were to be found in Africa, Asia and the Caribbean.

When the usual circular arrived at our office, I studied what was on offer. The normal tour of duty for long-term attachments to the Foreign Office was three years. I applied for two posts: one in New Delhi, India and one in Kingston, Jamaica. I saw that the post in Jamaica offered far more career development as there would be only two officers responsible for all immigration matters, while the post in Delhi was much larger and offered fewer opportunities for personal growth. I also noticed that the post in Kingston would be opened up to officers with families. Previously it was deemed to be such a high security risk that only single officers could go to Jamaica. The elections held in 1980 endorsed Mr Edward Seaga, a pro-American politician, as the prime minister. In the run up to the elections over one thousand people had been killed in Kingston alone as a result of political rivalries. The violence was now under control. It still was not a safe place to live without the fear of violence, but the risk had been downgraded by the

Foreign Office security experts to 'medium'.

You might think that it irresponsible of me to apply to take my family to live in such a dangerous city. However, I was convinced that my decision to apply was the right one and the choice of Jamaica was sound. I thought that if we were to change the course of our lives, that change had to be profound. I completed the form. My manager gave me a glowing reference and I sent it off. As the competition for places was fierce, I had little confidence that I would even get an interview. I promptly forgot about the application and focused on life. Some months later, much to my surprise, I was invited to appear before the selection panel which was comprised of two people from the Immigration Service and one from the Foreign & Commonwealth Office (F&CO). I was quizzed about my reasons for wishing to work abroad and the F&CO interviewer asked me about what I knew of the situation in Jamaica and why I was ready to take my family there. I had prepared myself well and knew a considerable amount about the political situation, the immigration problems I would encounter in the High Commission and the security available for families. I was less well-prepared to answer questions about New Delhi. I left the interview reasonably happy with my performance but with no idea how the panel would judge me. Michelle knew that I was going for the interview but I had played it down, saying that it was just a routine assessment of suitability for working abroad in the future. I think that I wanted to protect her by not raising her hopes. I was also protecting my own ego from the stigma of failure.

One month later I unexpectedly received a phone call at work from a member of the F&CO posting staff asking me if I would take the job in Jamaica. Of course I was delighted but said that I first needed to consult my wife before I could accept. I telephoned Michelle at home but she was not there. She was at the house of a friend who lived near the sea, and was playing with the boys on the beach. Her friend called to her and said that I urgently wanted her to speak to me. When Michelle eventually came to the phone, I asked her if she fancied going to Jamaica with the boys for three years. I can still hear her on the telephone shouting, 'YES! YES! YES!' and she later told me that she had been dancing as she said this. The die was cast.

I had little idea about the challenges this posting would raise. We would be uprooting our family, travelling across the world to start a new job which would be under Foreign Office control, establishing the children in schools, trying to settle safely in a country famous for street violence and renting out our own home in our absence. The challenges seemed formidable but we were thrilled with the thought of beginning afresh. The Foreign Office told me that they expected me to be in the post in Jamaica within six months. The demands of preparation were considerable. I had to go to work in the Intelligence Unit at Harmondsworth, near Heathrow Airport, for three months and to Heathrow Airport, Terminal 3. Jamaica was a prime drug-smuggling route to the UK and we had serious problems with 'Yardies' – Jamaican criminals who dealt in arms and drugs. As background to my posting, I had to learn all I could about how they operated, what false documents they used to move in and out of the UK, and the crime gangs to which they were connected in the UK. I had to get to know which flights arriving at Terminal 3 from Jamaica caused the most problems and, once in post, what I needed to do in order to help solve them. I also had to familiarise myself with the workings of the Foreign Office, who managed the posts abroad, and learn how it interacted with the Home Office, who managed me. Michelle had to be briefed about what she could expect living in Jamaica and what security measures she needed to take in her daily life in order to keep safe. She was lectured about her role in supporting her husband and given tips on how to be a good Foreign Office wife. She would prove to be a rebel in this respect.

It was a hectic and difficult time especially as I was working in London during the week and at home only at weekends. This left Michelle often alone with the children and having to deal with all the demands of renting out our house and preparing for our move abroad.

I also needed to understand inter-agency rivalries as a background to my new post. The Home Office employed me but I would be seconded to the Foreign Office for three years. However, the Foreign Office wanted as little contact as possible with immigration staff as we created real problems for them. On the one hand they wished to maintain and develop good relations with the host country but, on the other, we would be refusing entry to some of its citizens who would complain bitterly about our actions: these would be highlighted in the media, especially if we refused an entry clearance or visa to a prominent person. The Foreign Office still considered itself as above visa and entry-clearance work. It was considered to be too low grade for them and indeed it often interfered with their job of selling the UK commercially, and influencing governments and their officials. Although the Foreign Office had to appear as helpful to us as possible, we Home Office secondees were disliked. Most Foreign Office staff detested working in the immigration section as they also considered that it did not enhance their career prospects. I entered this world and quickly saw that in terms of Foreign Office promotion there was clearly a glass ceiling that was almost impossible to break through if you hadn't been to the right school or university or didn't know the right people. I heard more moaning about this from F&CO staff during my time abroad than from the wind across Dartmoor.

The pace of change accelerated. Everyday we saw new demands and challenges until we were desperate to leave the UK behind. Andrew was still a baby aged fourteen months and the other children were excited when, finally, in April 1981, we set off on our Caribbean adventure.

18
Lamb Hot Pot

At last we were on our flight from Miami to Kingston Jamaica. We had nearly been refused permission to board. At the check-in desk I was asked by the airline representative how long I would be staying in Jamaica. I told him that I would be staying for three years, working at the British High Commission. He asked me if I had a work permit and I told him that I didn't need one as I had a diplomatic passport. He then told us to wait while he consulted his manager. When he returned he told me that if I didn't have a work permit we weren't allowed to board the plane as we would be refused entry and sent back by the Jamaican Immigration Service. Fortunately, one of the existing members of the High Commission staff was in our queue and overheard the exchange. He came forward to the desk and patiently explained that I didn't need a work permit as I was a diplomat and he vouched for me. After another hasty consultation with his manager, the representative issued us with our boarding passes. It was not the smooth start that I had expected.

My family was eagerly looking forward to a new life. I was also eager but quite apprehensive about the demands that I would face. I had made a promise to myself that once I was settled in I would find a new karate club and start training again as a beginner. I wanted a fresh start. I felt that although I had been training for years and had now reached the rank of fourth Degree Black Belt under Shihan Jon Alexander, a talented instructor who had guided me in his own way up the ranks of his style, I had little confidence that I was on the right path for my personal development in karate. I felt that apart from boosting my ego, I had wasted many years in the study of a karate system that had no real depth to it. It was a manufactured style, exciting in its own way, but with no historical connection to a real Master and no roots. I needed more.

My old friend, Mike Knight, had reluctantly taken over running the Za-Zen clubs in Kent. He too lacked confidence in the style he followed and had issues over its leadership. But at that time, as the plane landed at Kingston airport in the early evening near the infamous Port Royal, karate was the last thing on my mind.

Port Royal, the old pirates' haven of yesteryear is sited on a finger of land, on one side of the vast harbour. It is full of history. Out of fear of the Spanish invasion, buccaneers were lured by the British, who governed Jamaica, to Port Royal. We dangled the prospect of Spanish gold in front of them to encourage them to leave their stronghold of Tortuga in Haita. The aim was to mass warships in Jamaica to help discourage an attack by the Spanish. After peace with Spain in 1660, the same buccaneers easily acquired letters of marque that gave them the right to attack merchant ships. A 'letter of marque and reprisal' was a government licence authorising a person, known as a 'privateer', to attack and capture enemy vessels and bring them before admiralty courts for condemnation and sale. The British had many enemies at that time and so played a dangerous game in creating alliances with dangerous and unpredictable partners.

In the early 1700s Port Royal was a thriving port with nearly seven thousand people, beloved by just about every kind of human flotsam and jetsam that existed. Most notable amongst the pirates was Henry Morgan whose sacking of Panama ironically led to a British change of policy towards pirates. The new governor was weary of the pirates attacking even English ships so he attacked the pirates themselves with the introduction of a piracy law in 1681. The final blow to Port Royal came on 7 July 1692 when a huge earthquake and tidal wave tumbled two thirds of the port either into rubble or into the sea. Today it is a small fishing village with the remains of a fort and little else. There is much archeological treasure buried under the sea yet to be found so it still posseses an aura of excitement for me when I think about it.

At the airport, we were met by a representative of the High Commission who took us to Kingston. It was a hot evening and the windows of the car were slightly down, letting in cool air. We were excited. The roads were lined with traders as we drove out of the airport. We saw small shacks where you could buy spicy fish, exotic fruits and nuts. Children ran in bare feet along the road dressed in shorts and ragged T-shirts. We heard the boom of a driving bass as the sound of reggae music filled the night, floating out from dimly lit bars. We smelt the charcoal from the barbecues and the acrid odour of burning tyres as we came to the outskirts of the city. Youngsters clamoured around the car when it stopped at traffic lights: they tried to thrust their little hands through the car window as they begged for small change. It was hot and humid. We were taken to The Pegasus Hotel in New Kingston, about a five minute walk from the High Commission. This was to be our home until we found suitable family accommodation. It was a modern hotel, probably the best in Kingston, with a huge outdoor swimming pool that was very cold. We collapsed into our room, and awoke the next day in a strange new city. The first day of our new life together as a family. We laughed with the excitement of it all.

However, settling in wasn't easy. Firstly, our new car had not arrived. I had ordered a white Cortina estate and it was not expected to arrive for two weeks. The lack of personal transport was a big handicap for our family and we had to rely on lifts from others if we wanted to go out of the hotel. At that time, taxis were unreliable and sometimes just downright dangerous. It was not unusual to see passenger doors held on by string. We once got into a taxi which had half the floor missing with the road below visible to the passengers. We quickly got out again.

I grappled with the demands of a new job and Michelle looked after the boys as best she could, staying in the hotel. I was the new boy at the High Commission and was taking over the immigration section from a colleague who had spent the last three years there. Jamaica is so heavy with the promise of sex that it often seems to encourage people to throw away their normal caution. Consequently all sorts of illicit relationships were formed by those we knew within the High Commission and in fact my colleague had left his wife for a woman who worked in the building. His own life was in disarray. He was a morose and unhelpful guide for me, sarcastic and bitter. He had little good to say about Jamaica or its people.

The High Commission building itself was quite imposing but architecturally ugly with its sweeping flat roof and huge windows. I disliked it. It was uninspiring. I had expected more in terms of architecture in Jamaica, a country so bound up with our own history. After entering the grounds by car through heavy gates embossed with the royal crest and controlled by guards from the Jamaican police force, you drove to the back of the building and entered the underground car park. However, if you were being dropped off, your driver would let you out opposite the glass-plated main reception entrance which was reached by driving up the ramp. The chancery and commercial sections were on the top floor of the building while the passport and immigration offices were on the ground floor. This was a symbolic separation. There was a door for entry clearance applicants at the side of the building. I had my own office within the immigration section and opposite me, in his office, was the F&CO man who was having to do his penance in carrying out the loathsome entry clearance work. He was known as 'Jumbo' and was an ex-RAF man married to a woman called Paula. In fact he loathed working for the F&CO and referred to most of them as a bunch of tossers although he grudgingly conceded that there was the odd exception. He reserved his special venom for the security officers with whom he had worked in India. He detested their Masonic links which he considered to be sinister. He particularly disliked the two security officers within our High Commission, both Masons, who knew of his dislike of their organisation and were constantly seeking to report him for breaches of security. However, he was far too conscientious and wily an operator to be caught out by them.

Jumbo and Paula, who dressed like an earth mother wearing caftans and gaudy beads, were very good to us. They lived in one of the five small houses within the compound of the High Commission which were tiny compared to our own house in Martin Mill. To our horror, we discovered that it was proposed by the Administration Officer, one of the key posts within the High Commission, that we would live in Jumbo's house after a month when he was due to leave. Michelle and I did not want to experience Jamaica by living within a compound. An additional concern was the swimming pool close by to the houses: we feared that the children might well drown there as drowning accidents involving swimming pools and small children were all too common.

We were stuck in the Pegasus Hotel in a small room, living together while I settled into the job. It was difficult. Although it was a first class hotel with a calypso band constantly playing *Yellow Bird Up High in Banana Tree* in the evenings (how I hate that song) and it was clean with a huge swimming pool, it wasn't home. Also, we noticed after the first week that the maids were stealing the children's toys.

We really needed our own transport but our car still hadn't arrived from the UK. Jumbo and Paula really did their best to help us here and we still remember their kindness, but we felt isolated as strangers in a new country. If we left the hotel for a walk then we were the subject of intense scrutiny as all the boys had blond hair, as did Michelle. We hardly blended into the crowd. I was always concerned for our safety.

The F&CO staff were generally sympathetic, especially as we were the first family to arrive, but seemed uninterested in helping us to settle in. I was anxious for us to find a house that would suit us and to get the children settled into schools. I lobbied the Deputy High Commissioner (DHC) to put pressure on the administration section to come up with suitable accommodation. I finally convinced the DHC to agree that the house on the compound was too small for our family. Fortunately, a member of staff who had also recently arrived, had turned down a bungalow offered to him and his wife which was located about three miles away from the High Commission. The bungalow was situated within a Jamaican community. The wife of this new member of staff didn't want to live there as she thought that it was not up to the standard appropriate to her husband's grade and she was worried about security. We went to see it. Our car had now arrived and we were finally free to travel without being reliant on the kindness of others.

We drove up to 15 Widmer Drive, Kingston 6, and saw that the property was situated on the corner of the street which ran into the main road leading back into New Kingston. On that road there were shops made out of board with crude signs pasted on them advertising jerk chicken and fruit; reggae music was playing everywhere; barefooted children were running up and down the hill; cars honked at each other. It was noisy. It was vibrant. We loved it. The white gates to the bungalow opened on to a large front garden where grew a huge mango tree and palm trees.

There were many other varieties of exotic trees and shrubs around the garden. As you drove down the driveway you would mount a short ramp and park your car under the carport which had a door leading into the property. There was a white iron cage protecting the large patio area at the front but there was also a similar cage across the entrance door. High security. The assistant administration officer accompanying us explained that such cages were commonplace in Jamaica and were to deter attackers. The property needed a coat of paint.

We entered the front door to find that there was a medium-sized kitchen, maids' quarters and a large dining and sitting room with three big bedrooms adjacent to it. Access to the bedrooms was controlled by a locked iron-grilled gate referred to locally as the 'rape gate.' It was apparently commonplace for robbers forcing an entry into the property not only to rob the owners but to rape the women before they left. The gate would have to be locked at night in order to protect us. A dark reality for us.

We chose to ignore the horror stories and focus on the delights of escaping from the hotel. The children loved the garden which was enclosed by a wall surrounding the property and was a safe play area. We didn't pay too much attention to the décor or to the furniture, but we both agreed that the property was in a good position, close to the High Commission with plenty of room for the children to play and was essentially safe, or as a safe as could be expected.

As we were leaving, Michelle noticed a dirty looking animal asleep on the side of the porch. The assistant admin officer said that the dog on the porch seemed to belong to the house but that he would get rid of it as it was clearly filthy. The dog had barely moved a muscle and it looked half-dead. We said that we would keep the dog – we like animals. Later, Michelle and I washed the dog and he came up almost white. He looked like a whippet and I called him Dice which was the name of one of the bombers in which my Dad had flown. In time, Dice became part of the family and was a real character. Any bitch that was in season needed to beware of him. We have seen him climb a near vertical chain-link fence and escape from the garden in order to be of service.

On our return to the High Commission, I told the administration officer that we would take the bungalow once it had been painted. After some hesitation, on security grounds, he agreed to our having it. We were thrilled finally to have the promise that we could move in two weeks later. We would have a home again. We moved in as planned and our spirits soared. The helper – in Jamaica a maid was known as a 'helper' – who worked for us had worked for the family who had previously lived in the bungalow and she asked us to employ her. Her name was Icy and she had originally worked for the High Commission before she had had an accident in the kitchen which had left her scarred. She was a large proud lady with a gentle voice. She clearly liked our children and we said that we would like to employ her. It was a good decision as not only was she an excellent cook, but she ran our household very efficiently. Michelle was able to relax and pursue pastimes that she enjoyed. We were also asked to employ a gardener called Mr. Nelson. His previous employer had dismissed him as he had 'attitude.' He wasn't very good at taking orders from a woman. Mr. Nelson was only five feet four inches tall but he had the most enormous muscles on his arms that I have ever seen. He had his own hill farm. I interviewed him and asked him why he had left his previous job. He told me honestly that he hadn't liked the way the lady had spoken to him. She hadn't asked him to do jobs but ordered him. He said that he was his own man and would do a good job but had a right to be treated properly. I liked him, Michelle liked him and the boys liked him. I said that he was hired. We got to know him really well and he would do anything to safeguard our family. He was a man to be reckoned with: he told me that he had once killed a man, chopping him with his machete, when he had tried to 'thief' a goat from him on his farm. In Jamaica this was not unusual. Mr. Nelson wasn't much of a gardener and once fell out with Icy when he claimed that she had tried to poison him with her soup, but our home was starting to come together and Icy and Mr. Nelson were eventually reconciled.

We could now really start the job of getting our family settled, but this proved to be far from straightforward. Andrew was too young to attend school but we looked for schools that would be suitable for Gareth and Alex. The school recommended by the High Commission was the Priory School in New Kingston. This school had a mixture of children of diplomats and local children from wealthy backgrounds. It was run on American lines and seemed easy-going. When we first visited the school, it looked like something out of the John Travolta film, *Grease*, with the cast singing, *Summer Days, Drifting Away*, as provocatively dressed girls smooched up to smart fast-talking dudes standing outside the school and smoking cigarettes. We couldn't see our boys fitting seamlessly into this environment and didn't care for it ourselves. Nevertheless, in the absence of a suitable alternative, the boys attended the Priory School.

We were astounded when we received their first term school reports. It seemed that they were child geniuses as they achieved straight As for all their subjects. These were not the children we had nurtured. Although our sons were bright enough it was evident that the reports had been written to encourage parents to continue to pay for the expensive tuition. We later got an insight into how the school was really functioning when Gareth came home one day and said that the teacher had left the class in the hands of a student to take the music lesson while she went for a driving lesson. The student had written the word 'fuck' as many time as he could on the lines of musical notation shown on the blackboard. An interesting approach to music. I think that if we had left them there they might have been educated as gangsters but, not surprisingly, that was not what we wanted. After some further investigation I found a school called St. Peter's and St. Paul's Catholic School which was not far from where we lived. It had old-fashioned values which included uniforms for students and rules governing their behaviour. Our two blond boys stood out in a sea of black and brown faces and they had their problems integrating but they left that school three years later with a solid education which enabled them to engage with our own school system on our return to the UK.

Jamaica was a fascinating place. Michelle and I leaned heavily on each other emotionally as we experienced a

Gareth, Alex and Andrew ready to start their school day.

different culture: addictive music was played 'yard' style with basic booming rhythms; there were food shortages in the supermarkets; aggressive begging by young well-built males hampered your progress as you walked through the streets; beautiful Jamaican women, elegantly dressed like models, walked to work in a proud and haughty manner; Rastafarians[1] smoking spliffs with their dreadlocks looked cool and aloof in their multi-coloured hats; cars and buses in poor repair hurtled around corners cutting through pedestrians like a hot knife through butter. You would often see youngsters on roller skates hanging with one hand onto the back of packed mini-buses as they careered dangerously around corners.

There were cloudless blue skies and hot balmy evenings. The smell of rain crept into your nostrils before it arrived from the hills that ringed Kingston and then suddenly the rain tumbled furiously through the gullies flooding the streets in which boys splashed and played. It was chaotic, colourful and exciting. Music could be heard everywhere. Jamaicans talked loudly and aggressively to each other with expansive hand movements. Often you would think that a fight was about to break out between people holding a conversation. It was commonplace to see farmers or land-workers walking along with a wickedly sharp machete dangling from their hands. The police were called Red Stripes as the uniform they wore had a red stripe running down the trouser leg. The best Jamaican beer was also called Red Stripe. Marijuana or 'weed' was illegal but nevertheless it was openly smoked throughout Jamaica. White rum was a powerful drink and was used not only for drinking but also for medicinal purposes. Jamaicans are very superstitious and so there were still pockets of dark magic to be found on the island among people living close to a vibrant Christianity. Jamaican churches were happy places, full of singing and laughter, but the God that the preachers gave to the congregation in their sermons was a vengeful God should laws be broken or disobeyed.

I started to settle into the daily rhythm of the High Commission (HC) but it was made clear to me by my colleagues that they thought that immigration was the equivalent of pond life within the F&CO environment. Nevertheless, our immigration section was the happiest section of the HC in which to work. We had a Jamaican whom we called 'Mac' whose responsibility was to organise the orderly presentation of applicants. He had worked in the High Commission for many years and was a trusted employee although later I found out to my cost that he was corrupt.

In my second year at the HC a passenger in possession of an entry clearance issued at the High Commission arrived at Gatwick Airport on the Kingston flight and was detained by the immigration authorities who did not believe her story concerning the reason for her visit. I was contacted in order to explain the basis on which the entry clearance had been issued. When I checked, I found that her entry certificate had been stolen from our supply and that the counterfoil had been made to appear as if the certificate had been spoiled and discarded. Additionally, when I went back through the past issues, I found that this was not the only time fraud had taken place. An investigation revealed that Mac had been responsible for obtaining these entry certificates by deception and his knowledge of our system, gained over the years, had allowed him to cover his tracks. He was eventually sacked and a major review of our administration procedures took place. I really felt sorry that his association with the High Commission had to end in such an unpleasant manner as he had such an engaging personality and was well liked by all. Who knows what drove him to risk his job and pension?

Our audio-typist was another Jamaican lady called 'Icy'. She was an amply built lady who held strong opinions on morality and these opinions were reinforced weekly through her church visits. We dictated our statements into a recorder and she would spend her days typing up the recordings made by the officers about applicants for entry clearances who would have been refused permission to travel to the UK mostly on the grounds that they were not genuine visitors or did not meet the requirements for settlement. She would type up our statements which then become legal documents subject to scrutiny by the appellate authorities if an applicant chose to appeal against a decision – mostly in settlement cases.

Within the office were three local women, all expatriates: one from Scotland, one from Australia and one from Essex. These women had led interesting and colourful lives and were either in Jamaica because of their husband's employment or for personal reasons. All of them were lively conversationalists, especially Sheila from Essex who was a man-eater in her spare time. It was a lively office with a full and noisy waiting room of Jamaican applicants keen to secure entrance to the UK.

Dealing with Jamaicans was a real challenge for me. Of course there were the usual tricksters who made up stories about their backgrounds, seeking to convince me that they had a job and settled life to return to after their two week holiday in the UK but the fact was that the Jamaican economy was depressed and few local inhabitants from a lower economic background had sufficient funds to leave Jamaica simply for a holiday. I learned that in Jamaica it is not uncommon for people to hold down two or three jobs just to make ends meet and if you visited relatives abroad, you would not expect to pay for anything during your visit When I interviewed an applicant, I would often be told that the money for the trip was saved by 'trowing a pardner' or that's what it sounded like. A group of neighbours would get together and pay weekly into one central fund which was held by one trusted person and God help him or her if they didn't take care of the money. In Jamaica retribution would be swift and merciless. When a contributor needed funds, he would take the amount needed and then just keep paying back into the fund until the debt was repaid. The community supported itself without the need for banks. The system actually worked quite well but, as a young immigration officer, I took some convincing that this was a legitimate way of funding a holiday.

You have to immerse yourself in the culture if you are to understand the people. It certainly wasn't unusual for me to be shouted at if I refused an entry clearance to someone: I was often threatened. In fact this happened to me on an almost daily basis but I soon got used to the tempestuous nature of Jamaicans.

I was often offered gifts by applicants when they returned from a visit. This was their way of thanking me for believing their intentions were genuine. An enormous lady, twenty-five stone plus, who said that she spoke to the spirits of the dead and was a medium of renown in Jamaica, had previously visited the UK but had exceeded her permission to stay by three months. She had therefore been illegally in the UK. She came back to me four months after her return in order to ask to if she could visit the UK again. Normally I would have refused her an entry clearance but I saw no harm in her and gave her another chance, emphasising that she must keep to the rules this time. She went over for the visit and was back within the time permitted. I was surprised when Mac said that she had left a present with him in order to thank me for my trust in her. The present was a three foot by four foot picture frame which contained a detailed tapestry crafted in lace depicting The Lord God Himself surrounded by angels with trumpets. My name had been embroidered in the middle of this work and linked to the Lord proclaiming me to be *Blessed Mr Jones*. I have been called many things in life but never that. It must have cost a lot of money but I had to give it back to my benefactor as we could not accept gifts otherwise it might be gathering dust now up in my loft as certainly Mrs. Jones would never have displayed it on any wall of ours.

The characters within the High Commission could have appeared in a Dickens novel. The High Commissioner (HC) was Mr. Drinkall, The Deputy High Commissioner (DHC) was Mr. Beveridge and one of the communication staff was Mr. Tippett. Surely there was a joker back in London who was grouping these postings to Jamaica by surnames connected with drink? As it happened all of these men were masters of the drink. The HC was a dapper man who was serving out his last posting. He intended to settle in Jamaica after his retirement. Years later I heard he had been murdered during a robbery at his house which was near Irish Town, about four miles outside Kingston. Rumours were that the post of HC in Jamaica was given to retirees who had an expectation of making as much money as they could from their final posting in order to cushion financially their departure from office.

His number two, the DHC, was a small man who looked perpetually frightened. His wife was very kind to us. She was clearly weary of Foreign Office life and how serving diplomat's wives were expected to support their husband's protocol-bound life. We almost immediately broke the invisible protocol rules which govern life abroad in diplomatic missions when Michelle, who met Mrs. Beveridge at a 'Witches and Bitches' meeting – the short-hand used informally to describe the weekly meeting of diplomats' wives – invited her and her husband to have dinner with us. Michelle never gave it a second thought, but there were gasps from the women present as it just wasn't the done thing. Nevertheless, Mrs. Beveridge accepted the invitation and she and her husband came to dinner with us some weeks later. I had nothing much to gain from seeking the DHC's patronage for, although he was my boss at that time, my future lay with the Home Office. The evening proved to be both relaxing and entertaining: Michelle is a good cook so we ate well, played music that they liked and spoke freely. The DHC's wife later said that it was the best evening that they had enjoyed since their arrival in Jamaica.

Within six months both Mr. Drinkall and Mr. Beveridge had departed. A new HC arrived, Mr. Smallman, who looked and acted like a bishop. He was full of bonhomie and had a clerical air about him.. His number two, the DHC, Jeremy Jasper, cut a tall, slightly stooping figure with a cultured deep voice. His Indian wife was a large lady who wore saris which exposed rolls of fat dancing gaily around her midriff. Jeremy was my new boss, and if he ever made a decision without first extracting a piece of fence from up his rear end then I certainly didn't see it. When asked anything, all he would say was, 'thank you for bringing it to my attention'. His job was to make sure that the High Commission ran smoothly and he relied heavily on his administration officer (AO) to keep on top of matters.

The AO has a very powerful role to play within a mission. He or she controls every facet of mission life and there is nothing that can be achieved without his or her agreement. Normally AOs are selected for their wide experience. By the time they have reached the age of forty, however, their promotion opportunities are very limited. Thwarted ambition can mean that the AO may well be bitter, twisted, mean, nasty or possibly shady. Our new AO was Terry Evans and had served previously as AO in Chile. He once boasted to me that he had made at least half a million pounds from that posting. He was a large man with a wide forehead and heavy hooked nose. He spoke with a broad Geordie accent. He chain-smoked and was believed to hold a senior position in the Masonic Order. Naively, when we arrived at the HC, Michelle and I thought that we were part of a team. We had the youngest and largest family and probably had to deal with more problems on a daily basis than most. It was certainly recognised that to work in immigration spelled trouble for you but that was my daily responsibility and I accepted it. What I couldn't accept was the invisible barrier that seemed to separate Home Office from F&CO staff.

General talk amongst theF&CO staff in the HC cast doubt on Evans' real reason for his regular trips to Miami. Rumours were circulating that he might be manipulating currency exchange rates and importing and later selling goods brought into Jamaica under diplomatic privilege. I had no way of knowing if the rumours were true but I was surprised when he once told me that he was on track for easily exceeding his Chilean experience on the money-making side and he had the best of every luxury in his large villa and pool. His wealthy appearance seemed well beyond his rank within the mission. I didn't trust him one bit and he didn't like me.

The distribution of some meat was to become a catalyst for change. We were all members of the HC commissary which imported goods from the UK and sold them at close to cost price to HC members. This kept our overall food costs down but also let us have access to UK goods rather than having to rely on local goods which were often in short supply. It was a fair and most helpful system, especially if you had a family like ours. The commissary accountant was on the HC staff. He was a small, wiry Scotsman with quick darting eyes. He had a cunning and furtive look about him that said he was a survivor. He was an obsequious and knee-crooking knave when he was working for the colonel. He was deferential while in the colonel's company and absolutely vitriolic behind his back. The adjutant's wife was a large lady with a rolling gait who had that resigned look in her face which reflected years of having been an army wife. She was grimly determined to take advantage of any-thing that she could and, unfortunately for us, she was in charge of running the commissary. One day Michelle was in the HC commissary shop which was located downstairs in the High Commission. She opened up one of the freezers and saw that there were lamb joints in it, as well as other meats and cheeses: all sorts of goodies. I love lamb: it's my favourite meat. Michelle was just about to take a lamb joint out when the adjutant's wife tore across the room at the speed of an Olympic runner and nearly slammed the freezer lid down on Michelle's fingers. Michelle was bemused. The adjutant's wife hastily explained that the meat could not be sold to Michelle as it was part of an order bought from the Australian Commissary and it was now all allocated.

That night, Michelle told me what had happened and I set about carrying out an informal investigation as it all seemed irregular to me. I quickly discovered that a consignment of goods had been bought by our commissary from the Australian commissary and that the goods had been allocated to nearly all the members of the HC except us. Strange. Here we were on a low income with the biggest family in post and also members of the commissary and yet we were not included in the distribution.

I decided that we needed to explore this further. I wrote to the adjutant, who was also the commissary accountant, asking him to give me a list of the order and its distribution within the HC. You would have thought that I had thrown a banger into a barrel of gunpowder. He stormed into my office demanding to know why I wanted the information. He said that he was responsible for the accounts but I wouldn't understand them as he used a military accounting system. I told him that it must mean that it was simpler to understand as I knew the military liked simplicity. He said that they had tried to contact us in order to allocate us some meat but we had been away the previous weekend and therefore had not answered our phone. In fact we had not been away. He explained that they had to distribute the goods quickly and he went on and on. I said nothing but just looked steadily at him watching him shift awkwardly from foot to foot. I thanked him with barely suppressed contempt for his explanation.

I knew that some of the HC UK-based staff were members of the Masonic Order and attended the local temple which was located near to the HC. It was no secret as Terry Evans, the security officers and others could be seen regularly leaving together for their lodge meetings, dressed in their dinner jackets and walking across the road to the temple. I had heard from friends who worked for local companies outside the HC that commissary goods could be bought if you had the right connections. There was speculation that having a Masonic connection might well be helpful. I had no way of proving or disproving such rumours but the reselling of such goods for a profit was, of course, illegal.

Evans certainly didn't like me. I wondered if the reason why we were not included in the distribution of the order was that we were judged to be outsiders. I thought that this was ridiculous. I couldn't have cared less about a leg of lamb but I was appalled by the lack of principle. It was worrying the way the commissary mission was being run. I consulted some of the HC staff whom I thought that I could trust. They were embarrassed about the way the distribution had been organised and were apologetic.

Although I would have preferred a smooth life, as I had quite enough on my plate representing the Home Office and dealing with the media and the HC on the daily grind of immigration matters, I was not prepared to run away from what I believed was worth fighting for. I thought that the worst they could do to me if I made a fuss would be to send me home. I decided that I would attack the whole of the commissary system. I was as sure as I could be that the HC and DHC were honourable but that they simply avoided asking too many questions of their staff as long as their employees were doing their jobs satisfactorily. I also sought the advice of one of the high-ranking diplomatic staff who previously had worked for the Security Services in the UK and was now working as a diplomat. He was aware of the shady practices within the HC. He thought that I was doing the right thing to be a whistle-blower but couldn't get involved personally. He wouldn't specify the reasons why.

Michelle and I discussed the possible consequences of any action and she gave me her full backing. But how was I to expose the questionable practices? I needed a ruse. I knew that the AO and his followers would already have covered every angle concerning the distribution. Therefore I wrote to Jeremy Jasper asking him to call a meeting of the commissary committee because there was information that I needed to lay before them. I did not specify the nature of this information but hinted that it might be embarrassing for the mission. The DHC called a meeting and invited me to attend. The committee seemed hostile. The wee adjutant jumped the gun even before Jeremy had officially opened the meeting to say that if this was just about us not getting the goods, his wife had tried very hard to contact us to ask if we wanted to buy some meat but she simply hadn't been able to get hold of us. He repeated the same old tired explanation. I said nothing until Jeremy asked me to explain what this was about. It was then that I dropped a bombshell.

I explained that I had just finished playing squash in the Liganea Club in New Kingston and had been in the bar having a drink by myself after my partner had left. Next to me was a club member who had engaged me in conversation about squash but who had then asked me if I was interested in selling him some goods from the commissary. He understood that some others diplomats within the HC were doing this and said that he would give me a good price for whisky, especially Black Label whisky, but also any other goods. I told him that I wasn't interested and didn't understand why he was asking me to supply him with these goods. I asked for the names of those that might be engaged in illegally selling commissary goods but he finished his drink, shrugged his shoulders and walked off.

It was this experience that I wanted to bring to the committee's attention. I had been concerned about the handling of the meat order and surprised and disappointed by our treatment, but this was insignificant compared to the information that suggested abuse of privilege. Of course I couldn't prove that there was profiteering taking place but there was a stunned silence and the wee adjutant started blathering again until Evans silenced him and agreed that it was serious situation He asked if I could produce the man who had approached me.

I said that I certainly would trace my informant if asked by the DHC and I looked at Jeremy who now clearly saw that a real nest of vipers would be uncovered if we went down this route. What if it was true and I did produce the man? There would have to be a major investigation which might involve police investigators being sent out from the UK. It would reflect very badly on the HC. He said that the HC and he would come down hard on any member found to be profiteering and that it was illegal to profiteer. I suggested that a simple scrutiny of the accounts would show if anyone had been buying a disproportionate amount of goods which could not be used for personal or entertaining use. The wee adjutant was again spluttering and saying that his military method of accounting was difficult to understand for the layman and that it might be difficult to spot this information.

The DHC had to find a way out of this. He suggested that the committee co-opt me as the family representative. I agreed to this as long as the committee accountant would show me the accounts and explain the system to me. Jeremy was now presented with this situation and sought to find a diplomatic solution. He ruled that the adjutant had to stop using an accounting system that was esoteric and not easy to follow. With immediate effect he was to use the same accounting system as the HC. He would need to work with the HC accountant in order to make any changes, and present the accounts to the committee within one month.

Jeremy was head of the committee and therefore had oversight of the accounts. If he demanded a breakdown of the distribution in simple terms, the commissary accountant would have to give it. Once this was done, the accounts could be open to scrutiny. He had also directed that the commissary and the HC accountant work together. The HC accountant worked to Terry Evans. By coincidence he was a new arrival who also accompanied Terry and others on their lodge nights. Unfortunately I never did discover who were the recipients of the meat order and what goods were being bought by HC staff. I never saw the original accounts. I was not on the circulation list of the new set of accounts either. My impression was that the wagons had been circled. I had had enough.

At the very least my ruse had affected a change in the accounting system, making it more transparent. I suspected that I would now be *persona non grata* within the HC.

What followed came as no surprise. All the committee, except Jeremy, froze me out. They would talk to me only when they had to on business matters. They would ignore me on a daily basis. Evans would try to block or frustrate any administration matter that came to him from me. I noticed that the two security officers were increasingly patrolling our section and trying to find breaches of security. It was clearly a ploy to punish me for attacking them. It was pathetic. It made my life difficult but Michelle and I had each other. Fortunately, we had also started to build a circle of friends outside the HC. This cold shoulder approach went on for about four months, with increasing harassment from the security officers. But sauce for the goose is sauce for the gander. When I went into the HC on a Sunday to complete some work, I was delighted to find that the door to the immigration waiting rooms was open as was the door leading into my office and no-one was about. I immediately shut them and waited for Tom, the ratty-looking security officer, to appear. He was astounded to find me there and I said that I was just about to telephone the DHC, who was head of security, to report a serious security breach. He was furious and in a real corner. I asked him for his opinion as HC security officer. He told me he had been taking some chairs out of my waiting room as he needed them for a pool party and had just left the doors open for five minutes. I had him. A breach of security is absolute. Five minutes or five hours makes no difference in terms of the offence.

I asked him what I should do and he suggested that we should deal with it between us with no harm done. I asked him to explain why he had intensified his sweeps of our immigration section which coincided with the commissary committee meeting. He didn't reply. I suggested that a return to normal security checks would be helpful and said that I would think about my action. Not reporting the offence was an offence in itself but, practically, the breach of security was minor. I left Tom stewing until Monday morning when he came to see me. I logged the breach within our immigration section in order to cover myself but didn't report it up the line. It was interesting how the intensity of his sweeps on our section immediately dropped to normal levels. However, I felt that I was now fighting on two fronts on a daily basis. It was not pleasant.

Sometimes I would be so exhausted from my work at the HC that I would come home, get changed into running shorts and trainers and just blast off up the hill adjacent to our road in order to clear my head. I felt that if I didn't have such a physical outlet then I would explode. This run was the run from hell. It was up a steep hill and, as I reached the first bend, I would hear the sound of a large, cross-bred Rottweiler dog as he smelt me and started his run around the back of the shacks on the hill. My heart would start pumping as I increased my jogging pace to that of a sprint. My aim was to get to the bend on the corner where there was a little shop by the gully before the dog.

There were always three or four men sitting on the wall opposite the shop. They would cheer me on to beat the dog who was snapping at my heels – or at least I think that's what they were doing . Usually, I would run thirty feet up the hill just past the shop before the dog would finally give up the chase. By this time I had definitely forgotten about the challenges of the day. Often the men would clap as I tore up the hill and then ran on for about a quarter of a mile or so in the heat. When I reached the top, I recovered my breath as I stretched out looking down at the view of Kingston spread below me. I found it strange that the dog would never bother me on the way down the hill.

Just past the shop, sitting on the gully wall, there would be a poorly dressed elderly man with his grey hair woven in to twisted dreadlocks. He had white teeth that looked far better than mine and very good for his age, and a kind face. He tended about ten goats who grazed at the roadside but they were never there when I started my run. On my return, I would usually stop and talk to him and found that he had lived in the UK many years before. We would discuss just about any subject for five minutes and he had a considered opinion on politics, religion, and sport. I really enjoyed talking to him and looked forward to our chats which gave me an insight into life in Jamaica. I even began to understand his heavy Jamaican accent although I sometimes missed a sentence or two if he became excited. At Christmas, I would buy him a bottle of Scotch and a carton of cigarettes which I told him were for him to enjoy and were not to be sold on. I wasn't really worried what he would do with them but it was important to me that he knew the gift was for him. I made sure that I logged that I had given the gifts as part of goodwill as I knew that I was still under close scrutiny. The smile on his face when I gave the gifts to him was delightful and he once gave me hug which really surprised me. Jamaica was often full of surprises. Some of those surprises were not pleasant.

We were about to head off in our car to the north coast, which was our favourite beauty spot, when a madman tried to 'chop' me. 'Chop' is patois for to cut with a knife, axe or machete. Our favourite place on the north coast was the Port Antonio area where Noel Coward had his villa, Firefly. We had the gates of our house open in preparation for leaving and I was loading up the car while Michelle was getting the children ready. I thought that our dog, Dice, was running about in the garden behind me when suddenly a madman, brandishing a wicked looking machete, appeared at our gate from nowhere. He was foaming at the mouth and waving the machete at me alleging that my dog had bitten him. As evidence of this he showed me two deep scratch marks on the back of one of his legs. I was trying to keep him away from the house and my family when our domestic helper, Icy, came out and started to cuss (swear) at him. He went berserk, attempting to get at her but I managed to keep him away from Icy and sent her back in. I eventually persuaded the attacker to drop the machete to his side and to stop threatening me with it. He asked me for money in order to go to the hospital to have his legs treated.

Now a Jamaican crowd would just build up from nowhere and suddenly there were about ten men and women around us in a ring. The madman was still ranting at me and the situation was tense. I kept my eye on the machete and was prepared to hit him if he made a sudden move towards me. I asked the crowd what they thought I should do about his allegations. They said that it was scam. He was well known for scoring his legs with a nail and then blaming a dog for biting him. He would intimidate the owner into giving him money. I asked the crowd what I should do, explaining, that I was afraid for my wife and children. Two men got hold of him, one wrenched the machete out of his grip and they drove him off, even throwing his machete after him and cursing at him.

He picked up the machete and started to walk back towards us but thought better of it and then disappeared. I thanked the crowd for their help and shook hands with as many of them as I could. They disappeared like magic giving me time to shut the gates just as Dice, came trotting back through them. I had been sure that he was in the garden. Had Dice bitten the madman? I wasn't sure but believed that the marks had looked too clean and parallel to be dog bites.

This was a fine example of Jamaican crowds being fair in their judgements but life is not always as kind. Adverse situations like that can happen so quickly in Jamaica and, if you don't have your wits about you, events can get very nasty indeed. One of my friends, a Scouser who was the manager of the local paper factory in downtown Kingston, was driving his wife and son to the university beach, about twelve miles outside Kingston going east on the south coast. It was noon on Sunday and we were following him in our car. He was travelling at about twenty-five miles an hour on the main road that ran near the sea. The road had wooden shacks on both sides and there were plenty of people about, talking and relaxing. Suddenly, a young boy aged about eight years old, ran out into the road in front of him. He was chasing a football. My friend tried desperately to avoid him but the boy bounced off the front of his car and lay still in the road. I stopped my car quickly and ran to the boy. My friend was distressed. He was saying that the boy had 'just run out' in front of him and there was nothing he could do to avoid him. I checked the boy over. He was breathing, seemed alert but his leg looked broken. Within seconds, a large hostile crowd of Jamaicans had gathered and I could sense that we were in trouble if I didn't quickly take control of the situation.

The crowd was not interested in what had really happened. They had a sense of outrage that the boy had been hit by a fat white man in a large car. I could hear the crowd getting noisier. I quickly asked them to bring me a relative of the boy and a man came forward, saying that he was the boy's uncle. We shouldn't really have moved the boy but I immobilised his leg as best I could and told the uncle that we had to get the boy to hospital fast if were to prevent any further damage to him. I asked him if he would come with us . We lifted the boy into my friend's car and I instructed the uncle to tell the crowd what was happening and also to tell them that we would take care of the lad. I then told my friend's wife and son to get into our car and urgently said to Michelle that she must get out of there fast and return to our home.

The crowd was now standing all around the car and we couldn't move unless it dispersed. I again asked the uncle to explain to the crowd that we had to get the boy to hospital and that his uncle was going with him. I asked someone to let his mother know where he was and to get her to come down to Kingston hospital as soon as she could. I said that we shouldn't hesitate or the boy's leg might become worse. I pushed my friend out of the driving seat – no mean feat as he was a big man – and he clambered awkwardly across into the passenger seat. I didn't want him to get out of the car as I feared that there would be violence. I jumped behind the wheel, turned on the engine and eased the car around in a circle to point the way back to Kingston. People were everywhere but they moved slowly, still looking into the car. Tension hung in the air and sweat was running into my eyes, making me blink. I told the uncle to lean out of the window and tell the crowd to get out of the way as we needed to hurry. We sped off in a cloud of dust and, looking back in the mirror, I saw that the road was blocked with the crowd staring after us. I heaved a sigh of relief. I was so glad that we had managed to get away unscathed

Fifteen minutes later, we arrived at the hospital. The boy was alert, inquisitive and looking around as we carried him into the hospital. In fact he seemed to be unhurt apart from a badly swollen knee. I was starting to think that his leg might not be broken after all. We waited in the casualty department. You have no idea what the waiting area of Kingston hospital is like unless you have actually been there. It seemed like a disaster recovery area. Hot, sweating people were sprawling on chairs or sitting on the floor. Some men were holding bloodstained rags over head cuts; others were bent double and quietly moaning. Everyone looked to me as if they needed urgent attention. The TV series that show a patient on the trolley surrounded by doctors and nurses quickly giving medical commands while drips are set up on the move were not a reality here. The administration staff were in fact moving as if they had lead boots on and seemed uninterested in just about everything. Hardly any nurses were to be seen and there was a smell of blood and urine in the hot stale air. I remembered that this was just Sunday lunch time. God alone knows what Saturday nights must be like. I created a bit of a fuss using my diplomatic identity in order to ensure that the boy was seen quickly.

He was examined by a doctor within an hour which was little short of a miracle. The leg was not broken and apart from the swelling and bruises, the doctor said that he was otherwise fine. I insisted that we got the boy's full address and details as well as those of his uncle. My friend gave his uncle some money for the taxi and any medication and then we left the hospital.

My friend was exhausted and I felt weary. He just wanted to go home and put the day behind him. I told him that his troubles would just be starting as now we had to go and report the accident to the police. If we didn't do so, and the family filed a complaint and looked to sue him, he would have a very hard time fighting it. After all, the accident had not been his fault. Reluctantly he agreed and we drove to the central police station on a very hot August afternoon.

The officer at reception was hot and bored. He listened to what had happened but was uninterested. He said that as long as the boy was well there should be no problem. I insisted that he took a statement but he couldn't be bothered. I then had to play my diplomatic card again and insist on speaking to his inspector about his attitude. We would have to wait for his arrival. I used the names of high-ranking police contacts with whom I had dealings on immigration matters to convince him that potentially I could make trouble for him. Eventually, we managed to spur the officer into action and my friend gave his statement and signed it. I witnessed it. The whole process took about three hours and it was exhausting.

What happened next? Within two days, the boy's family sent a 'collector' to see my friend at his factory. The collector, true to his name, tried to extort money from my friend. However, as my friend had already reported the accident to his insurance company he was able to give the collector the name of the insurance contact, explaining that it was now out of his hands. The matter wasn't settled for a long while. My friend received nasty threats for months and at one point he feared that he would receive a 'hit'. In Jamaica life was cheap. You could buy a gunman downtown at that time for US$50 (£30) and no questions would be asked. If you wanted someone out of the way, it was very easy to arrange. My friend worked downtown near the waterfront, close to Trench Town, a very tough area of Kingston. Fortunately for him, his factory employed a lot of locals and it was in their interests to keep him safe. The word went out that he should be left alone but he still had to make a one-off payment to keep the peace and he suffered sleepless nights for at least six months. If we hadn't taken the action that we had, my Scouse friend would have been mercilessly bled financially by gangster Dons who controlled crime in Kingston. The dollar is king in Jamaica.

Terry Evans. He just wouldn't go away. He took every

opportunity to disrupt my life and would often come to see me in my office and explain with a smirk on his face why we couldn't have an item I had requested for the office. We had to fight for everything. However, it wasn't all gloom and doom. The grand Christmas party *chez* Monsieur Evans was one to remember. The Evans were hosting the event and had chosen to invite nearly everyone from the HC because the guest of honour was a visiting baroness. The villa was ablaze with light and Christmas sleighs, Santas, and crackers could be found in every corner. The pool area had waiters dressed in their best whites, scurrying around serving canapés and drinks of every description. Soft music wafted across the blue water mixed with the sounds of glasses tinkling, and light laughter. There was a party mood in the air. In the entrance hall stood a magnificent ten-foot high artificial Christmas tree imported from Miami. The decorations must have cost a fortune: there were glass bubbles displaying Christmas scenes with snow falling reflected in the light of hundreds of candles. The tree had a fairy on top of it. We all looked enviously at the tree. Michelle and I had a branch of pine at home that one of our forestry friends had kindly found for us to use as a Christmas trees. Jamaica didn't grow the sort of Christmas trees that could be found in the UK. We had decorated our branch with lights and tinsel to make it Christmassy. The children liked it.

Jim worked in the communications section of the HC and was known for his love of drink. When he eventually left his apartment to return to the UK, the landlord found that he had used his barbecue inside the apartment ruining the ceiling with black smoke. He liked to barbecue when he was drunk. Neighbours sometimes found him asleep in the flowerbed. However, he was sober when required to do his job and therefore given some leeway.

At the Evans' Christmas party, Jim was already drunk at 7.30 p.m. and guests were still arriving. The baroness was scheduled to say a few words at 8.00 p.m. after which the buffet would be served. Evans had spared no expense for this buffet and you could see the table groaning with lobster, crayfish and many other kinds of fish beautifully presented on silver trays. There were plates of beef and chicken and I wouldn't have been surprised to see a roasted swan next to the ice sculpture. Yes, there was an ice-sculpture. There were mounds of chilled profiteroles, ice cream and pastries of every description. Evans intended to impress everyone with his beneficence and he was doing a good job of it even though we knew that most of the cost would fall on the UK taxpayer.

Jim had been exploring the Evans' villa and came to join a small circle of us chatting near the Christmas tree. He said that he had looked in one of the villa's rooms and discovered at least ten full-size fridge freezers lined up like soldiers. He speculated on why Evans would need this number of freezers. It wasn't hard to guess. Jim was swaying and giggling. At 7.45 p.m. the Evans' small dog appeared. It was a terrier of some description and was wandering among the guests who were feeding it from their plates and making a fuss of it. Until, that is, it wandered up towards Jim. The dog stood by Jim's foot and I don't think that he was fond of dogs as he tried to move it away with the side of his foot, a gentle enough shove. He was holding a plate full of canapés and a large glass of red wine. The dog growled. Jim looked down at it and attempted another shove. Suddenly the dog made a grab for Jim's leg and caught hold of the trouser material shaking his head from side to side. Jim was infuriated and stood on one leg while attempting to throw the dog off with the other by vigorously shaking his shoe. This was no mean feat as he was also balancing a plate and a glass. His balance might also have been slightly shaky because of the amount of drink that he had already consumed.

It all happened in slow motion. Jim's back was towards

the Christmas tree as he hopped backwards with the dog hanging on to his trousers with great determination. Jim's arms windmilled backwards, throwing the plate of canapés up towards the fairy and the red wine in a graceful arc up towards the white walls where it spread like blood from *The Texas Chain Saw Massacre*. Jim, with his considerable bulk, fell into the tree hitting the tree stand as he disappeared beneath a crash of glass baubles and tinsel. The fairy toppled from the treetop and bounced on the floor in front of us. Seconds before all you could hear was the sound of clinking glasses and laughter. Now there was silence except for the soft music playing.

Mrs. Evans stood in her posh frock with her hands over her face. Terry Evans looked very much like he was about to have a heart attack, he was so angry. Jim crawled forward shrugging off the glass and tinsel. He attempted a smile and then mumbled something about the dog biting him. Evans 'helped' him up and frog-marched him to the front door and outside. He looked murderous by this time. I know it was not very charitable of us but we all felt that some sort of justice had been meted out that evening. I think that the baroness mentioned how sorry she was to hear that the tree was ruined.

Evans continued his vendetta against me until the end. When leaving your diplomatic post, it is customary for you to seek permission from the host government to sell your car once you have paid any import taxes. All diplomats did this as a means of making some money legitimately at the end of their stay. I was advised to do the same. You needed to submit an application to the Ministry of Foreign Affairs through the administration section in the HC in order to get approval. This process needed to begin some six months before leaving Jamaica in order to give the wheels of bureaucracy time to turn. I submitted my application six months before we were to leave but, some weeks later, when I checked with the administration section, I found that my application had not even been sent. I complained to Evans about this. He came to see me with his customary smirk. He told me that there was a logjam in the Ministry of Foreign Affairs and therefore he couldn't push my application through the system. He was having to prioritise applications. He then said that I should prepare to ship the car home as there would be no alternative if he couldn't get the application through in time for my departure. He laughed and said that he was sorry but implied there was nothing he could do.

I was furious about his action. He was lying but I couldn't prove it. It seemed like he would get away with this abuse of his position yet again. A week after his visit I received passport applications from the Ministry of Foreign Affairs for gratis entry clearances. This was usual. I asked my staff to prepare the passports and stamp them with the visas. I knew that Evans was in Miami at this time. I went to the admin. section and saw one of the secretaries. I asked her if I could have back my application to sell the car. She found my file and returned it to me. That lunch time I personally returned the passports to the Ministry of Foreign Affairs. I saw the Minister's secretary and asked her if the Minister could do me a favour by signing my application to sell the car. As it happened, I had previously met the Minister and so when he consented to my request saying that it would be ready to collect at 4 p.m. that afternoon. I mentally punched the air, but outwardly calmly thanked him for his help. That afternoon I obtained the document I needed and the next day I arranged to pay the car import tax and get the final documents I needed to enable me to sell the car. I already had a buyer.

I finalised the sale and told the buyer that I would hand the car over to him the week before we were due to depart. I returned the stamped document to the secretary and asked her to put it back in to the folder pending further administrative action. She did this. I waited for Evans to come to see me again with his aim of gloating over me. Sure enough, one month before we were due to leave, he arrived in my office. He started the conversation by asking how our preparations were going for our return home and I told him that we were well prepared and looking forward to going back to the UK. He then said that he was sorry but that he had tried to do everything he could in order to get me permission to sell my car, but the Ministry were just not taking any more applications at that time. He was smoking a cigarette as he lounged in the chair and looked up at the ceiling smiling. I told him that he shouldn't worry but should be happy that I had saved him some work. I explained that I had already sold the car and that all the paperwork had been properly completed. He jerked upright in his chair. His face reddened. He flew out of the office and went back upstairs only to reappear ten minutes later. He was absolutely furious with me and said that I had had no right to go behind his back. I said that I didn't know what he was talking about as clearly he had been trying to help me and all I had done was walk the application over. The Minister was more than happy to sign it and there was no mention of any logjam. I was happy if he wanted to complain to the DHC or the Minister himself for that matter. I asked him why he was acting so irrationally. He swore at me, stood up and banged the door shut as he stormed out of the room. I smiled.

But what became of Terry Evans? He admitted eight charges of false accounting and was jailed for nine months. The prosecution showed that Evans had been using High Commission money in Jamaica and putting it into his US bank account to buy Jamaican dollars on the black market. He restored the money at the official and much lower rate, pocketing the difference. At the Crown Court, Southwark, London, on 15 April 1992 he agreed that he used part of the money to supplement the HC's budget but also profited personally from transactions from 1984 to 1986.

NOTES FOR CHAPTER EIGHTEEN

1 – The 'Rastafari movement' or 'Rasta' is a religious movement that arose in the 1930s in Jamaica. Rastas worship Haile Selassie I, Emperor of Ethiopia (he ruled from 1930–1974) as God, also known as 'Jah'. The Rastafari movement rejects western society which is called 'Babylon,' from the metaphorical Babylon of the Christian New Testament. It proclaims Africa (also 'Zion') as the original birthplace of mankind, and from the beginning of the movement the call to repatriation to Africa has been a central theme. Awareness of the Rastafari movement has spread throughout much of the world because of its association with reggae music made popular by Bob Marley, the singer and songwriter.

19
'STOP OR I'LL SHOOT'

After we settled in our home, I joined the Royal Jamaica Yacht Club. I bought a small dinghy from a colleague who was leaving the HC and at weekends we would take our family out of the heat of Kingston and spend Saturday or Sunday sunbathing, swimming or sailing at the club. The club was not far from Port Royal, near the airport, and it still thrives today. It was a lively club, full of wealthy or privileged people from all walks of life who shared a common love of sailing, and possibly drink. The boys loved to swim and Gareth enjoyed the freedom of exploring the marina and its surroundings. They had little real freedom to roam elsewhere in the city of Kingston as it was far too dangerous.

At the club, they had adventures. Gareth was nearly chopped to bits by the propellers of a powerful motorboat and had to swim under its engines in order to escape injury. He was swimming in the sea with a friend, knowing that we had expressly forbidden it and he almost drowned playing on a half-sunk boat when planks disintegrated under his feet. We discovered these incidents only recently when exploring the past with him. But I had quite a few adventures of my own when sailing in that vast harbour and underestimating its tricky winds.

The night was clear and the stars shone brightly in the inky blue sky. The hills that surrounded Kingston harbour twinkled with lights from the small houses and shacks that were built on the slopes. Kingston was lit up and looked calm and peaceful as we set out from the marina to take part in a moonlight race. The full moon was clear and shone an eerie light across the dark harbour. The wind was blowing softly, just enough to fill the sails, as we slowly moved out of the marina and into the harbour. There were six of us on our yacht which was twenty-five feet long and had a small cabin. The owner was a friend of a friend who had invited Michelle and I to join the party. One of the young women on board was pregnant. Only the owner and I were really capable of sailing the yacht. The others were partying, enjoying a drink or two while we followed another eight yachts out to the starting line which ran parallel to the yacht club. Nobody took this race seriously. It was a social occasion and after an hour and half sailing we would head back to the club for some supper. The evening was warm and we chatted together, enjoying our slow sail around the harbour.

We were returning to the marina on the final leg of the race. I was steering and we were lying a comfortable last in the race. The wind had increased slightly so we were now making good progress before turning back around the marker buoy and home. It was a comfortable sail. I looked over my shoulder and saw a searchlight shining from about half a mile away on a boat that was quickly approaching in our direction. It seemed to be moving too fast to be a fishing boat and, worryingly, was coming directly at us. I told the others to keep their eyes on it – we wondered where it was heading. As it approached, the searchlight raked our sail and then flashed at us forcing us to shield our eyes. It was hard to see the boat itself but it seemed like a powerful motorboat. I started to worry, fearing that there might be drug-smugglers onboard the motorboat bearing down on us. Suddenly, the boat altered its course and manoeuvred to a new position thirty feet behind us, on our left. I could now clearly see a man standing on the foredeck. He was pointing a gun at us. Someone using a loudhailer then gave us orders: 'We are armed police. Stop the boat immediately or I'll shoot. We intend to board.'

I was astonished to hear this and immediately we all became alert. We had a jib (front sail) and a mainsail flying. Two of the women had previously been relaxing on the foredeck, one of whom was so heavily pregnant that she

My first boat, a Mirror Dinghy, actually upright for a change.

couldn't move quickly. The wind was blowing on to the port side of the boat. The only way to bring the boat to a stop would be to turn her into the wind but if I made this manoeuvre too quickly then I might endanger the women on deck. The other option was to drop the mainsail and I told the owner to prepare to get the sail down fast, but even then I knew the yacht could not stop as quickly as a power-boat with its powerful engines. I decided that I had to talk to the boat captain.

It sounds completely daft now but I turned to face the man with the gun and shouted out, 'British High Commission. We are in a race. Can I speak to the captain? Whats the problem?' The dark boat pulled close to us and a man, whom I believed to be the captain, stood at the boat rail. He could almost touch our boat. He asked me what we were doing and I told him that we were in a race. I said that we were based at The Royal Jamaican Yacht Club. He asked me why we did not have any stern lights showing. I hadn't been aware that the rear lights were not working and the owner immediately apologised, explaining that the wiring was faulty and that the bulbs must have blown because of this. The captain said that his crew were on the lookout for drug-runners and had spotted us moving slowly but not showing lights.

In fact we did have our port and starboard lights showing but admittedly the light from them was poor, so their interest in us was not unreasonable. He said that he wanted to search the boat. I asked him if he could accompany us back to the marina. I explained that we had a pregnant woman on board and that it would be safer for us if the search was done at the marina. He went into the wheelhouse and then returned to the boat rail saying that we could proceed but that we must fix the stern lights as soon as possible. I thanked him and then said, in an effort to lighten the situation, that we had now lost the race because of their intervention. He smiled and offered to give us a tow back into the marina but, unfortunately, the club rules didn't allow for this. Throughout our exchange, the policeman holding the rifle aimed at us had never dropped down the barrel of the gun. They were clearly ready for trouble. The powerboat's big engines roared as the boat swung away from us and sped off into the night, leaving us swaying in its wake.

We were quite subdued as I steered the boat back towards the marina. However, I relaxed a little too much and misjudged the approach towards the marina, lost my concentration and brought the yacht too close to the bank. The yacht slid to a halt as we stuck firmly in the mud. The owner and I then had to jump overboard, with ropes attached to us, and manhandle the yacht back into the main channel. It was hard and difficult work. We finally arrived back in the marina and brought the yacht safely to her berth. We were dripping wet but fortunately had no bullet holes in us. After cleaning up we joined the other crews at the bar. Our race position was confirmed by the judges. We had posted the worst time for such a race and were definitely last.

I preferred to sail in small boats. They are much more fun as you sail closer to the water and this gives you a real feel for the speed. You also have to make sailing decisions quickly so it is a great way to improve your skills. I upgraded the small dinghy to a 'Wayfarer' which is a fibre-glass-hulled sailing dinghy, often used for short sailing trips as a 'day boat'. The boat was just over fifteen feet long, broad and deep enough for three adults to sail comfortably for several hours. I bought it from a diplomat who was leaving Jamaica. It came with a trailer so I would be able to tow it home and work on it there. The boat was fast and great fun to sail.

My sailing companion, David, who worked for a Jamaican company, was an adventurer who was always keen to race the boat and see just how fast it would go. We would often capsize in the harbour and there was always the possibility of sharks cruising near the rubbish that could be found there, so getting back into the boat quickly was a priority. I always felt fear when the boat turned over and we went into the water.

One Saturday morning, we entered a race that was open to all classes of boat and therefore the eventual result was based on a handicap system. The smaller the boat, the more points you would accumulate if you finished. The weather in Kingston harbour can be very difficult as the winds swirl around the hills and meet warm air from the sea, causing testing conditions for sailors. We didn't like the conditions – the wind was blowing strongly and the waves in the harbour were three feet high with white crests. We discussed withdrawing from the race but eventually decided to take part. It was a triangular course that would take you across the three mile wide harbour, north towards the hills and then back to the marina with the wind behind you. Once we had started, the sailing was exhilarating. Our boat raced through the water, cutting through the waves at real speed. We took turns to take the tiller and steer the boat. When you were not steering her you would hang out of the boat balanced on a trapeze – the name given to a wire that comes from a point high on the mast to a hook on the crew member's harness at approximately waist level. The aim was to keep the boat as upright as possible by keeping your feet on the side of the boat and leaning backwards out to sea. It was a wild ride and we whooped and laughed as we sped through the waves. However, the wind was getting stronger. I started to get worried, as to make a mistake and capsize in these adverse conditions would spell real trouble for us. We managed to sail safely around the buoys and make it to the last leg of the triangle but we had very nearly capsized at least five times. I had had enough sailing and just wanted to get back safely as the conditions were worsening.

We aimed for the marina and had the wind behind us

and the sails spread either side of the boat. This is a really difficult point of sailing as you leap from crest to crest in a crazy slalom. The skipper has to be quick and agile in order to prevent the boat's stern moving across the wind in which case the boat would quickly capsize. David was the skipper taking the last leg and he was a very good skipper. I was glad that he was at the tiller as I did not think that I had sufficient experience to navigate home safely in the conditions that we faced. We were both silent as we knew just how dangerous it was to sail so close to the rocks on the shore where the waves were now pounding and foaming white but the wind had blown us there and it was almost impossible to increase our distance. As long as we maintained our course, we would be safe. Suddenly a wave lifted the transom – the stern of the boat – and, as it did, the wave also lifted the rudder from the pins that held it to the back of the boat. The rudder, tethered to the boat by the securing rope, then flew up into the air and crashed down into the water. We were now rudderless.

The boat raced down the waves and plunged bow-first into the pounding sea. The bow was at such a steep angle that David was flung forward from the rear of the boat and hit me. We both fell overboard away from the boat and we watched as the boat flipped onto its side and the mast hit the water. The whole boat then turned upside down, sinking little by little under the fury of the waves with its buoyancy tanks barely keeping the hull from submerging completely. This was bad news indeed. Waves crashed over us and the water stung our eyes. We both knew that we had to swim to the boat and use it as our life raft. The rocks were perilously close and we knew that if a wave picked us up and smashed us into a rock then we would be seriously injured, or worse. We were coughing as we had swallowed water and David had a cut on his head which oozed blood. We were both pale-faced. I turned my head quickly, looking around for any evidence of sharks. I was scared. Our bulky life-jackets made swimming difficult and the wind was blowing the boat away from us faster than we could swim to it. We were making little or no progress and tiring badly.

Suddenly, the boat came to a halt as if the mast had snagged on an underwater obstacle. We now had a chance to swim towards the hull and both of us battled desperately against the wind and the waves. We made it. We hung on grimly to the hull and looked at each other, both glad to be in one piece. Although I didn't like the fact that our legs were dangling in the water, I thought, and hoped, that it was probably too rough for sharks so close to the rocks.

We had been concentrating so hard on reaching the upturned hull that we hadn't noticed the sixty foot snow white powerboat that was approaching us at speed. It started to slow down when it was about two hundred feet away and then began to manoeuvre into the wind ten feet in front of our boat. I could clearly see the name of the boat on the stern, *Black Dancer*.

A large black man was now standing in the stern of the boat and he spoke to us in a broad Jamaican accent. He asked us if we needed a tow back to the marina and we said that we did. He then threw across a rope which David caught and hung on to while being pulled across and helped onto the stern of the boat. I thought that the man who was helping us was a member of the crew as he threw a line to me and told me to make it secure to our boat, which I did. He then threw me another line and pulled me across and onto the stern together with David. We were shivering and the wind was whipping up the waves even more fiercely. Our saviour knew his seamanship. He made a signal to the skipper who was steering the boat and we slowly edged forward under power which brought our dinghy towards the stern. I wondered if our mast would snap under the water but the boat came slowly forward until we could touch its bow. The crewman asked me if I wanted to turn the dinghy upright now that it could be steadied.

In all honesty, I think that I would have preferred to have the dinghy towed as close to the marina as possible as I really didn't want to get back on it. I was feeling cold, wet, and weak. But I thought that it would be stupid not to take advantage of the help that had been offered.

I tied a rope around my waist, slipped back into the water and then climbed on to the hull. The centreboard of the boat, which helps balance the boat under sail, was sticking up vertically and I moved towards it. I faced out across the harbour as I eased my feet down the hull until they were on the side of the boat and I was hanging on to the board. In this position, I brought my full weight to bear on the centreboard as the counterforce to start the boat turning upright. The wind was blowing directly at the stern of the boat and pushing the bow towards Black Dancer. At first I thought that the mast was again stuck thus preventing the hull from turning but then I felt the centreboard start to move slowly from the vertical to the horizontal position. This meant that the mast was starting to move up towards the surface. It was slow-going and I was getting thrown about. I felt absolutely exhausted. David asked me if I wanted him to climb over and help but I was worried about the two of us getting into trouble again. At least I had the rope around me and I was tied to Black Dancer so I was safe from drowning.

Slowly, agonisingly slowly, the boat started to right itself and, as the centreboard started to descend back under the water, the mainsail on the mast began to appear. Once I saw this, my fatigue left me. The trick now was to roll into the inside of the dinghy just as it righted itself. If I misjudged the placing of my weight, then the boat would simply roll over the other way and sink into the water once again. This often happens and can be terribly dispiriting when you are cold and wet. I think that David and the crewman helped steady her as I rolled over and into the boat.

The noise was incredible. The jib – the front sail – was

flapping and the mainsail had again caught the wind and was spread out to the side, forcing the boat to sail forward. I had to get the sail down. It is no easy matter to drop a mainsail in adverse conditions as you have to release the tension on the wire first by releasing its rope from the cleat – a fixing where ropes are tied. My hands were shaking and felt cold. I managed to free the rope. This allowed me to drop the sail but the boom which held the foot of the mainsail was moving around dangerously. If the boom hit my head, it could kill me or knock me unconscious. I held it as best I could and then grabbed a handful of the mainsail and started to pull it down the mast-head. Once I had the sail down, I knew that I would be able to get the water out of the boat as the boat would be more stable. The sail started to come down the mast really fast and I felt elated but then the sail suddenly jammed. I knew that I would have to hoist it up again and then try to pull down on the sail as hard as I could in order to overcome the snag. The boat was full of water and my feet were caught up in ropes and wires. Time seemed to be standing still for me even though probably only about ten minutes had elapsed since I had regained the boat. I was now feeling really weak. I pulled the sail back up slightly and then stood up, grabbed it in both hands and just fell with my weight on to it. It came down with a crash. I knew I had no more to give and yelled to David that he would have to bail the boat out now. I asked for the crewman to pull me back on to the Black Dancer. I was completely exhausted.

Once I was back on the stern, I talked to David about bailing out the dinghy but the crewman interrupted me. He said that the Black Dancer would go ahead slowly once he had secured the bow of our dinghy to its stern by raising it higher so that it was on the powerboat's transom. He explained that the water would simply pour out of the dinghy's stern so there would be no need to bail it out. I was too tired to argue about it and thanked him. He signalled to the skipper to go ahead and his strategy worked just as he had predicted. Our boat emptied of water as we travelled to the marina which was only ten minutes away.

Black Dancer stopped just outside the marina but I asked the crewman if the skipper would take us into the inner harbour. He said that they would leave us close to a pontoon and that would have to do. I asked the crewman if he could thank both the skipper and the owner of the boat for the rescue and for his expertise in getting us safely back. He then told me that he was the owner. I was absolutely speechless. What a lesson in life that was for me. Black Dancer roared off. We tied up the dinghy and made our way to the locker room for a shower. We fully intended to have a drink at the bar after our adventure and I was disappointed not to be able to offer the hospitality of the yacht club to our rescuer.

When we arrived at the bar, a ragged cheer went up from the assembled company who had been able to watch the drama unfold. I asked the commodore if he knew who was the owner of Black Dancer and if I might see him later at the club. He replied that we had just been rescued by the biggest gangster and marijuana dealer on the island and he had been previously denied club membership because of his sinister connections and dealings. I was shocked to hear this. But I didn't care who he was, he had acted as one sailor to another in difficulty, and that was all that mattered to me. During the following week, by various means, I managed to track him down and speak to him on the telephone. I told him who I was and where I worked. I also told him that I knew about the background to him being *persona non grata* at the club. I told him that I simply wanted to thank him again, as one sailor to another, for looking after us in such difficult circumstances. He seemed genuinely pleased to hear from me and said that he had been happy to help out. He never sought to take advantage of his connection to me at the High Commission and I never saw him again.

On a different occasion, on a fine Saturday morning in June, David and I decided that we would drive my car and take my dinghy on its trailer down to the yacht club and spend the morning sailing. Michelle and our boys, together with David's wife and family, would drive out later and we would all meet up for lunch. There was a decent, steady easterly wind blowing and so we would be able to get the boat really racing along. I was looking forward to the sail as it had been a long and difficult week at work. David came around to our house at 9 a.m and we set off. We reached the club about thirty minutes later, put our clothes and valuables in the locker room and then backed the trailer and dinghy down the ramp and into the water. We then busied ourselves preparing the rigging, hoisting the sails and checking the trapeze which we would use in order to balance the boat once we had gained some speed. There were hardly any other boats to be seen on the water and we set off from the marina with the wind blowing across the side of the boat, the optimum condition for sailing. We spent half an hour not far from the marina entrance tacking and practising different manoeuvres and then we decided that we would make a fast crossing across the harbour towards the prison shore and then turn and sail back.

The harbour is wide and so there would be plenty of time to settle into a steady sail. I took the tiller and David was hanging out of the side of the boat on the trapeze. We were really flying with a fresh breeze powering the sails and a moderate sea. The boat was surfing across the waves and the sun beat down on us. We were laughing and just enjoying the day. We had just passed the halfway mark when the boat hit an object. There was a loud bang. We didn't lose any speed and we thought that it must have been simply a partially submerged buoy that marked a lobster pot. There were many such buoys in the harbour. We were unconcerned.

However, I noticed that shortly after the collision the boat started to handle differently. Instead of flying along and jumping from wave to wave she had now started to be less responsive as I moved the tiller. I told David to move inboard and eased the jib to take some speed off her. The situation deteriorated. Something was badly wrong now as the boat had started to roll in an uncontrolled manner. My heart began to hammer and we discussed what the problem might be. We decided that water had entered one or both of the buoyancy tanks that run the full length of the dinghy. These tanks would keep her afloat if she should capsize. My mind went back to the bang that we had heard. Some sharp object must have put a hole into the side of the boat. I knew that the boat wouldn't sink as the buoyancy tanks had solid foam blocks in them that would keep her from sinking if she was holed, but clearly water was pouring in. With one side of the boat filled with water, we were becoming dangerously unbalanced. We were also slowing down.

We were now rocking and in danger of capsizing. We were about six hundred yards away from the prison shore. It would be impossible to turn the boat around and sail back to the marina. Our only choice was to beach the boat on the rocky shore. The prospect of doing this filled me with dread. The prison shore is not a place in which to be stranded. Jamaica's principal maximum security prison, the General Penitentiary, was near the harbour in downtown Kingston at the back of Norman Manley Boulevard. In 1983 it held over a thousand prisoners, including dangerous criminals. The area surrounding the prison was known to be dangerous and for a foreigner to be there was just asking for trouble. Two white men with a holed boat landing in territory where even uptown Jamaicans were scared to go had disaster written all over it, but what choice did we have? I knew that the central police station was not too far away from the shore and so I thought that our best plan would be to head for there. David then said that he had his wallet with him. He had forgotten to take it out of his pocket. The wallet contained US$50, 200 Jamaican dollars (£40) and two credit cards. I was relieved to hear this as I knew that, provided we could get up to the main road, we should be able to flag down a taxi. We would then have to go back to the club, get the trailer and drive back to pick up the boat. I thought that we would have to ask the police for protection when we did this. It was a confused plan but I had a lot on my mind.

Fifty feet, now forty feet, then thirty feet out from the shore, we dropped the sails and the waves carried us on to the stony beach. There was no-one about and we sighed in relief. However, it would be impossible for just the two of us to carry the boat further up the beach, even though it was made of fibreglass. The sun beat down on us. Standing at the side of the boat talking to David, I noticed that we had company. I guessed that there were now ten boys and men standing in a horseshoe shape in front of the boat. I thought that I needed to explain to them what had happened to us and told them that we had hit a submerged object, perhaps a lobster pot buoy in the harbour which had holed the boat. We now needed help to carry the boat up the beach to the road. I said that we would pay them if they would help us carry it. Much to my surprise, they surrounded the boat on either side and together we lifted it up and began to walk slowly up the one hundred and fifty yards towards the road that ran parallel with the shore. As we were walking, a youngster shoved his hand into the boat, grabbed our bucket and ran off with it. We put the boat down about ten feet from the road. I knew that we would be able to pay them using David's money. In a flash, another youngster, about eighteen years of age, put his hand into David's pocket, stole his wallet from his shorts, and ran off.

Without any thought for his own safety, David ran after him at full pelt. I shouted at David to stop and let him have the wallet but he was sprinting after the youngster who was aiming for a tenement building. There was nothing I could do to stop him. I feared for his life. I asked the bystanders, who had now been joined by a least another ten men, who the thief was. No-one replied. My mind was furiously racing, thinking about what I should do. At that moment, an old American car came to a halt at the kerbside and someone wound down the driver's window. I recognised the driver as a Jamaican I knew from the karate club where I was training in uptown Kingston and I walked over to talk to him. He had another three Jamaicans in the car. I told him what had happened and asked if he could help me. The bystanders were now starting to walk towards his car. He told me to get to the police station as fast as I could, slammed the car into gear and roared off just as a couple of the youngsters began to throw bricks at the back of the car. I now was really stumped for a plan of action. I was surrounded by tough-looking Jamaicans, had lost David, had no money to pay for the help but it was David's absence that scared me most.

The crowd parted and one of the men walked towards me. He was about six foot three, wore wrap-around sun glasses, had scars on his face and was wearing a vest, jogging bottoms and new white trainers. If ever there was a man in charge at the prison shore it had to be him. I spoke to him and explained what had happened. He said nothing. Miraculously, David appeared walking slowly towards the boat and holding out his wallet. My spirits soared. At least he was alive. He told me that he had chased the youth and cornered him on the landing of a tenement building. The youth had pulled a knife on him David had told him that he didn't care about the money but that he just wanted the credit cards back. The youth had pulled out the cash, flung the wallet on the floor and ran off, much to David's surprise and relief. I just couldn't believe that David had risked his life for two credit cards.

I decided to see if I could negotiate with the apparent

leader of the group. I asked him if he could arrange for our boat to be looked after and be kept safe while we went and got the trailer for it. If he could arrange for some men to help us lift it on to the trailer on our return then I would pay him for his help. He asked me how much I would pay. I said that I had US$50 which I could bring back to him. He told me that he wanted US$100. I said that I would see what I could do. I asked him if he could get us a taxi, thinking that he would refuse but he spoke with some of the group and a taxi appeared at the side of the road within five minutes. David and I jumped into the taxi and headed back to the yacht club.

We were tired and I was scared. Life is cheap in the ghetto. I told David that I would now have to return and try to get the boat back. I would understand if he had had enough for the day. To my relief, he said that he would come back with me. He was a good man to have in crisis, apart from occasionally being head-strong. Yes I was scared of what might happen when we returned but I was determined to get the boat back.

I managed to get together US$60 and we jumped into my car and drove back to the prison shore. I knew that we were taking a big risk as my car had diplomatic plates showing and was fairly new. It could be car-jacked and we could still be harmed. It is really strange, but somehow I had confidence that it would all work out. I have absolutely no idea why I had this confidence and we should just have driven to the police station and asked for help. I also knew that the men guarding my boat would hate police involvement and would perhaps turn on us if we chose that course of action.

I had no intention of abandoning my boat. Thinking about it now, I realise that it was a stupid decision as no boat is worth the risk of losing our lives. When we arrived back on the prison shore, I was astonished to find that the boat was still there as I half expected it to have disappeared.

The leader was not to be seen but eight or nine youngsters were leaning on the boat. Some of them were smoking ganja. I decided to take command and told them that we were now going to lift the boat on to the trailer. Once again to my surprise, they helped us lift the boat and we put it on to the trailer without a problem. We secured the boat with ropes. The big man suddenly appeared. Smoking a cigarette, he strolled slowly and menacingly up towards me. I thanked him for his help and took out US$60. I asked him if he knew the youth that had stolen David's wallet. He didn't reply. I then told him that the wallet had contained over fifty US dollars when it had been stolen. I said that if he could find the thief who stole the wallet, then that money, plus my US$60, was his. I handed over the money to him. He stared at me. I felt a shiver run down my spine and, on impulse, I reached out for his hand and shook it. I thanked him for all his help, looked at David and turned to walk back to the car. The hairs on the back of my neck were standing up. I got into the driving seat, just as David got into the passenger seat. I turned the key in the ignition and the engine started. I engaged first gear, shut the door and let the clutch out. The car bounded forward with a lurch as we took up the strain of the trailer and boat. I kept my eyes fixed on the road ahead, expecting a brick to hit the car, or worse. Nothing happened. I asked David to look behind to see what the big man was doing. David turned and said that he was still standing in the road and looking at our departing car. My body felt like jelly. Nearly all of me was shaking with the effort of keeping my adrenaline under control. David had closed his eyes.

We drove back to the yacht club and parked the car. Michelle, our boys and David's family were playing in the swimming pool and the women were relaxing with a drink. Michelle said, 'Did you have nice sail?' We looked at each other and ordered a beer.

After and hour or so and a swim, I felt as if the whole

episode had been a dream I told Michelle that David and I would now go home with the boat and meet them later. I had had enough adventures for one day. We set off. Neither of us spoke about the incident which each of us was replaying in our own mind. I couldn't believe how we had come out of it unscathed. I was still thinking about how stupidly brave David had been to run off after the thief in such a dangerous area. I also wondered what my friends from the karate club were doing in that area. What had they thought would happen to me when they had roared off? We were half way home and the car engine was idling as we waited beside a red traffic light. I felt dozy. I had the window down and was listening to music on the radio. On the side of the road opposite me I noticed that there was a barber shop. All was calm. In an instant, the situation changed. I heard a loud cry as if someone had been hurt. A man staggered backwards out of the barber shop holding his face. He had blood streaming down his cheek and an open wound. I could see his skin flapping where it had been cut. Close behind him another man followed, brandishing a gleaming knife which had a six inch blade. They were both only about six feet away from my car. I had had enough. I slammed the car into gear, ignored the red light, and hurtled across the road with the trailer rocking behind me. There were cars braking in order to avoid the car and trailer and honking furiously at us. I sped off up the road. It was scarcely credible. We arrived home fifteen minutes later and I parked the trailer and boat in my garage. There was a hole the size of my fist near the bow of the boat in the buoyancy tank. David and I went out on to our patio, took the lid off a couple of Red Stripe beers and sat down. David looked at me steadily and said, 'Don't bother asking me to sail next week, Roger. I'm busy!'

Why hadn't the men in the car from the karate club helped me? I later found out that they had been driving on the main road and had spotted me standing on the shore.

Normally they wouldn't have dared drive down to the shore road but they thought that it was vital that I should be warned to get to the local police station as fast as I could. They said that it was so dangerous that even their karate skills would be useless in that environment where most of the locals carried knives or guns and would fight intruders to their territory. Just how we escaped unharmed from our predicament still remains a mystery to me.

20

BLACK BELT WITH A BROKEN WING

After the initial excitement and wonder of arriving in Jamaica, we began to settle into a daily routine. Gareth and Alex attended a primary school and Andrew went to nursery school. Michelle had a good circle of friends and was really enjoying life. I was very busy at work but had learned how to cope much better with the demands of the job. We were leading a regular existence.

I decided that the time was right for me to begin looking for a local karate club in order to start training again. On reflection, I started my search with the wrong attitude as my expectations were low. My first visit was to a school run by a 4th degree black belt in the Shotokan style of karate who was clearly talented. His students trained hard and his standards were as good as anything I had seen in the UK. The Taekwondo School, a Korean martial art which is highly focused on using kicking as distinct from punching methods, was run by a Korean, Mu Yee. He was just starting to establish his club and had been a top referee and exponent of the art in Korea. He invited me to take lessons with him which I did for a while and he was an exceptional athlete. He was also a hard taskmaster. He later married an American, Sally, who worked at the US embassy. She also had a 1st degree black belt in Taekwondo. She told me that Mu Yee didn't think that her skills at breaking were up to standard and once he had locked her out of their house until she had broken the pile of tiles and bricks left outside their door. She did succeed in breaking them but her revenge was sweet. She locked him out in a different way until he apologized. Women always win in the end.

All the instructors I met were most helpful and friendly and I had many offers to start training full-time with them. A Jamaican friend told me that there was a Seido Karate Club close to where I worked and he suggested that I should take a look at it. I had never heard of Seido and wrongly prejudged it, thinking that it was probably some half-baked local style of karate, but one Monday evening I went along to assess it.

The *dojo* (training hall) was in Annette Crescent in Upper Kingston. The club trained in a bungalow which had been modified for use as a small gym. There was an open part at the rear which had a raised wooden floor where group training took place. I noted that there were signs in Japanese, weapon racks and posters of karate which all added to the feel of a serious martial arts school. When I saw the students training, their skills knocked me sideways. Their sheer energy and commitment was breathtaking. I held a fourth degree black belt grade but the green belts – mid-ranking students – looked more skilled than I was, and certainly fought harder.

I looked at how complex the movements were as the students exchanged techniques with each other. I had never encountered such movements previously. I had the strongest feeling that I had found a place in which I could learn skills and develop my character. The instructors showed great respect for the students and the students in turn were respectful towards both the dojo and their seniors. I felt strangely drawn to this place. Inevitably, I wondered if I would be in for a hard time as the only white person training in the dojo. Would I be resented for my colour and status? The students were tough-looking and muscular. Would I be in for a beating? Many negative thoughts went through my mind as Sensei Errol Lyn, the club leader, asked me about my background and intentions before he invited me to return the following Monday evening to begin training.

That Monday came and I felt both excited and anxious. I had no illusions about the road ahead and although the Seido Karate structure seemed different to me, I felt that at least I had some previous knowledge on which to to rely. Even so, I couldn't help feeling like a beginner. I entered the dojo wearing a plain white karate suit *(gi)* and a white belt which signified that I was a beginner in Seido Karate. *Sensei* (the Japanese term for 'teacher' or 'instructor') Errol welcomed me and introduced me to the instructors and the students. It was a warm evening and the open-sided dojo was surrounded by sweet smelling flowers. I wished that Sensei Errol had not mentioned to the students that I was black belt in a different style of karate as I had wanted to start training without feeling the need to impress anyone. But he did mention my history. I noticed that two of the larger instructors took a special interest in me when he talked about my past and they looked at me intently.

Naturally I was nervous but I tried not to show it. Sensei Errol put me under the care of a green belt student and told him that he was to show me basic Seido techniques. These techniques were similar to my own experience and so I was quickly able to copy them. However, I struggled to keep up with the pushups which were done on first or second knuckles against the hard wooden floor. I noticed that I had skinned my knuckles, leaving them red and raw. After an hour, Sensei Errol said that we would have a *kumite* (free-fighting) session. I watched as the students limbered up, throwing fast kicks and combination punches. They looked fit and quick. Sensei Errol emphasised that students should spar with me only lightly, as this was my first session, so I thought that we would be points fighting, which is fast movement but very light contact to the face and body. The Jamaicans had a different interpretation of light contact. Very few students had protective equipment on their hands and feet. Some wore gum shields but some didn't. You were not allowed to punch fully to the face area but you could kick to the head and punch and kick to the body.

My first fight was with my green belt instructor who was a young man aged about twenty. He came at me, throwing punches and kicks from all angles. There were twenty students fighting in the dojo so our room to move was restricted which was just as well as this meant that my opponent couldn't use the full extent of his kicks against me. He hit me hard and I felt it. I thought that I had better step up my game if I was to survive the first night. One of my favourite techniques is a foot sweep followed by a kick or a punch to the body. I waited until he had committed himself to attack by putting his weight on to his front foot in preparation for throwing a kick with his rear leg. I distracted him with a feint to his face and then I swept his foot from under him, punching him hard in the chest on his way down to the floor. He hit the floor and an area cleared around us. I gave him my hand and pulled him up. He nodded to me, acknowledging the technique. Sensei Errol called for us to change partners. We bowed to each other and as I turned for my next fight I saw one of the largest instructors, *Senpai* (Senior) Tony Robinson, who was six feet three and towered over me. He pushed my partner away and stood in front of me. I swallowed nervously. He was wearing boxing gloves and I was wearing light sparring gloves. He had legs that looked as tough as tree trunks so I knew that he was going to be a handful and that it would be difficult to sweep such legs from under him.

Sensei Errol called for us to begin but I heard him advise Senpai Tony that he should take it easy. Much to my surprise, he didn't hit me too hard although I took a few unintentional hits to the head. My opponent was so tall that even if he had aimed at my body, his gloves would have hit my head first. I fought him hard as I didn't want him to think that I was intimidated by him, but I knew that he was

Training with Sensei Errol up in the Blue Mountains.

coasting and simply testing me out.

We changed partners quite a few times that night. After forty five minutes of fighting, we stopped. I was exhausted and dripping with sweat from head to toe. My gi was wringing wet but at least I had survived the first night. My body felt bruised and I had a cut lip and some bruising to my eye but, apart from that, I was fine. As we changed in the locker room, the students were friendly to me but I couldn't understand much of what they said and I had no chance of understanding the fast patois language in which they communicated with each other. This was my first real taste of what it felt like to be an outsider. Sensei Errol came to find me just as I was leaving the dojo. He asked how I had found the training session. I was honest with him. I told him that I had found it hard and that their style of fighting was harder than I was used to. He laughed and said that the free fighting session was just a light warm up but he encouraged me to return. He said that I would get used to it.

I thought seriously about returning to the dojo. I had my job to consider and I would need to seek permission to train with a local club as there were potential security issues. It was tough at the Seido Karate Club and it could get tougher for me. I could get seriously hurt training with these men. I wrestled with a parade of excuses, all drawing me towards a softer option and I was tempted. However, I thought that if I was honest with myself and wanted to improve my skills and knowledge then this was a challenge that I could not ignore. To train at the Seido Club would be a unique opportunity for me to develop personally, get to know Jamaicans outside the High Commission, and learn about Jamaica and her culture. Sensei Errol was a highly talented instructor and I thought that he would stop me from getting seriously hurt, at least until my skills had improved so that I could fully take care of myself. I decided to return and join the club the following Monday. I fixed my mind on my chosen way forward and banished my doubt.

Training with the Seido Club became a regular part of my life. I recall so many strong images of the dojo: warming up outside in the rear garden heavy with the scent of the brightly coloured flowers; the intense heat of the hot and humid summer as sweat ran down my forehead on to my nose, stinging my eyes and forming pools at my feet; the *thud, thud, thud* of fists striking the *makiwara* (padded wood used to develop striking techniques) which were fixed on to the metal posts holding up the roof; the posts becoming hot as the day progressed; the closeness of the bodies in kumite; men fighting hard and hurting each other; powerful and determined men who enjoyed the thrill of training hard; the hand slapping between students after an intense training session when I could just about barely raise a smile or even walk out of the dojo without feeling that my legs were made of rubber.

The influence of Sensei Errol Lyn, who was a handsome man with facial features that reflected both a Chinese and Jamaican heritage, was profound. He never raised his voice but would guide students in such a focused way that less than one hundred percent effort was unthinkable. In the summer months, we would train at the camp in the cool Blue Mountains about one hour's drive north of Kingston. We would sleep in a dormitory that smelt of wood smoke and was set in a valley where the heavy and heady smell of coffee beans drifted down to us on the wind from the plantations. We would plunge into the icy pool beneath the waterfall. The water felt so cold that your body would instantly spasm and your teeth would chatter until you adjusted to the icy feel. We would then quietly meditate, kneeling by the stream while listening to the chorus of chattering birds. It was a magical time.

In the evening, it would be party time but no one touched alcohol. We would entertain each other with songs and skits and laugh at the comedians in our group or applaud the dancing and singing students before collapsing into bed early in the evening. I felt that I was fully accepted as a member of the Seido Club.

I recall one journey, driving home from camp, that could have turned into a nasty incident. We were driving on narrow mountain paths that wound across the mountains with steep descents on the open sides, when our convoy was stopped at a tortuous bend by ten aggressive and threatening men. I was told by Sensei Errol to stay in the car as our club members got out including Dirty Harry, a tall, lean and rangy student with legs like whipping steel coils. Tension hung in the air as insults were traded at high decibel levels and threats were made. The men wanted money in order to let us pass. We refused to give them even a dollar. It became a Mexican standoff. I could feel the electricity of potential violence crackling in the air as the mean-looking leader of the robbers shouted insults and threats at us but his men finally backed down and let our convoy pass. There would be no mercy on that route for lone travellers but our party just laughed off the incident. I can still see the gleam of the late sun shining on the machetes that dangled from the long arms of the would-be robbers as they watched us drive away.

After twelve months of training regularly once or twice a week, I felt at home in the dojo. I had adapted to the heavy contact style of fighting which was so different from the style that I had previously been used to which was faster and lighter. Free-fighting sessions involved heavy body contact and kicks to the head area. While punching to the face was forbidden, accidents regularly happened if you didn't protect your face properly. It would not be unusual for students to end up in hospital with broken noses. Bruised or broken ribs were also commonplace. Grappling would be permitted if you went to the ground and if there was space on the floor in which to move, but it was generally discouraged. Sometimes I would go home after a free-fighting session and Michelle would say that my body looked like it had been hit by a car: the skin on my torso would be dark from purple bruises. Michelle wondered if I was being targeted simply because I was white but I assured her that black bodies in the locker room looked just as bruised.

I was intrigued about the history of Seido Karate. I learned that our chief instructor was none other than *Shihan* (Master) Tadashi Nakamura, the top student of the legendary Kyokushinkai Grand Master Masutatsu Oyama. Shihan Nakamura gained worldwide fame for representing Japan in Thailand where he defeated one of their top fighters in the famous Lumpinee Boxing Stadium as part of a three man team sent by Grand Master Oyama. Grand Master Oyama had vowed that if the team returned defeated from Thailand then that defeat would become a matter of dishonour for him and he would commit *seppuku,* a ritual suicide carried out by disembowelment. He meant it, of course. The team returned victorious and Shihan Nakamura became a national hero in Japan. On 15 October 1956 Shihan Nakamura had also completed the one hundred man kumite. This is one of the most extreme forms of testing your fighting spirit as it involves one hundred contests of up to two minutes duration. You must win each contest. The list of those who have successfully met this challenge is short. It is unbelievably demanding. My chief instructor was indeed a formidable fighting master.

The Seido system that I had found in Jamaica started to make sense to me and I appreciated the roots of Seido through the Kyokushin Karate tradition. I learned that Shihan Nakamura had formed Seido in 1976 following a break with Kyokushin Karate. I was delighted to find that fate seemed to have steered me towards a karate system with so much history and integrity.

The Human Face of Karate, written by Master Nakamura is an excellent martial arts book and gives the reader real insight into the history and philosophy of the Seido Karate system.

Previously, in the UK, I had had experience as a karate referee. A little over one year after I had started training with the Seido Club, Sensei Lyn announced that he would host the West Indies Open Invitation Karate Tournament which was to be held in the New Kingston Hotel, not far from the British High Commission. In view of my previous experience as a referee, he asked me if I would take the role of chief referee. I have to say I was not looking forward to the job but I felt under pressure to accept it as it was a real honour to be invited to take part. Many styles competed against each other on the Sunday of the tournament and the standards were high. The fighting was fast and furious with Kung Fu (Chinese Martial Arts) exponents leaping into the air with their red waist sashes twirling as they demonstrated their athletic kicks while the more down-to-earth Japanese karate competitors in the styles of Shotokan and Wado Ryu relied on sweeping their opponent's feet, using a front kick to the body and a reverse punch to the head to get them through the bouts.

After a gruelling day in the knockout rounds the fighters were narrowed down to the finalists who would fight in the evening. The tension which had built up over the day was now highly focused on the final bouts. The crowds that came to support the fighters were fearsome. Everyone seemed to be shouting out a strong opinion. If a referee made an unpopular decision then all hell broke loose. Men would leap from their seats and run down to the ring in order to bang on the canvas if they wanted to make a point, or stand on their chairs shouting insults at the unpopular referee. The whole scene was noisy, colourful and felt electric. It also felt very threatening and dangerous. I was not looking forward to refereeing the finals.

I started with the women's final. I don't recall the styles the fighters represented but one woman was a heavyweight

(Miss Heavy) who weighed in at about two hundred pounds and the other (Miss Light) was much lighter at around one hundred and sixty pounds. Both meant business.

The opening round saw both fighters feinting to draw their opponent forward and to look for exposed openings. So far so good and I could hear that the crowd were still choosing sides and the noise levels were reasonable. Then Miss Heavy lashed out with a front kick to the body that caught Miss Light in the stomach but she immediately countered with a reverse punch to the head. I awarded *Ippon* to Miss Heavy. Ippon is a full point in Japanese scoring terminology. The aim of the bout was to amass as many points as you could in the one and a half minutes available. Miss Light then moved around the ring still feinting with her hands and waited for Miss Heavy to try the same move which she did. This time Miss Light beat her for speed and threw a roundhouse kick (a kick in which the kicking foot is snapped outward in a motion from the knee) that proved to be a solid hit to the side of the face but the kick was well-controlled. Ippon. The score was even. Miss Heavy thought that she had been hit too hard and complained to me about but the crowd booed her and I told her to fight on as I thought that the kick had been delivered with good control and respect for her safety. I considered that she was using the break in action in order to break up the other fighter's rhythm and was in fact unhurt.

I could almost see the red mist coming down in front of her eyes as she then used her weight to sweep Miss Light's front foot off the canvas. As Miss Light stumbled, she was hit hard on the jaw and fell to the canvas. Miss Heavy had clearly committed a foul and I gave her a warning, deducting half a point from her score. The score was now Miss Light one point and Miss Heavy half a point. The crowd was shouting loudly and had chosen their favourite fighter, Miss Light. I could hardly hear myself speak in order to give instructions to the fighters as the noise was so loud. I called both fighters together and lectured them about the need to control their blows. They both glared fiercely and muttered in patois at me. I assumed that their comments were far from complimentary. I restarted the contest and both fighters circled each other. There were clashes between them but I did not award any points as the techniques they used were messy. Suddenly, Miss Heavy dashed in and threw a front snap kick at Miss Light which hit her below the waist. It was not a deliberate foul in my opinion but more a misjudgment of aim. Miss Light looked in some discomfort but did not go down to the canvas and looked ready to fight. I warned Miss Heavy to keep her kicks higher but sensed that we were now in for trouble.

I restarted the contest. There were thirty seconds to go. Miss Light lost control. Fuelled by energy derived from her belief that the low blow was deliberate, she threw a left back-fist strike high towards her opponent's face in order to force her guard to come up and then, with her right hand, smacked her opponent straight in the mouth, splitting her lip. Blood flowed from Miss Heavy's mouth. I jumped in between the fighters and parted them disqualifying Miss Light. I knew that both fighters had lost their ability to control their power and if they were to fight on, serious injury would result. The crowd went crazy. It didn't like my decision. It liked the underdog and had liked Miss Light's last blow. It liked the blood. I awarded the contest to Miss Heavy and both fighters left the ring without shaking hands. It had been a dishonourable contest fought in a bad spirit and as such would not enhance the reputation of martial arts. The booing continued and I felt exhausted but I still had another two finals to referee. The experience was proving to be even worse than I had expected.

In view of the crowd's adverse reaction, I spoke to Sensei Errol and asked if he was happy for me to continue. He suggested that I use the microphone to explain the background to my decision which I did and the crowd seemed to settle down.

The next final for me to referee was the men's heavy-weight final. I expected this to be a really interesting contest between the Seido finalist, who had only one arm, and a fighter from the Shotokan style of karate. However, after the bout began, it became apparent to me that the Shotokan fighter was not giving his best performance and was patronising the Seido man by staying away from and moving around the ring. It was almost as if he felt that he felt sorry for his opponent's disability. I knew that this was not his normal way of fighting. I stopped the fight and spoke to him. I pointed out that, however well-meaning, it was an insult to his opponent not to try a one hundred per-cent and that his opponent, who had battled his way through the earlier rounds to get to this final, needed no favours. I told him that I would disqualify him for lack of fighting spirit and that I would tell the crowd this. He nodded his head to me and immediately looked more aggressive as his eyes narrowed. Sparks then flew.

The Seido fighter threw fast roundhouse kicks and hook kick combinations (a kick that uses the heel of the foot on the extended leg to hook backward toward the body) to the head while the Shotokan fighter favoured a deep stance, spreading his weight across both legs and then suddenly countering the kicks with powerful punches thrown by his rear hand towards his opponent's body. They were very evenly matched and the crowd were split in their support for the fighters. When the timekeeper called a stop to the contest, neither fighter had gained a decisive point. I ordered a thirty-second sudden-death extension which meant that the fighter who gained the first point would win the contest. There was a lot at stake now and both fighters were breathing heavily. The Seido man's kicks took a lot of energy to throw and I guessed that his physical reserves would be lower than those of his opponent.

The extension round started. Both men circled each other warily. The Seido fighter threw a feint punch with his front hand in order to draw up the guard of his opponent and then tried to hit his torso with a roundhouse kick, but the Shotokan fighter saw it coming and moved out of range. He then stepped forward in a blur of action and launched a back-fist strike to head level forcing his opponent to lift his hand to protect his head, dropped his body and hit his stomach area with a perfectly timed punch to the midsection. There was no doubt in my mind that this blow was a match-winner. I stopped the contest and declared the Shotocan fighter the victor. The match had been a well-fought contest with each man showing good respect for each. The fighters showed their mutual appreciation by hugging and exchanging 'high fives'. I now felt as if I had been through ten rounds with Mike Tyson and was dripping with sweat but it had been a good fair fight and one in which the crowd had appreciated the efforts of both men.

A men's open-weight final is always eagerly anticipated by the crowd. This was to be a clash between David and Goliath. The Seido fighter appeared muscular, small and fast while his opponent appeared tall and heavyset but with an excellent physique. On paper it appeared to be an uneven contest but I knew the Seido fighter's skills were amazing. He could easily jump and kick to a height of six feet and above, demonstrating perfect control. It promised to be a fascinating contest. At the start of the contest, the big man waded straight in and unleashed top-heavy kicks from his rear leg that seemed as if they would cut his opponent in half when they made contact. He tried to follow up his kicks with strong punches to the body. The smaller man jinked left and right, moving quickly around the ring and frustrating him. The Seido fighter looked for openings and circled both ways around his opponent in order to keep him off-balance. Suddenly, he jumped into the air at face height and released a punch from his rear right hand. It was a perfect score and I awarded him the first Ippon point. The crowd loved watching his technique and were shouting further encouragement to him. The noise level was rising. After a roundhouse kick thrown by the bigger man failed to connect, the Seido man jumped and threw a reverse back spin kick that looked as if it had been choreographed in a martial arts film. He feinted with his lead hand in order to force his opponent's head back and obscure his sight. He then spun through one hundred and eighty degrees, releasing the power in his leg. His foot hit his opponent's head but it hit in such a controlled manner that no injury resulted from the blow. The crowd was now standing on chairs, cheering as the Seido man took a two point lead.

The big man remained calm. He feinted as if he was going to throw a left front kick but cleverly used the same leg to sweep away his opponent's back leg, taking advantage of the reach that his long legs gave him. Quickly he followed up his sweep by hitting the Seido fighter with a reverse punch before he reached the canvas. It was a very well executed technique and I awarded him a full point. The score was then two points to one in favour of the Seido man. However, when the Seido combatant jumped up from the canvas, I could see that the kick had damaged his calf muscle and that his mobility, which was his greatest weapon against the power of his opponent, was now drastically reduced. He had to be fast to evade the power that he knew would be coming his way. He also knew that he had to extend his lead if he was to win as simply defending was not an option. Summoning his spirit, he created an opening and flew at the big man, using roundhouse kicks to the ribs with his good leg and fierce face punches. The noise was deafening and the fight seemed to me to be in slow motion. I seemed to float in a detached manner, watching the fight unfold before me but I could still see every move, almost before it happened. This had never happened to me previously and it felt very strange.

The Seido man's opponent was now being forced into the corner but he had been taking all the blows on his shins and arms. I separated the pair as no point had been scored. The Seido man was tiring fast having hoped to score and his opponent sensed his weakness. There were forty seconds of the fight remaining. The big man feinted with a front jab and again swept his opponent's back foot from under him, catching him with a good reverse punch as he lost balance. Two points each. The noise level was now incredible. I asked the timekeeper how long was left and he shouted out that there were only thirty seconds remaining. I restarted the fight. The Seido man knew that unless he attacked at once then he would lose the championship. He was desperate to secure the final point and launched himself at the big man, actually leaving the canvas and jumping into the air as he threw yet another reverse punch at his opponent's face.

It was a brave move. However, his opponent had seen it coming and moved to the side while at the same time throwing his own punch out at head height. It was a superbly judged blow, showing great control, and it caught the Seido fighter high on the temple. I awarded the winning point just as the timekeeper rang the bell. The championship was over.

Both contestants threw their arms around each other and the crowd applauded wildly. The combat between the two warriors had been thoroughly good and fairly contested in an open and honest manner. It was an excellent example of how such a contest should be fought. I congratulated the winner and commiserated with the loser. I was delighted to leave the ring. Sensei Lyn kindly presented me with a trophy for my efforts and as I received it from him, I asked him if he could guarantee that he would never ask me to be chief referee again. He smiled.

I learned a lot from refereeing that tournament and

have some idea of how top boxing referees must feel under intense public scrutiny. The memories of that day are quite vivid even now. It was a great experience and although I have refereed in Jamaica at many tournaments over the years since then none have been as electrifying as those open championships.

After our first year, our dear friends John and Elaine Doust, together with their children Laura and Sam, came out to stay with us for a one-month holiday. Gareth was about the same age as Laura, and Alex and Sam were firm friends. Their family had only just arrived when I threw John the keys of my car and asked him to drive me to the open championships in New Kingston and then pick me up later at night. There are not many men that I know who would have taken that challenge of driving in Kingston at night but then there are not many men with a spirit like John. At that time, he was a banker working for Coutts & Co in London. Elaine had known me from childhood and was a great friend of Michelle. John is pretty much fearless. The only problem with their visit was that they were on holiday and I was at work. I can't recall how I actually managed to get through the month and work at the same time as we rarely got to bed before two o'clock in the morning and we attacked the Red Stripe beer with commendable enthusiasm. John quickly acclimatised to the Jamaican lifestyle and we had some wonderful weekends with our families together up at the beautiful north coast, particularly Silver Sands in Trelawny where for the weekend you could rent villas with fabulous views of the blue sea and the golden beaches.

We used to rent a villa near Port Antonio where, as I have mentioned earlier, Noel Coward had his villa, 'Firefly,' which has spectacular views of the island. From there it was possible to enjoy the Blue Mountains, and the riot of green vegetation on the hills near the blue sea. I would like my ashes to be scattered in the gardens of Firefly or my coffin to be taken to the top of the hill and thrown over the side, although it wouldn't quite reach the sea. I would probably favour the former method of disposal in order to avoid frightening the locals.

One particular weekend, together with John, Elaine and our young families, we stayed in a beautiful white villa close to Firefly. The weekend involved an almost total lack of parental responsibility and the potential destruction of a petrol station, me, John and my car. The children played on the nearby golden sand while we lazed on the beach drinking Appleton's Gold Label rum with Desnoe and Geddes ginger ale, Red Stripe and other heavenly concoctions. Somehow the children had found a boat to play in and we let them use it as it was floating close to the beach. They had great fun jumping in and out of it. Andrew was only about two years old at this time. He loved the water and splashed about wearing his water wings. We had put Gareth in charge of the children as he was the eldest but we were also keeping an eye on them. We hadn't totally abrogated responsibility. It was an ideal afternoon until Michelle noticed that the boat that we had believed to be anchored had drifted away from the shore and was now floating out to sea. The children were still using it to jump from into the water and had no idea of the potential danger they were in. It was an awful time as one moment they were close to us and the next moment they were dangerously distant. Panic ensued, but John and I swam out to the boat and eventually we got them all back to the shore safe and sound.

Even today, Michelle and I still wonder how we could have been so stupid as to have let them go out in the boat without first ensuring that it was safely anchored but someone must have been watching over their safety. The children thought nothing of it of course and considered it a great adventure. Life can change in a heartbeat.

That evening we had a barbecue but we had used up all

the calor gas and so the next morning we had nothing to cook with. We could not find the spare canister that was supposed to be somewhere in the villa. I decided that we would drive to the nearest garage and buy a replacement. John and I located a garage up on the hill about three miles away, just outside a small community. It was rundown with shells of cars around it and worn-out tyres abandoned on the grass verges near the pumps. Exhausted dogs lay panting under the shade of the few sparse trees near the petrol pump which had a broken indicator.

A Rastaman was leaning against the door to the battered concrete building that seemed to serve as a shop. He was smoking a spliff. Not just any spliff but one that was at least twelve inches long. Of course there is nothing unusual about a Rastaman with a spliff as smoking *ganja* (marijuana) is part of the Rastafarian religion and the 'erb' is used in the daily worship of God. I asked him if I could buy calor gas and indicated the empty cylinder that I was holding in my hand. He wandered over and took it from me. I didn't even know if he was actually connected with the garage. I started to become concerned for our safety when I saw him meander over to the calor gas tank which had a sign above it saying, *Strictly No Smoking* and put my canister down beside it. We watched the hot ash from his spliff floating down towards the container. It was Sunday morning at ten o'clock and it looked very much like our man hadn't been to bed. His eyes were so red that they looked like rubies, giving him a vampire look. As he began to fill up my canister, I wondered if he had recently read the safety procedures sheet. Both of us hid behind the adjacent tree until he had completed the task. It must have been a miracle that prevented the fumes from the cylinder igniting. I had been certain that he would cause the whole of the petrol station to explode but he looked at us as if were idiots to be hiding behind that tree. We paid him and left, glad to be in one piece.

We had a great time in Jamaica with John and Elaine, Laura and Sam. However, Jamaica hit John hard. On his return to the UK, he found himself suffering from a strange sickness. In the morning, he would settle into his chair in his office reviewing the day's work ahead but then he would drift off back into the Jamaican experience. In an instant, he would experience himself sitting on a chair in our patio area, staring at the shifting hues of colour on the hills behind our bungalow and watching the clouds drift by in a blue sky as he felt the warmth of the day settling on his body. As he let his mind roam free, he could smell the rich and heady aromas of our plants in the garden. Inevitably, he thought of the attraction of an ice cold Red Stripe beer that would be within easy reach in the patio fridge. This was of course a great way to start the day in Jamaica but a world apart from the realities of commerce in working for Coutts & Co. John needed to be as sharp as a tack at least until lunchtime when worldly matters could then be dealt with at The Lamb and Flag pub, close by in Rose street. John told me that it took him at least one month to recover from the Jamaican experience. He was lucky. Some never recover from it.

We loved to have friends visit us even though it would play havoc with my working life. So many relatives and friends came to see us including my mother, Michelle's brother, Peter, who was frisked at Montego Bay airport as he looked like a drug runner, and Michelle's step-father, Bob. He had served in the army during World War Two when apparently he was taught to drive a lorry and sell cigarettes and nylons at a personal profit. He had honed these skills during his service in Italy and brought them back to the UK where he set up a recycling plant of unofficially obtained goods at the factory where he worked. Bob could get you anything you needed, at a price. He met Eve, Michelle's mum, at a social function and eventually moved in with her and her children, Michelle and Peter. What attracted Eve to

Bob is still a mystery to Michelle but I have to say he was a great grandad to our children even if he did have many faults. Bob loved to buy presents. At Christmas time in our house you couldn't move across the floor without bumping into one of the enormous electronic cars or fire engines that would need a power station to keep them charged up. Bob would arrive with so many presents that there would no room in the car for passengers. He was a very good-hearted and generous man but could be a very frustrating person to those who cared for him.

He always had plenty of cash in his wallet, a big car and a smart answer for everything. He could be irresponsible and thoughtless. Bob, Eve, Michelle and Peter, with the addition of their Alsatian dog, Anna, were in a car which was being driven along the motorway. Anna was making signs that she wanted to pee. Bob immediately understood the problem and acted with commendable vigor. He simply stopped the car by driving it on to the hard shoulder of the motorway, opened the door on the motor-way side of the car and let Anna jump out. Eve and Michelle were screaming at Bob and trying to make him see how stupid his action had been but Anna then had her pee and jumped back into the car from the other (safe) side. Bob completely failed to see what the fuss was about, and amazingly there was no accident.

He loved fish, and not only the swimming variety – he had been known to eat fourteen fish fingers for his tea. He built a big pond in the back garden of Eve's house and filled it with carp and other varieties, spending a lot of money in buying only good stock. One hot summer day, he decided that the pond needed to be cleaned out. His solution was to fill a children's paddling pool with clean water, net the fish and put them into the pool. He cleaned out the pond but, as it was getting late, he decided that he would transfer the fish back the next morning. It never occurred to him that fish needed oxygen to breath. It never occurred to him that putting about thirty fish into a paddling pool might stress them. They all died during the night. Bob was really upset and was at a loss to explain how it had come about. After all, they had only been crushed together overnight without room to move and without oxygen. He was really indignant about their loss. But little really phased him, except when one of his relationships went wrong and gave him a heart attack.

When he came to stay with us in Jamaica, he dressed the part of an Englishman abroad with his cream suit and tan shoes. I once took him to a diplomatic party hosted by a US colonel who lived in a magnificent villa with the most beautiful pool. Bob took in the view and surroundings within a glance and said, 'It's all right here, innit?'

He could be a show-stopper as he moved between the groups talking to the diplomatic community. They really had no idea what to make of him. However, he could make some interesting statements and once told the US ambassador that he had a 'cushy life out here' just before he asked the colonel who was hosting the party to tell him how much 'it' had all cost.

I spent most of my time steering Bob into calmer waters but his determination to make the most of the free cognac often made this a tricky task. His capacity to wind up Michelle was infinite. We had rented a wonderful villa on the north coast at Sans Souci. We wanted this trip and the villa to be a highlight of his holiday. The villa was on three floors and had a spectacular view out across the bay. It had an elegant interior with marble floors. Michelle was excited and hoped that Bob would appreciate it. It had cost a lot to rent the place. The children were also excited to be there. We opened the door and Michelle went in first. It was dark and cool. She then went down to the patio doors and flung them open with a flourish. The vista was beautiful. A clear blue sea stretched in front of us. There was a flawless sky above and the villa was flanked by small cliffs on either side of the bay fringed with gently swaying palm trees. A golden beach stretched out below us. Michelle turned and looked at Bob expectantly.

She said, 'Look at that view – the beautiful Caribbean sea.'

Bob spent a minute or so looking at it and then turned to her with a shrug of his shoulders and said, 'Yeh, it's all right'.

Michelle took a deep breath and exploded telling him that for a man who lived in a **** hole in Woolwich where you had to wade through rubbish daily, his lack of enthusiasm was not appreciated. In fact her response was bit stronger than that. The penny finally dropped and in Bob's brain, cogs whirred and gears crashed. He realised that he might well have said the wrong thing. He mumbled something that sounded like, 'It's very nice', but the damage was done and I believe that Michelle never forgot his lack of appreciation. I think that Bob did appreciate the length that Michelle had gone to, to make him happy, but he was just 'one too cool dude' at that time and had made a big mistake.

Time was galloping along. The political situation in Jamaica had stabilised over the time we had been in Jamaica, with the Prime Minister, Mr Seaga, gaining continuing support from the US government for his policies. Food and drink were plentiful in the shops and the post-election tenseness lightened. Tourists, the lifeblood of a small island with limited exports, started to reappear in the resorts and further afield. I had got used to the daily immigration workload at the High Commission. My FCO colleague was Brian Lester Smith. With his Foreign Office background he cared little about immigration matters. Brian had many talents and was an historian with a great interest in the flora and fauna of Jamaica. He was very knowledgeable about military matters and had worked in a wide variety of posts within the F&CO He was a most useful member of the HC and could turn his hand to almost anything. Unfortunately, he was a challenging man to work with. He either worked at breakneck speed, issuing entry certificates, the Commonwealth equivalent of visas, to applicants without due diligence, or he found interesting people to talk to, and spent hours doing so. The staff used to ask me to deal with the difficult cases, and as these were plentiful in Jamaica the applications would pile up on my desk. We worked out a modus operandi and became friends. Brian and his wife, Vlad, now live in the Czech Republic and Michelle and I have visited them and enjoyed their hospitality. In fact our son, Andrew, and his wife, Caroline, were married in a castle in the Czech Republic and Brian and Vlad were there as guests. However, Brian still has the capacity to infuriate Michelle with his ceaseless probing of society's ills and his gloomy outlook.

Of the several friends we made in Jamaica, some of the closest were Nick, Sue, and their children, Ellie and Tom, whom we met in Kingston. Nick was working as an exchange teacher and we met him at a diplomatic party. He was one of the few guests there who was remotely interesting and as a historian and Marxist, he was very knowledgeable and could be challenging. You must know your facts if you want to take on Nick in a debate.

Nick viewed travel in Jamaica as a project and used to hire an old car from Pappa Jack's Auto Shack in Kingston at weekends. He would then ask one or two Jamaican friends to accompany him and his family in the car and the party would leave Kingston to explore the island. His aim was to visit every village that was shown on his map of Jamaica. The family and friends used to arrive back at Nick's and Sue's small house, which was close to ours, looking like the survivors of a trip across the desert on a camel: parched, weary, red-eyed and unable to stand up straight without lurching to the side with leg cramps. Nevertheless, Nick was not a man to be beaten and just about achieved his aim before he left. As a mark of our friendship, Nick, Sue and their family once came to spend Christmas day with us and left the house four days later when the food and drink ran out. We are still close friends today,

So much happened during our time in Jamaica which will always have a special place in our hearts. Jamaica has the capacity to bring out every emotion in you in just one day. Michelle recalls one heart-stopping incident that definitely was potentially life-threatening. Gareth was not at school as he had been ill and Michelle needed to buy lettuce for a dinner party that we were giving that evening – of course there was more than lettuce on the menu. She drove down to Liguanea Plaza which was close to our home and parked the car, intending to shop in the Hi Lo Supermarket. Just as she left the car, holding Gareth by the hand, three gunmen ran out of the jeweller's shop which was almost opposite the car. Clearly, they had just robbed the shop. Hot in pursuit were armed police firing shots from automatic weapons across the plaza at the fleeing thieves. Michelle grabbed Gareth and ran to the Hi Lo Supermarket just as they were locking the doors to prevent the gunmen from entering. She was worried not only about the bullets but had thought that the gunman might hijack her car as she was standing beside it with the car keys in her hand. Michelle ducked into the supermarket with Gareth, aiming for the back near the freezer compartment. She intended to take refuge there if the gunman entered the store. This was quick thinking under pressure, on her part. In contrast, the majority of Jamaican women in the store had their noses pressed up to the window to watch the action as bullets whizzed across the plaza. At any moment, a stray bullet could have killed or wounded a bystander but that didn't seem to matter to the Jamaicans who preferred to see the action at first hand. The police killed the three gunman. One stray bullet creased the head of a little girl but she was otherwise unharmed.

Michelle rang me later at the High Commission to tell me that she and Gareth had been very close to a shootout but were unharmed. She seemed quite calm about the whole incident and said that she didn't need me to come home. I felt really disturbed about how close my wife and son had been to death as I knew how irresponsible the police could be when pursuing gunmen. They used to shoot without consideration for bystanders who were often killed in crossfire.

Our three years in Jamaica passed quickly and we were shortly to leave and return to the UK. I remember that after training one evening, Senpai James Crooks asked me what I would be doing on a Sunday in four weeks' time. I told him that I had arranged to take a party to climb the Blue Mountain Peak overnight on the Friday and that we would return on Saturday. He advised me to cancel it. He told me that I would need all my strength for the Sunday morning as he was inviting me to take my *Shodan* (first degree black belt) in Seido Karate on behalf of the club. I was speechless. I had trained with the club over the years without any thought of advancement. I knew much of the Seido syllabus as I had worked at every level of it but my skills and knowledge were far below that expected of a black belt candidate. I expressed these concerns to James but he said that the committee had considered all aspects of the promotion and had allocated him to work with me to get my skills up to scratch. This would be a formidable task as I knew how serious the Seido gradings in Jamaica were. You had to fight every step of the way for your promotion, and many failed.

A problem struck me. I had committed myself to the Blue Mountain climb and had organised a party of eleven people to accompany me. I couldn't let them down. Despite my misgivings, I would have to take the climb and do the grading. Over the next four weeks, I prepared as best as I could and tried to cram the extensive syllabus into my mind. James came to my house and helped me prepare. The students also helped me at the dojo and my skills started to improve significantly.

In order to pass the promotion you had to know all the basic techniques to a high degree, be able to demonstrate the complex self-defences, show a mastery of fighting skills, with and without a partner, execute the *katas* – increasingly complex patterns of fighting moves against imaginary opponents – and finally fight everyone in the dojo, including the teachers. The thought of it all began to overwhelm me and the fear of injury was ever-present.

On the Friday before the promotion, I met our party at five o'clock in the evening outside the High Commission and we drove up to the base camp at the foot of the mountains. The Blue Mountains form the longest range in Jamaica and the island's highest point, Blue Mountain Peak, is over seven thousand feet. The mountains get their name from the blue haze created by the mist from the high rainfall they receive. If you are lucky, on a clear day from the summit you are able to see both the north and south coasts of the island. Additionally, you might also see the outline of Cuba, one hundred and thirty miles away. I had walked up to the summit previously and had been fortunate enough to see some spectacular views from it. It is a challenging but exciting walk as you climb up the paths which take you through lush vegetation, towering trees and over five hundred species of flowering plants, more than half of which are unique to the island. Over two hundred species of birds live in the Blue Mountains. The heady scents from the vegetation and the smell of coffee beans that waft over you as you climb are wonderful.

Two hours after leaving Kingston we parked the cars at the trail head and walked to the old wooden building that was known as Whitfield Hall. We had paid for basic accommodation, bunk beds and a wash basin, in order to rest until we set out on the trail at one thirty in the morning. The aim was to arrive at the summit in order to see the beautiful dawn. It wasn't easy to rest as we could hear large rats scurrying about nearby but we dozed until it was time to leave.

At one o'clock in the morning it was black and cold. Torch lights flickered around the walls as we pulled on our clothing. Our bodies were stiff and cold and our muscles were protesting but I encouraged the party to stretch out. Conversation started between us and we shared coffee. The children were wide-awake and excited. The hike would be seven miles. We had torches, but the night was unusually black and, when we walked down to the track that leads to the start of the climb, I lost my bearings and missed the small opening to the path. After about fifteen minutes I realised my mistake and turned back much to general barracking from the group but it is quite easy to miss the opening in the darkness. We had out eldest son, Gareth, then aged ten and his friend, Stuart aged nine, hiking with us as we finally began the walk to the summit.

Flashlights flickered on to the rocks at the side of the path and the way up was narrow and steep, especially as we came to the section known as Jacob's Ladder. Michelle had worn her trainers but the constant rubbing of canvas against her toe started to aggravate her skin and her toe was becoming sore. The party slowly made its way upwards. The forest seemed to hem you in but as you looked above you could see the sky twinkling with stars with a magical quality. Sometimes faster moving hikers would overtake us, exchanging a few words as they did so. You could almost feel the dawn approaching and we quickened our tired legs, anxious to be at the summit for dawn's arrival. Michelle asked me for what seemed like the twentieth time, how far we had to go. I knew that her toe was causing her problems and so I was encouraging her but she was becoming irritated as I said again that it would not be much further. Finally, we arrived at the summit but there was a fine mist all around us and visibility was poor. I felt disappointed as I had been full of hope that we would see a spectacular dawn.

It was cold on the summit and the little forestry hut built there was crammed with hikers taking shelter. The smell of ganja smoke from the overnighters hung in the air as a slow fire burned in the hearth. In an instant, the clouds parted, the mist seemed to burn off and a magnificent blazing golden sun appeared against a blue sky filling the dawn with light and warmth and giving us a momentary but unsurpassed glimpse of the island. The sun vanished as fast as it had appeared and that magical moment gave way once more to thin rain.

We took some breakfast together and the mood in the party was positive even though we had not seen the view for as long as we had wished. Now we had to retrace our steps for seven miles down the mountain. It was a completely different experience and we were able to see the richness of the mountain in plant, bird and tree life. The views were wonderful. We walked down steep trails through eucalyptus trees, bamboo and tree ferns. The morning was coming to life as birds called happily to each other and the sky was clearing. It was easy to see that some parts of the trail were dangerous and that the slow, steady pace that we had taken overnight had been the right way to proceed. Michelle and her friend, Alison, another member of our party, were both surprised at the height to which we had climbed.

We had one heart-stopping moment when we lost Gareth and Stuart who had run off enthusiastically down the path as it levelled out. We were worried because it was easy to get lost in these mountains as sometimes the paths turn and cross each other. I ran down the hill after them and called out their names as I was really concerned for their safety. Initially, they did not answer, but eventually I did catch them up. They had just run down the path like the wind, enjoying their freedom. There was no harm done. We arrived home about midday. Apart from Michelle's sore toe – she had resorted to ripping off the top of her trainer to allow the toe to poke through – there were no other injuries and we had all enjoyed the challenge. I was tired. Taking charge of a party is always testing and, as I soaked in the bath, I thought that the very last thing I wanted to do the following morning was to take a Seido Karate promotion.

Sunday arrived and, still stiff and with those familiar butterflies fluttering in my stomach that signalled the start of having to cope with my fears, I arrived at the dojo in the cool six o'clock morning air. Mr Chin, the caretaker, an elderly gentleman, greeted me with his usual politeness. Sensei Lyn, Senpais Tony Robinson and Oscar Lawson, the two dojo hit men, also greeted me in good humour. Sensei Lyn told me that I would be taking my promotion with another student who couldn't speak. I got changed into my karate gi in the locker room already full of other students changing into gis and there I met my partner for the first time. He was from a club in Mandeville. There was much good-natured banter and fast patois exchanged between the students and directed our way. We eyed each other nervously and acknowledged the banter of the black belts as the dojo slowly filled up. My nerves were starting to vibrate. I had no idea what I would have to do specifically in the grading so my mind raced away going through the endless possible demands until I mentally shouted at myself to stop worrying. I would need to take one step at a time, forget about mistakes and keep in the moment: technique before strength, spirit before technique.

The black belts lined up and we were invited to join them at the back of the open-sided dojo as formalities were completed. Sensei Lyn spoke briefly about what he expected from us and then the tests began. I really don't remember much about grading as it seemed to pass in a blur but there were a barrage of demands for us to demonstrate our spirit by doing pushups on our knuckles, fingers or thumbs, *yakusoku kumite* (prearranged sparring with a partner) *kihon kumite* (practice moves for fighting, a bit like shadow boxing) self defences, more push ups, and *katas.* We were asked to demonstrate the moves both on the left and right side, eyes open and eyes closed. I wasn't as sharp as I had hoped I would be but I managed to keep up with the pace. My companion really knew his syllabus but was taking a bit more heat than me when he made a mistake. Perhaps they expected more of him. We were allowed a drink break after every hour and two hours had already passed. The heat of the day was starting to warm the dojo which had a tin roof. You can imagine how hot we were in that environment.

Sensei Lynn told us to put on our gloves for *kumite* (fighting). We had no protection on our feet. Sweat was running freely down our faces. I shook hands with my partner, shared a drink with him and we once again kneeled at the dojo entrance awaiting our invitation to join the black belts. I deliberately didn't look at the numbers of the fighters who were waiting to test me as I knew that however many there were, I would fight only one at a time. I stared straight ahead.

The first fight started. I bowed to my opponent. I thought that we might exchange a few blows while we were warming up. The shock of the uppercut to my chin and a leg sweep that bounced me off the dojo floor and left me outside the dojo in the gravel set the scene for me. I climbed back on to the floor and thought that anything went in this promotion and I had better be prepared for the worst if I was to survive. It was rough and it got rougher. There were no half measures. We fought the black belts one after another with hardly any break. There was not much room in which to move your opponents around so I decided that I would try to stay really close to my opponents and use hook punches to the body and leg sweeps to keep them at bay. I was doing quite well using this tactic. I was taking some punishment to the body but I was not letting the kickers use their full range and I had already caught a few fighters off-guard by sweeping both their legs from underneath them.

My companion was still moving fast but I could see that he was being relentlessly cornered and made to fight his ground. He was taking a lot of hard hits.

I think that I was in my twelfth fight when disaster happened. My opponent was to be last year's club champion. He was tall and rangy with whip-like kicks and terrific flexibility. He was a real handful. I knew him well and was relishing this fight as I had thought out a way to take the sting out of his kicks by changing stances and fighting him from a right-handed stance, keeping my lead leg outside of his. This can cause quite a few difficulties for kickers and open up possibilities for sweeping the legs and counter-punching. He threw quite a few slow kicks towards me, gauging my tactics and then, just as I was changing my stance, he shot out a side kick *(yoko geri)* aiming towards my ribs on the right side.

I saw the kick coming and twisted to my left. I thought that I had angled my body enough to deflect the kick with my right arm but I was badly wrong. I misjudged the downward block of my arm against the kick and met the kick at right angles. This was a really bad mistake. I felt the impact of the kick on the arm, specifically the ulna bone which is the lower bone of the arm located on the side of the little finger. The bone snapped about four inches above my wrist. I automatically changed sides, putting my left side forward in order to protect myself. I was now fighting him with one hand as my right arm was dangling uselessly but I didn't feel much pain. Sensei Lyn called for the bout to stop. He examined my arm and asked me how I felt. I knew the arm was broken as I could feel the ulna bone grinding against the radius bone, which runs parallel to it. I asked him if I could strap up the arm and continue grading.

He wanted me to stop but I felt bloody-minded and I was determined to carry on. He consulted the other seniors and they agreed that I could continue.

I strapped the arm up as best I could by tying a karate belt around it and then securing the belt over my head in a loop. I fought on. Even now I can't believe how foolish it was to do this and I would never permit my own students to act in a similar manner as there is a high possibility of long term injury to the arm, apart from the dangers too of internal bleeding which could lead to collapse. But sometimes these things happen. Sensei Lyn then told all the students to fight me with one hand and to avoid the injured arm. If I had thought that there would be sympathy for me then I was wrong. The black belts continued to fight as before and punched hard with their one arm or kicked to my stomach or my head. How I survived the fighting is still a mystery to me as I really don't remember much detail except for the endless bouts that I faced. Finally, the *kumite* was over and I thought that the grading would be over as well but it was not finished yet. We were both exhausted but were then told to complete *Sanchin Kata* – an isometric pattern of movement that focuses on internal tension and breath control. The black belts tested us with our eyes closed as we completed the moves but those thigh kicks were the last thing that we really wanted. We completed the *kata* breathing hard and raggedly. In all honesty, my body felt mostly numb and no bit felt worse than any other, including my arm. The grading surely must be over now I thought.

'Last fight,' said Sensei Lyn and I thought that he must have been joking. We could both barely stand up but the last fight was to be against each other. We must have looked a comic sight as we circled each other surrounded by black belts. My companion was the last person I wanted to fight but I thought that if I attacked hard to his centre then it would soon be over. I remember feinting to his face with a

With Sensei Errol Lyn after my sword demonstration at my final night in the Seido dojo. Senpai Tony Robinson, first man second row left, is now head of Seido in Jamaica,

left jab and, as he walked forward, just throwing myself to the right in order to deliver a back kick to his stomach. I misjudged the kick. Instead of my kick hitting him in the stomach area my leg whipped around in circle at head height and hit him straight in the face. Blood exploded from his mouth and he dropped to the ground almost unconscious. I felt dreadful for causing him such injury. I was so tired that I dropped to one knee whilst the black belts helped him up and he got to his feet. They cleaned up his face. Thankfully he had not lost any teeth and was just shaken up with a bloody lip. We collapsed against each other after the formal bow that ended the fight.

There are no photographs of that promotion and I am glad of it. At that time no-one took photographs of such events in the same way as they do today. We would have looked a sorry sight. Our gis were ripped and torn. Dried blood had soaked into the fabric creating dark stains on their front. We were so exhausted that we could hardly stand up. All the black belts warmly congratulated us on completing the promotion and there was a great atmosphere in the dojo as Sensei Lyn tied our new black belts with one gold strip embroidered on to them around our waists signifying that we were First Degree Seido Black Belts. Quite frankly the belts were the only things holding us together.

Sensei wanted to take me to the hospital but I said that I would look after myself. I simply wanted to get home. I remember driving myself home in a daze, steering and changing gears with only my left hand which was a real challenge in itself. I staggered through our door clutching my new black belt in my left hand. Michelle could see that I was beaten up but I tried to make light of my condition. I didn't tell Michelle that my arm was broken but explained that it was damaged but I would go to the hospital the next day for treatment. It was a poor decision. I had a hot bath, dosed myself up with pain-killers and went to bed where I found myself in agony throughout the afternoon and most of the night as every time I moved in the bed, the fractured bone grated on the sound one. It was a very rough night.

Early on Monday morning, I went to a private hospital where a doctor set the arm in plaster. Despite the injury, I was determined to be back in the dojo that very night and I drove there myself there with the intention of training. Michelle thought that I was mad. Sensei Lyn wouldn't let me train and, after explaining to the class what had

My first impression of the World Seido Karate HQ in New York.

happened at the grading, he advised me to rest the arm for at least a month.

It took six weeks for the bone in the arm to heal but I never stopped training and was back in the dojo the following week. I even learned to play squash left-handed and the height of success for me was when I beat my usual squash partner in a friendly match. He didn't take the loss very well.

We were fast approaching the end of our stay in Jamaica. On my last night at the karate club, Senpai James Crook helped me perform a sword display which was very well received. The club generously gave me gifts to remember them by. I presented Sensei Errol with a Japanese sword *(Katana)* as a mark of my profound respect.

I matured in Jamaica. I learned so much about myself and others. I am profoundly grateful to my Jamaican brothers and sisters in the Seido Karate Club for their time and effort in helping me with my development. As I review my time spent training in the dojo, it sounds hard and rough, and indeed it was, but it was the same for everyone. There were no favours or favourites in the dojo and your skill and spirit marked you out.

I know that on many occasions I had been protected from serious injury by the consideration of some of the fighters in the dojo whose fighting skills were simply astounding. They could have done real damage but they looked after me in their own way. The head of Seido Karate in Jamaica now is Jun Shihan Tony Robinson, and he was one of the first men that I met and fought in the dojo. He was an awesome fighter then and

With Kaicho Nakamura
at the Seido HQ.

even now, at his age, he still commands great respect for his fighting skills. I keep in regular touch with him and whenever I visit Kingston, Jamaica, I still bump into fighters I knew in the dojo so many years ago. Fighting is so honest and the friendships developed by fighters are lasting. You always know if you win or lose no matter what spin others may put on the outcome. In my experience, when old fighters meet there is almost a spiritual insight into each other that seldom exists outside the ring, a real feeling of warmth and respect for the trials and challenges faced in their career of fighting.

Michelle had also matured over the three years we had spent abroad. She had blossomed into a confident and lovely person who could mix easily with people from all walks of life. She had worked as a volunteer in an orphanage where she saw the heartbreak of abandoned children and, at one time, she seriously thought about adopting a delightful young girl whose name, coincidentally, was also Michelle. My Michelle was now a good Mahjong player and could certainly hold her own within FCO diplomatic circles. Our children, Gareth, Alex, and Andrew had grown up too and benefited from having being educated in a foreign culture. They had a refreshing innocence and zest for life that seemed somehow different from similar youngsters of their age at home in the UK. Andrew could almost speak patois and had a Jamaican accent. We knew that, as a family, it was time to move on but our hearts belonged to the Blue Mountains.

We left Jamaica in 1984 and headed back to the UK via New York. This was the first opportunity I had had to meet *Kaicho* (Grand Master) Nakamura, founder of the World Seido Karate Organisation, who knew of me through Sensei Lyn. When I first entered the dojo on the first floor of 61 West 23rd Street, not far from the infamous Chelsea Hotel where Nancy Spungen, the girlfriend of the punk rocker Sid Vicious of the Sex Pistols, was found stabbed to death, I was impressed by its beautifully cared-for golden burnished floor which led down to the Seido Karate calligraphy that adorned the *Shinzen* – the spiritual centre of the training hall. I felt as if I had stepped back in time in Japan.

The dojo was crowded. There were so many students and so many black belts. Kaicho introduced me to his instructors and students just before the midday class and a few of the Jamaicans who had known me in Kingston came over to greet me. It felt good to be made so welcome there. Kaicho later took me out to lunch and we discussed my future. He had spoken at regular intervals with Sensei Lyn about my training in Jamaica and had supported my candidacy for black belt. I told him that I wanted to continue training in Seido but as there were no UK clubs it would be hard for me to do so. Kaicho suggested a compromise. He was satisfied with my commitment to Seido Karate and thought that my previous experience in running my own dojos in the UK would be most helpful when I came to open the first Seido dojo in England.

I was shocked. Usually, a black belt of the first rank would be insufficient to merit the honour of opening a new dojo but I was gratified that he thought that I would be able to take on the responsibility of representing him. He told me that I would need to travel to the Seido HQ every year in order to receive instruction and to correct my faults. I asked him for time to think and to discuss this future commitment with Michelle. I knew that we would have so many challenges ahead of us when we returned to the UK. We would have to move from Dover to near Heathrow Airport, where my new job would start. We would have to find a suitable house and settle the children in new schools and establish new roots for our future. I would not be able to start a Seido club until my family were settled. Nevertheless, Michelle encouraged me to accept the challenge and said that she would support me. Once we were settled, we would look for suitable premises and open up the first Seido Karate Club in the UK. This aspect of our future was decided.

Jamaica, the country and her people, live on in our hearts and our lives were changed for the better by our experience of living there. Once again we were starting out on an adventure in our life. But we were strong together and had matured and grown with each other and felt confident that we could meet the unknown challenges that we would face in the future back in England.

21

NEW ROOTS AND CHAOS

When we returned to the UK we knew that we would have to devote time to looking for a new place to live. We now had to resettle and we knew from past experience how difficult this would be. I didn't want to work at Heathrow Airport, preferring instead to work at Gatwick Airport. We liked the idea of living in Sussex with its pretty little villages and ease of access to the south coast. Before we left Jamaica, I wrote to the Chief Inspector of Immigration, asking him if I could be posted to Gatwick on my return. My letter set out powerful arguments that I hoped would influence him but all to no avail. In his response he acknowledged that I had done a very good job in Jamaica but explained that my knowledge and skills would be put to better uses at the pressure point of the UK for immigration, Heathrow Terminal Three. On a map, we drew a ring around London Heathrow Airport, aiming to find a maximum travelling distance of twenty five miles from home to work.

There was no appeal against this directive and we still had our family home in Martin Mill near Dover, Kent. Consequently, we would be separated again until I could find us a new home. I found accommodation in Twickenham, near Heathrow, with an old friend, Colin Parfitt, who thirty years later died in tragic circumstances when he shot himself following an extended bout of depression. It was hard to see why he chose death over life as he was a kind and gentle man with much to offer. It was difficult being separated from each other as Michelle had to be responsible for resettling the children, while I would be living the bachelor life at Heathrow. The bachelor life was unattractive. After the initial euphoria of being able to go out every night and drink six pints of ale before coming home to the flat, where I would eat fish and chips, have a whisky nightcap with Colin, go to bed and then repeat the process the next night, the family life became very attractive indeed.

I missed Michelle and the boys but had little time to dwell on their absence as the work at Heathrow was very intense. The UK was having real problems with an influx of Africans, particularly Nigerians and Ghanaians, Pakistanis, Indians and Bangladeshi nationals arriving and seeking entry as visitors even though they had no intention of ever returning home. The UK's response was to seek to impose a visa control on those nationalities but this involved a wide range of negotiations with the governments of their home countries. Our intentions were leaked and this created a panic and inbound planes were packed with would-be immigrants. The arrival hall at Heathrow Terminal Three would be heaving with humanity and the system to manage them worked like this: if an immigration officer thought that the passenger merited further examination then that passenger would be given notice that a further interview was required.

A second immigration officer would interview the passenger and then make a recommendation to a chief immigration officer about whether or not that person should be granted or refused entry to the UK. Interpreters needed to be involved and there would usually be children with the family who needed care, feeding arrangements to make, luggage to examine and so on. It was almost impossible to speed up the process without sacrificing its integrity. The number of arrivals began to overwhelm us. We started to use the grant of temporary admission to the

UK as a way of getting those detained out of the airport as fast as possible. We would set a date for their further examination in one or two months. With this approach, the detainee would need to have a sponsor who was reliable and this meant that we would also have to interview the sponsor. This caused further problems. The numbers increased to a point where it became impossible to operate any real control as the entire system was grinding to a halt. We were told by our senior management not to investigate the *bona fides* of the sponsors but to just let the detainees go to anyone with an address. We rarely checked that the addresses even existed, such was the pressure on us to get the detainees out of Heathrow. Only the worst cases were detained and so the UK had a huge influx of immigrants who just disappeared and never returned for their second interview. We had no resources to follow up these disappearances.

The inspector in charge of immigration at that point was a very charismatic character called John de Llanos. He was desperately pushing our HQ to accelerate the introduction of a visa regime for the five main countries for potential immigrants to the UK: India, Pakistan, Bangladesh, Nigeria, and Ghana. His tactic was to reflect what was happening at ground floor level up the line in graphic detail as well as to manage a few leaks but the situation remained farcical. He bestrode the floor like a captain on deck knowing that there would be a point of collapse in the immigration control which would hasten the introduction of visas. Immigration officers were worked off their feet and could barely keep pace with the demands. On some nights you would come on duty at six o'clock in the evening and be given about thirty passports to 'sort out'. This meant that you sat down and examined those passports and the accompanying notes which had been hastily compiled by the initial interviewing officer and you would then have to make a decision about whether to grant entry to the passenger. Picture a typical detention area at Terminal Three on a Saturday morning after the arrival of the Nigerian flight. The detention room was a small space overseen by the security firm, Securicor, responsible for bringing the detainees to the immigration officer and for arranging for their care. Of course, with so many detainees, it was almost impossible to keep to a structured system. Babies were howling, children crawled across the floor, pregnant women seemed to be everywhere and demanding food and care. Many Nigerian men would be shouting at the top of their voices demanding to know why they had been detained when their friends had been given entry. Interpreters, in short supply, were run ragged. The whole area resembled a combination of a railway terminus and a psychiatric hospital. The noise was incredible. Tempers were frayed and staff were barely civil, even to each other. Often the background notes of the first interview relating to the passengers would get mixed up and, as the interviewing officer, you would be asking a passenger to confirm the reason for coming to the UK and expressing surprise that he or she had changed their story so quickly. Naturally, we would stop the interview once the discrepancy had been discovered but we had become battle-hardened and nothing surprised us.

This chaotic situation prevailed for nearly two months until, eventually, a visa regime was imposed on the five previously mentioned countries. The regime drastically cut the number of arrivals and automatically created a situation whereby anyone who wanted to visit the UK would first have to apply to the British High Commission, usually in their country of origin, for pre-clearance to travel. This shifted the bottleneck away from the UK and stemmed the flow of potential immigrants. But at what cost to the UK? I think the complete breakdown of our immigration control, not only at Heathrow Airport, where the pressure was the worst but at all ports of entry around the UK, is the root cause of many of the social problems that we encounter today. I have noticed that every time our immigration control system breaks down, the government of the day creates some sort of, often hidden, amnesty over a period of time that allows migrants to settle here. The system of processing asylum applications, for example, is tortuous and has been abused by economic migrants who realise that they have no basis to remain in the UK unless they make a false claim of persecution in their own country. Many years can pass before their application is resolved, by which time they may marry and have children thus making their eventual removal almost impossible.

Once the Home Office realises that there is little prospect of fully dealing with the mounting asylum claims, suggestions are made to ministers that an 'amnesty' of some kind needs to be offered to make the numbers more palatable. This creates a long term problem as the people-traffickers quickly pick up on our weak solutions and know that they can exploit the system. The result is that they find more and more creative ways of securing entry for their customers in the knowledge that only a small percentage of migrants will be removed. There is a really difficult social balance that needs to be maintained if we are to be a successful and fully integrated country that thrives on the energy that a properly managed immigration policy can bring to us. People who want to stop immigration hark back to Nazi Germany in 1939 when no one in their right mind wanted to migrate to Germany. Democracy costs us dearly but so far I can't think of a better system and there will always be those that take advantage of it. Getting the balance right has taxed the brightest minds in the country and no one has found a solution yet probably because a solution doesn't exist. The immigration portfolio for ministers is one of the hottest potatoes there is. Once you are given the job, you just want to get out of it as quickly as possible as you know for certain that disaster awaits you. This is why the Home Secretary's job is possibly the most difficult portfolio to manage and a good Home Secretary is worth his or her weight in gold. The pits are deep and hidden everywhere. You only have to look at the casualty list of Home Secretaries who have fallen on to the immigration sword to see what a challenging a job it is.

You might understand just how difficult it was for me to work at Heathrow, drive down to Dover to see my family when I could, and house-hunt on my free weekends. It was a demanding existence for both Michelle and me. She had to cope with the everyday needs of the children but she hardly every complained as she knew that we needed to pull together to make things work in the long term for our family. I despaired of finding a suitable home. I went to visit a large semi-detached house which was next to a sports club in Holmer Green, about four miles from High Wycombe. The house was a post-war build but had an extension added to the main structure. The vendor was getting a divorce from his wife so wanted to sell the place as quickly as he could. The kitchen was enormous but quite bare and there were five bedrooms. It had a big garden and all the space we needed for our family. The property was opposite a local school but not ideally situated as it was close to the main road. It ticked most of the right boxes. I arranged for Michelle to come up one weekend to view the house. We were shown around by the vendor but when we went into the extension which contained the fifth bedroom, Michelle noticed that the room seemed odd. The floor seemed to be sloping down. The vendor said that his brother was the builder who had put up the extension. He said that although his brother was a good builder, he was a poor decorator and had misaligned the wallpaper which gave the illusion of a sloping floor.

Although the house was spacious and seemed to meet our needs, it lacked soul. However, by this time we were so exhausted by the search for a family house that we discussed our options and I asked Michelle if she wanted to move to

Holmer Green. I listed all the reasons why the property would suit us and Michelle agreed that we should move there. We made an offer on the property, well below the asking price, and subject to a full-scale property survey. At last we had somewhere to bring the family together again. Two weeks later, I was home in Dover for the weekend and we were considering moving dates when a letter from our surveyor arrived. The letter contained a full report which stated that basically the house was sound except for the extension which had not been properly built and in fact was one inch lower than the original structure. We now understood the feeling of the sloping floor we had experienced in the fifth bedroom. The story given to us by the vendor about the wallpaper was disingenuous. I read out the relevant parts of the report to Michelle and said that we would not take the house in this condition. I was sad for her as I thought that she had her heart set on it. Imagine my surprise when she told me that she had never liked the house and was delighted we were not going to move there. She explained that she had said that she liked it only because she could see that living apart and searching for a family house was getting me down. She had just wanted us to be together as a family again. I didn't really like the property either but thought that she did. We opened a bottle of wine to celebrate not getting the property! Bizarre. It was incredible that we had both sacrificed our aspirations to please each other and had both been totally wrong in our judgements.

I returned to the job of searching for a family home with renewed determination and within a couple of weeks I had found a property on a newly built private estate outside High Wycombe in a village called Hughenden Valley. It was a smaller property than we were used to but was nearly new, located in a cul-de-sac which was safe for the children to play outside, near good schools and within walking distance of the local pub. When I first took Michelle to see the property, again her spirits dropped. We drove through High Wycombe, which had abandoned shopping trolleys littering the roads, past rows of dingy and poorly maintained properties on the way to Hughenden Valley. It was a depressing sight until we reached Hughenden Park with its stately oak trees and interesting history – Queen Victoria visited Benjamin Disraeli who was the British Prime Minister of England in 1868 at his house located within the grounds. We were in the country. Michelle's spirits started to lift. She liked our new house which had four small bedrooms and a tiny garage but the property was neat and felt like home. We thought that we could be happy here and, even though it wasn't fully finished and the estate was still covered with rubble and planks of wood, we saw its potential. The main drawback was that the estate agent told me that the house was under offer already. I do not like the principle of gazumping but I was desperate to settle my family and secure our future. I told the estate agent to contact the vendors and say that I was an immediate cash buyer. Luckily the Home Office could offer me a bridging loan until we sold our own house which didn't actually happen until two years later. The offer was accepted and at last we had a future in Buckinghamshire together as a family. Our new neighbours Rob and Pauline Allen were friendly and welcoming. In fact Rob was so welcoming that he insisted on pouring me half a bottle of brandy just to settle us in. The local pub had a large garden where children could play. It was the right place for a fresh start and we both felt excited by the prospect of living in the valley.

On 2 January 1985, we moved into the house which we called Pine Grove after one of our favourite places in Jamaica. We enlisted the help of our neighbours. I told them that there was some heavy lifting to be done but didn't tell them the weight was contained in a baby grand piano. I had bought the piano from a Scottish friend and it had real history. It was originally a 'travelling' piano used by touring theatrical groups in their productions and could be dismantled. It had last been played on stage in Canterbury, Kent, by Fenella Fielding, an English actress popular in the 50s and 60s. My friend James was a larger-than-life Scotsman and he had bought the travelling piano at an auction. He couldn't play it but simply liked its looks and history. The piano was out of tune but I used to tinkle on it when I went to visit him and his eccentric family.

His wife, Jane, was a disorganised woman with a sad history and she was inclined to live in a fantasy world. Their five children were a challenge, to say the least. James told me that once when he was in their house, which was near the beach in Kingsdown, he had been reading in the conservatory while the children were climbing and playing in an apple tree in the garden. He had glanced up to see one of his boys, aged about nine years old swinging from the tree. It is not unusual for boys to swing on trees except that this boy was swinging from a branch by his neck! His long scarf had caught around a branch as he fell towards the ground. The scarf had jerked the boy suddenly upright and his face was going blue as he hung there being strangled. His brothers were on the ground watching him and wondering what to do next. James, spilt his coffee, rushed out of the house and into the garden, grabbing the boy's legs to take the weight off his neck. He disentangled the scarf and lowered his son to the ground. The boy was still breathing and James' heart was racing like a formula one driver on the starting grid. He was just about the call for an ambulance when the boy jumped up and joined his brothers, apparently none the worse for his experience.

The events in James' and Jane's house would take a book on their own to chronicle I remember a time when Michelle was on the phone to Jane who said, 'Sorry, must go, as the cockatoo has bitten off the budgie's foot.' Their youngest boy was very strange. Although he was intelligent, he pretended to be stupid. Sometimes he would talk and sometimes he wouldn't. He was hugely manipulative. Once, while Michelle and Jane were having coffee in the house they smelt an acrid burning and heard the sound of a fire engine. The boy had been flinging all his plastic toys on to the grate and setting fire to them. Perhaps a neighbour had seen the black smoke and called the fire brigade. They had to put out a chimney fire and the house could easily have been burnt to a cinder as pieces of burning plastic had fallen on to the carpet. The smell of the burnt plastic was awful. Michelle was advised that it was not the first time the boy had set light to items in the house, including his bed clothes. The boy, aged only four, would sometimes put on his overcoat, ready to go to school but decide to walk down to the sea and walk into the waves fully clothed while throwing stones. His mother would have to rush out from the house and drag him back from the waves.

The family eventually moved to Leicester and it was there that I went to pick up the baby grand piano from their new house. James had previously given it to me as he didn't want to take the piano and knew that I liked to play. I recall arriving at the door of their new house and being greeted by Jane. James was at work, the boys were at school and only their youngest was at home. She invited me in, apologising for the state of the place explaining that they were still moving in. Jane was a genteel lady with a sweet disposition. I had just entered through the front door and the removers were bringing furniture into the house. The youngest was upstairs, leaning over the rails on the landing telling us all to, 'F*** off.' Jane looked up at him and said, 'Please don't be rude, darling. Why don't you come down and meet Roger whom you knew in Dover.' The boy came down the stairs and looked at me. I put out my hand to greet him and he lunged forward, aiming to kick me in the groin. This was not the friendliest of greetings and apparently, was not unusual as, according to Jane, only the day before he had kicked the visiting vicar in the groin. Still the vicar was not a martial artist and I am. I saw the boy's intention and decided to make it into a game. As he darted forward, I moved to the side, scooped him up with a laugh and said playfully, 'Good try.' I put him gently back on the floor. He shot up and furiously attacked me again and the same thing happened. All the time I was talking to Jane and saying, 'He loves to play, doesn't he?' Eventually, I said to the lad, 'Come on, you can do better than that.' After the fourth rush at me, he was getting a bit fed up with his lack of progress so he then rushed back upstairs to his place on the landing where he proceeded to scream, ' C***, c*** ,c***.' at anyone who came through the door. Jane, who clearly had no control over him whatsoever, asked him not to swear. When he ran out of breath he disappeared into his room, doubtless hatching some dark plan which involved my demise. I never saw a child like him and, although his parents were the most loving and understanding people you could ever meet, they were odd in a social sense. I hope that the boy eventually found tranquility in his life, but he was a raging storm when I knew him.

With the help of the removers, I loaded the piano into the van that I had hired for the day and brought it back to Hughenden Valley. I directed the neighbours' efforts as we manoeuvered it down the alleyway, past the garage, around the back, into the garden and through the door into the dining room where it filled up the room leaving barely space for the dining table and chairs. Michelle was not too pleased about this but I felt that I was linked to the piano and didn't want to give it up, even though it was clearly too big for the room. The piano story has a tragic ending. Some years after I took possession of the piano, James moved back to Scotland, taking Jane and the family with him. He seemed to have undergone a personal crisis as he was found in his car having committed suicide using a pipe connected from the exhaust into the passenger compartment. He left his wife and family in a farm house in the middle of nowhere. Michelle went up to stay with the family after this tragic event and helped look after the children. No one could work out why James had killed himself. Shortly before his death, he had converted to Catholicism and had withdrawn a large amount of money from his savings and donated it to the Catholic church. We lost touch with the family but my heart goes out to Jane and the five boys for the pain they must have felt at the loss of their father. He was a most intelligent and funny individual who didn't make friends easily. He dominated the family, never even letting Jane buy her own dresses. There are secrets about his life that may never come to light, but I hope that the family has found healing in its own way. The stigma of suicide is a terrible curse on a family.

We had made a good decision about where to live. Gareth, Alex and Andrew went to Kingshill Primary school which was close by. It was a Church of England school which was very well run and highly regarded in our area. Gareth had previously been attending the Dover Grammar School but when we moved to Buckinghamshire, he had to sit the 12+ exam as he was not automatically assured a place in a grammar school in this county. He failed the test by a small margin and we appealed against the decision.

The appeal itself was a farce and loaded against the appellant. The adjudicators did not take into account that he had previously been doing well at a grammar school, had been uprooted from it and was trying to settle down at his new school. The fact that he was only a few points short of the pass mark showed that he had coped very well with all the disturbance to the pattern of his life. They didn't take this into account, they were simply seeking ways of turning down borderline applicants to avoid overloading the selection system. We appeared before the representatives on the board but the answer was still negative. We then looked at St. Bernard School which was the local Catholic

Secondary School. The school had a good reputation and, as I was a Catholic, my children were eligible for selection.

The interview with the headmaster, Mr Duckham, was extraordinary. He wore a dark three piece suit and displayed a pinched face expression that some might say looked almost Dickensian and spiteful. We accompanied Gareth on the appointed day and he was interviewed by the headmaster first. He was asked to do some mental arithmetic and to read out loud. He was also asked what papers his parents read. The significance of this is still a mystery to us. We were invited into his study. Mr Duckham interrogated us about our life in Jamaica – I am sure that he could have led the Spanish Inquisition – and then he asked if we had any questions.

I had previously done some research on crime in the High Wycombe area and knew that a drug problem existed. A number of dealers were operating in the area and I felt that they represented a threat for students in local schools. I asked him if the school had been troubled by dealers trying to sell drugs to students, explaining that I knew that the town was a drugs target. He exploded. Gritting his teeth and with bulging eyes he hissed, 'Do you take drugs? If so, we do not tolerate that sort of thing here.' Whether or not he had deliberately missed the point I do not know, but he didn't answer my question and asked us what papers we read. We didn't like him, but he offered Gareth a place in the school. With hindsight, we should have seen his leadership for what it was. I have nothing against the school and I am sure that it has many fine teachers, but clearly this was a man who buried his head in the sand and ignored the threats now faced by so many schools : cheap drugs made readily available to students by pushers of their own age group.

Gareth started at St. Bernard School and, after the usual testing period when the new boy gets bullied, it became apparent to the bullies that he could easily hold his own in a playground fight. You don't go to school in Jamaica without being able to look after yourself. Gareth had a strong character and was highly energetic. He wasn't an academic and preferred to have fun. He really did kick over the traces as he was growing up and, again with hindsight, we probably gave him too much freedom. I remembered the restrictions my own father had sought to place on me and I believe I overcompensated when I was bringing up Gareth. He mixed with some boys who were troublemakers. He would concoct a story about going to the cinema with friends when he was actually going out clubbing. There were parallels with my own teenage years that didn't escape me. Schoolwork wasn't high on his agenda. We all went through a testing period over Gareth's teenage years but, to our amazement, he decided to stay on into the sixth form. That was a complete waste of two years as he was more out of school than in it. Aged eighteen, on his last day at St. Bernard School, he went on a bit of a wrecking spree in the toilets, including even ripping up his own school blazer. He convinced me that he didn't do it and I defended his behaviour when it was challenged by the deputy headmaster on the grounds that there was no evidence to show that Gareth had been the culprit. The school was glad to see the back of Gareth and the feeling was mutual.

We believed that Gareth was easily intelligent enough to study at university but having obtained a bagful of GCSEs and not much else, the commercial world, which promised money in his pocket and a girl on his arm, beckoned. His first job was in an estate agents where he worked about sixty hours a week for little money but this gave him a solid foundation in sales and now he could probably sell snow to Eskimos. His first full-time girlfriend became a nightmare for him. Her name was Anna and she had dark Italian looks. She was very pretty and lived with her mother and step-father. She had trouble written all over her and Gareth, who had by then wrecked at least two cars and was still pushing back his barriers, was still living with us. He was in love with her. They both walked on the wild side of life. We were stunned when, one Christmas Gareth, who was staying with Anna, her mother and step-father, phoned us to wish us a happy Christmas. He then mentioned that he and Anna intended to become engaged to be married.

We were speechless. Not long before this, Anna had taken an overdose of pills and ended up in Wycombe Hospital just after Gareth had told her that he was thinking of splitting up with her. This was not the basis of a sound relationship. I think that I wished them well and then hoped against hope that their plans would fall through. They did live together in a flat owned by Anna's mum, but Gareth later moved out, realising that their relationship was doomed to failure. There was hell to pay as Anna threatened him with just about everything you could threaten someone with, including committing suicide if he didn't stay with her. Gareth arrived home one evening, at the age of twenty-one with his suitcase in his hand. He was broke, had split up with Anna, his car needed fixing and life seemed in ruins. He was distraught and asked Michelle if he could come back him to live with us and get his life back on track.

Michelle welcomed him back but laid down rules: he didn't get his old room back as Andrew, our youngest, now had use of that, he did all his own washing and ironing and paid rent. The rules were obviously not too restrictive as Gareth stayed with us for another six years during which time we experienced another nightmare, Suzie. More of her and serial infidelity later. Parents would love to choose their children's partners and the Asian arranged marriage method of marriage choice seems to have quite a lot to recommend it, although our boys might not agree.

Alex, our middle son, was also at St. Bernard's but was of a quieter disposition than Gareth and did quite well there.

He left after his GCSEs and didn't want to go to university. Can your children trick the selection system? Well, Alex did. He told us recently that when he had taken his 12+ exam as a child he had failed it deliberately by selecting answers that he knew to be wrong. This is hard to believe if you don't know that Alex is very intelligent. His reasoning was that he didn't want to go to a grammar school where he knew nobody, but knew that if he failed the exam he could get into St. Bernard's where he had a brother. His reasoning was that he could fit right into the school and that his brother could take care of him. Later Alex went to Amersham College to do a Higher National Certificate in computer studies. It was an indifferent course and well below his capacity and he had to deal with quite a bit of racial abuse from students of Pakistani origin who would gang up on him to make his life difficult. However, Alex has always had a knack of making friends and he made friends with a bodybuilder of Jamaican origin who took him under his wing. His minder warned off the troublemakers and so Alex was able to get on with his studies in peace.

Once he gained his qualification, Alex decided to go travelling to Australia for one year. He worked anywhere he could when he needed money. We were astonished to learn that he trained as a orderly in a hospital looking after the elderly. The money was very good, and the job was worth doing. Good training for looking after us in our old age, perhaps.

It is strange how you worry more about your children when they are near to you at home than when they are half way across the world when you give barely a thought to the dangers that they might be facing. Our ignorance was bliss until we got a worrying telephone call from Alex in Thailand at about two o'clock in the morning. He seemed slightly drunk. He explained that he was in a bar downtown somewhere and had met a lovely Thai girl. He was going to go island hopping with her for a week. When he said,

'Don't worry, Dad, she's not a prozzie.' It did ring alarm bells with me and almost caused Michelle to faint. We constructed all sorts of scenarios, especially as Alex told us that he would be out of touch for some time on his travels. People disappear in such places. Apart from a dose of dysentry he got on his way back to the UK when he was broke and living in poor accommodation paying about fifty pence a day for food and a stained mattress, he came home safely. We met him at Heathrow Airport and, as relieved parents, we were delighted to see him. Although he had evidently lost weight, we saw the usual carefree Alex with his big open smile and good humour.

We were now firmly established in Hughenden Valley. All our family were either living with us or living close by. Michelle had a good part-time job at the Gliding Club which was about five miles away, our karate club had put down firm roots and we were running successful children and adult programmes and we liked our house and neighbours. Andrew, our youngest son, was doing very well at school and had secured a place at Southampton University where he would study Oceanography and Geology and eventually secure a good degree. We had made friends and we truly felt settled after our long stay abroad. Our relationship was strong. We felt lucky. But when you see that uncertainty is paradoxically the only thing that you can hold on to, it means that you cannot take anything for granted. Whilst the sky, sea and earth endure, every now and then the earth quakes to remind us that nothing lasts forever.

22
Intelligence Points the Way

June 1999. It is seven thirty in the morning I am sipping a cup of tea and looking at the empty arrivals hall from the chief immigration officer's (CIO's) office at Heathrow's Terminal Two. I had been posted here on promotion after a short time working at Terminal Three. All is quiet. My officers are waiting for the next flight of passengers to arrive at our control. My office has a glass partition which also allows me to see into the main detention room next door.

The detention 'suite' is for passengers who would be subjected to secondary examination by an immigration officer if they did not meet the formal requirements for entry into the UK. The suite has a female security guard on duty who has the task of taking care of the detainees and recording their movement in and out of detention. Unusually, I feel relaxed. Terminal Two deals with a wide variety of air traffic. We encounter passengers from all over the world as our flights from Europe connect worldwide. In my time I had encountered a wide range of problems, some life-threatening, including detained Iraqis trying to set light to themselves in front of me, in protest at their detention. I had had many other testing incidents including an interview with a deranged Greek army officer who produced a razor blade which he had concealed in his mouth and held the blade to my neck, threatening to kill me. I managed to talk him out of doing so as blood can make a nasty stain on your shirt. I dealt with a vampire: a national of Zaire, who was being put on a flight to Germany, launched himself at me in the van in which we were travelling and bit me on the neck. I removed his teeth from my neck, using my self-defence skills. Fortunately, the tests carried out on me later confirmed that my attacker didn't have Aids or Hepatitis C. A drunken Finn, who was waiting to be interviewed, lunged forward from his seat and grabbed my tie as I walked past him. He tried to headbutt me and kick me in the groin for no good reason that I could see except perhaps that he disliked my tie. I restrained him. I was battle-hardened and not much could surprise me.

I think that I hear a cry. I look through the glass partition room and see a detainee slitting his wrist with what looks like a jagged edge of glass. I see the guard has her hands over her face and is shouting. I put down my tea cup, rush out of my office and into the detention suite. The casualty is on his knees. He holds his right wrist with his left hand and blood is spurting from the cut. He shouts something that I cannot understand but he has dropped the cutting edge which looks like it was part of a broken glass tumbler. I pull out my handkerchief and grab hold of his bleeding wrist. I hold his arm as high as I can, telling the guard to call an ambulance. She is in shock so I shout at her again. She moves towards the phone. The man is moaning and shaking. I try to keep pressure on the wound as blood is still spurting out. He keeps trying to pull his arm away from me and so I pin him in to a corner so that he cannot move. I am wearing a white short-sleeved shirt and his blood is now running down my arm and soaking into my shirt.

The fight seems to have gone out of him and he begins sobbing and rocking his body back and forth which makes it doubly difficult for me to keep his arm high as well as keep up pressure on the wound. Help arrives as paramedics accompanied by police burst in through the door and take over from me. I stand up slowly and walk out of the door. There will be an enquiry. I have hours of paperwork ahead of me. Passengers have now arrived at the control and are being interviewed by staff. They watch me warily as I walk back into the CIO's office and a colleague asks me how I am. I look down at the blood on my shirt, the blood on my hands and the drying blood on my trousers. My colleague says that I have blood on my face.

That was the moment when I decided that I had had enough. Not because of the blood, not because of the emotions that can be generated by this sort of incident but because I was in danger of losing my humanity. I had no more feelings or care for this man than if I had been made of stone. I didn't stop to think about the despair that had reduced a human being to try to take his own life or at least to draw attention to his plight. I just didn't care. All I thought about was washing the blood off me and whether there was a chance of infection. But I was shocked by my indifference. I had lost my ability to care. Over the years I had dealt with tricksters, liars, cheats, drug couriers, bogus asylum seekers, economic migrants and dealt with them all without complaint – well almost. Little by little I had become desensitised to suffering. I decided that I needed to leave my job at Terminal Two if I was to have a chance of becoming human again. Paradoxically, my home life was happy and I had established a solid foundation for Seido Karate in the UK with clubs in Dover, London and High Wycombe. We had great instructors and there was a real feeling of progress as we built up our organisation. I needed to change my job.

Fate. Out of the blue I received a call from Andy Holden, a former colleague who had recently joined a new unit managed by Mike Smith, an immigration inspector. It was called the Immigration and Nationality Directorate Intelligence Section (INDIS). The unit was dedicated to producing intelligence to fight immigration abuse nationally and in a highly focused manner. The section had two CIOs but needed a third. The post had recently been advertised and Andy asked me if I would be interested in applying for the job. He warned me that the competition for the post was fierce. I rang the manager, Mike Smith, and discussed the details with him. I asked him what he wanted to achieve over the next five years. He replied that he wasn't even sure what he wanted to achieve next week. He told me that the Assistant Director in charge, Dave Wilson, wanted INDIS to be a flagship for the Immigration Service and somehow we needed to achieve this. There were many battles that would need to be fought and the hardest one would be to convince the Immigration Service that we needed to be intelligence-led.

I knew Dave Wilson's reputation for being a hard taskmaster who did not suffer fools gladly. He could be ruthless in his dealings with staff. He would be highly focused on what he wanted to achieve. In fact, I thought that he was just the sort of boss that would be needed to drive the unit forward as I knew that within the Home Office the higher management would be sceptical about INDIS' potential and that therefore obtaining resources would be an uphill battle.

I applied for the job and got it. I knew that I would. This was not conceit on my part but I just knew that INDIS was the right path for me. I was very happy. It was a new beginning. In karate we call this, 'shoshin' or 'beginner's mind'. It means having the ability to cast off the mistakes of the past and take a look at your life afresh. I had no background in intelligence work and didn't even consider myself to be intelligent. I had 'A' levels in English Literature, French and Spanish and a clutch of 'O' levels to my credit. However, I spoke French, Spanish, Portuguese and Serbo-Croat to a good standard. I believed that I had a sharp wit and an enquiring mind. But most of all, I wanted to learn and to help to develop a structure that was important in the fight against illegal immigration. The early days of settling into the job were exciting. The other CIO in the Unit was big

John Smith, a man I knew well and indeed he had started in the job with me. He was a pragmatist. Andy Holden was a sharp operator with a quick mind and political acumen. The inspector, Mike Smith, was the most amiable of men. He had a fund of stories about the Immigration Service and its staff together with a deep knowledge of enforcement issues but he too had no intelligence background. All eight immigration officers were fairly long in the tooth but brought with them specialist skills from their previous jobs. It was a lively and challenging environment in which to develop our credibility. But how could we be a national intelligence resource without a database?

One of my first achievements working for INDIS was to prepare a case for the funding of the first national immigration intelligence database. My colleague named the system 'Mycroft' after Sherlock Holmes' brother. You might think such an important bid for funding would have been painstakingly prepared after months of consideration. In fact the preparation was completed over one weekend. Dave Wilson told me one Friday that he had identified a source of funding for an intelligence database as long as we could meet a deadline with the correct documentation and get project approval from the board. We would have to achieve this by Tuesday so we had just three days to prepare documentation. I willingly took on the challenge as I knew just how important the database would be to our future. I rang a friend who worked in the immigration computer section and explained the problem: I had no idea which database we could use. He laughed and said that he had just bought a copy of a monthly computer magazine which had distributed a free database disc. He had reviewed how the programme, *Idealist*, stored data and thought that it would meet all our needs. I consulted a colleague working with me on the project and we sat together and looked at the screen shots of the database. Its name seemed appropriate as it looked ideal. It was simple to use and could retrieve data very quickly. It met our immediate specific needs and most of all, it was cheap.

That weekend we worked for up to fifteen hours a day to pull together the documentation needed by the Home Office for funding of this sort. The project template was so complex that it was almost unintelligible to me. Once again, fate lent me a hand. Creating a detailed document for a database system is daunting and demands specialist knowledge and expertise. I remembered that I had previously met the administration manager at the National Criminal Intelligence Service (NCIS) who had been responsible for all aspects of the funding bid and installation of their system which was far more complex and demanding than ours. I rang him and explained our dilemma. He was sympathetic and asked me to come to see him in his office at Vauxhall to discuss our needs. When we met, he gave me a copy of the documentation he had used for the NCIS bid. I couldn't officially use it but I could plagiarise it. I worked out that I could use its structure and format as the basis for our bid.

Together with my colleagues I began to put together the complex document that was needed to underwrite our funding bid. We would need to demonstrate that the system would save public money over a five year period. It was formulaic nonsense as it was impossible to predict with any accuracy the savings that would be derived from our intelligence database. By Sunday night we were exhausted. I had double vision from looking at the computer screen. At one low point, the software programme I was using crashed and I thought that I had lost nearly two hundred pages of work but, fortunately for me, my technical friends managed to retrieve the work. I had been almost in tears when the computer crashed but, in the end, we succeeded in creating the database within the tight deadline. By eleven o'clock on Sunday night we sat around the computer screen and stared at the document which proudly showed on the title page: *The Mycroft Project: An Intelligence Database for the Immigration & Nationality Directorate Intelligence Section.* It was professionally prepared and even I was impressed with the snapshots of database screens and technical jargon. We had clearly demonstrated savings to the public purse of over one million pounds within five years . Surely the board could not fail to release the funds for us?

Dave Wilson presented the bid to the Board and they agreed that funding could be released for the project. They said that the prepared document was of a high standard and that they could find no fault with it, however, it would have to be resubmitted by an external consultant who had the right qualifications to submit such a document to the board. What a waste of public money. We now had to employ an external consultant at five hundred pounds a day who would work with me for one week and produce an almost identical document in a slightly different format. I was incensed but the project got approval from the board and the hard work to implement the system could now begin.

Within two years we had developed the first UK immigration database for intelligence use and copies of it were distributed throughout the UK to all our intelligence offices at the ports of entry. Mycroft was later supplanted by a hugely complex intelligence-compliant system that was far better at safeguarding sensitive material but paradoxically, in my view, less able to provide officers with the information they needed to do their job.

Yes, we had our database and we had established a structure to take forward our intelligence needs but we still needed a major success against a key crime target. If INDIS was to be credible in the eyes of the Service, our senior management and partners in fighting crime then we had to think big. Operation Maybug was the outcome of such thought.

Operation Maybug was derived from the translation of

an unpronounceable Polish proverb that Andy Holden had memorised for some reason. The target of Maybug was a well known British racketeer of Indian extraction who had been bringing illegal entrants into the UK for years. As I discussed his activities with my team I realised that the way forward was not simply to disrupt his activities in the UK but also to provide intelligence that would lead to the break up, disruption and prosecution of those gangs and individuals intent on people-smuggling in all the countries en route. This sounds obvious, but at that time even coordinating operational action with our own police forces in the UK was highly problematic. To attempt to coordinate enforcement partners in other countries except by using Interpol, who managed international information exchanges, and Europol, who managed European information exchanges, was unthinkable. Additionally both of these organisations had their own agenda and were known to be leaky when it came to safeguarding intelligence. I thought that the best way forward was to go it alone.

People smuggling. It sounds fairly benign, doesn't it? But the reality is quite different. Once you have seen the nightmarish pictures of fifty eight Chinese, men and women, who suffocated in a lorry arriving at Dover from the Belgian port of Zeebrugge having been concealed in a refrigerated lorry filled with a cargo of tomatoes, you realise what a nasty business it is. The faces of these Chinese were so contorted with pain that many could scarcely be identified from their photographs. Their fingernail scratches on the metal sides of the lorry were testimony to the agonies they had suffered as they slowly suffocated. Seven suspects, including two Chinese nationals, were eventually arrested but the pipeline was controlled by Triad groups operating in the UK.

On arrival, the illegal immigrants would be ruthlessly exploited by the Triad gangs. It was not unusual for Chinese illegal immigrants to be chained to radiators and mutilated at the same time as their captors were speaking to their relatives on the telephone demanding more money to be sent if further torture was to be avoided. Tragedies occurred monthly but, occasionally some illegal immigrants had a lucky escape. For example, Hungarian police freed forty-six Asian and African illegal entrants from a locked van, rescuing them from suffocation. The van was stopped by a road patrol forty four miles east of Budapest. The illegals were sweating, short of breath and needed medical help. If they had not been found, they would have died of suffocation within an hour. The doors of the van had to be forced open as the driver insisted that he had no keys. The driver was a young Hungarian who showed no remorse for his actions. The racketeers and fixers care nothing for human suffering.

We can all appreciate the desire to improve our family circumstances but often the risks migrants will take are astonishing. I had real sympathy with their plight but, while I understood their wish for a better life, I did not condone their actions. I felt that the work we were doing was important to our country and the scale of illegal entry was, in my opinion, out of control. No one could estimate the number of illegal immigrants in the UK, but we all knew that nationally GP's lists were growing unaccountably bigger and hospitals were dealing with an increase in childbirth of foreign nationals, many of whom appeared to have no basis to stay in the UK. Communities were reporting increasing unrest caused by ethnic tensions. The pressure to house asylum seekers was causing local councils to report to the government that they had neither the funds to house them nor the places to put them. Tensions were rising as locals who had been on a council housing waiting list for years were leap-frogged by new migrants with large families. Anomalies in housing rental were coming to notice with councils paying thousands of pounds each month to house large families in expensive accommodation in London.

A well-balanced immigration policy is very difficult to construct. Illegal entry can cause a breakdown of the ability of social services to cope. During my time with the immigration service, I learned about young children being put on to aircraft with a 'carer' posing as a relative who would disappear once the immigration control in the UK had been reached. The abandoned child, usually from Africa, would then be taken into care by the social services and housed in temporary accommodation. Hundreds of children simply disappeared from such accommodation. We had information that abuse was happening in the form of forced child labour and sexual slavery, but there seemed to be little political will to tackle this awful problem. Once the children were in the UK and had disappeared, it was almost impossible to discover where they had gone. We knew that bogus 'uncles' or 'aunts' often turned up at the accommodation and claimed the child as their own. The immigration authorities typically were not informed of this change of the child's circumstances and then the addresses that were given were found to be false.

I saw one Home Secretary and Immigration Minister after another mouth platitudes about how the government was going to control immigration with clampdowns, only to later declare secret amnesties for both illegal entrants and asylum seekers: the Home Office could not effectively process applications and remove failed cases to their own countries. Pragmatism, not the law, ruled. The Chinese authorities played games with us. It could take up to two years to get a passport from their embassy for a failed asylum seeker. The Chinese were masters of bureaucratic delays. We succeeded in returning only a small percentage of failed Chinese asylum seekers.

I have seen policy decisions made by officials in the Home Office which, at the stroke of a pen, prevented investigations into either actively looking for illegal entrants or closing down bogus colleges. Once, at a meeting with mandarins, I demonstrated the extent of the problem of bogus colleges by producing evidence showing would-be migrants exploiting our lax rules. I was told by a mandarin that it was better to concentrate on attracting students to the UK, as the income from their studies outweighed the long-term potential difficulties of illegal entry. If the Home Office looked like it was was being overwhelmed by illegal immigration then civil servants would simply suggest a face-saving formula to the appropriate minister who in turn would try to bury the problem using political skill. For example, Adelaide House was an enforcement office near London Bridge. Its officers could regularly visit businesses where illegal entrants were known to be working. We had a weekly flood of intelligence informing us of the where-abouts of illegal immigrant workers. Our orders were to not arrest those unlawfully here if they came from countries where we couldn't return them because of military conflict or political difficulties. Such countries included Somalia, Iraq and Iran. No enforcement action would be taken against the illegals and the underground communities quickly realised that you could stay as long as you liked without too much trouble. Indeed, unless the police arrested you for a criminal offence other than illegal entry, you could do what you liked. This lack of an effective deportation policy was ludicrous and nearly all immigration staff spoke out against it as it seemed that illegal entry was rewarded rather than punished.

Furthermore, at a time of global unrest and terrorism, we had little idea of an illegal entrant's real identity. London was especially a potential powder keg as we had illegal immigrants and bogus asylum seekers walking the streets who had recently been fighting in war theatres. We had intelligence to the effect that Albanian crime gangs had taken over the sex trade in London: so vicious was their modus operandi that local villains couldn't match their ferocity.

Against this background it would have been easy to become disheartened but I felt that we could make a difference by tackling immigration-related organised crime not only at its heart in the UK but abroad. However, the Immigration Service badly needed to become more professional. For example, we had the power of arrest but Home Office policy prevented us from using that power except in conjunction with the police. In other words, we were operating under a comprehensive Immigration Act that enabled us to function in a variety of effective ways but we were not trusted to use the powers we had. The result was that when we came to work with the police or with Customs, we were considered junior players, tolerated but not of sufficiently high rank. We were also cut off from using the vast resources that the Intelligence and Security Agencies (MI5; MI6 and GCHQ) could bring to bear. They had been supporting HM Customs operations against drug smugglers for years. What we did have were officers within the service who were superb operators and could hold their own with any service if only they were allowed to fulfil their potential. We could scarcely get the police to come out on immigration raids with us if they had a conflicting priority and we nearly always needed their expertise in the subject of arrest and detention, producing evidence for court and raising prosecutions. In short, we were ineffective.

We had the intellectual capacity to function at a high level, we had the staff who could do it, but we had no backing from the senior civil servants in the Home Office who didn't seem to want a professional immigration service to be tackling organised crime. The view was that we should keep well away from dealing directly with crime and leave it to the police. I believed that INDIS could be the battering ram to break down the castle door and that we had to engage with the heavyweights if we were to be effective. I worked with colleagues under Dave Wilson, who was single-handedly fighting our corner with senior civil servants, to produce a strategy not only to engage NCIS (the National Criminal Intelligence Service) by attaching our staff there, thus quickly developing expertise in fighting major crime, but more importantly to engage the Security and Intelligence Agencies in the same way.

The UK has three main national intelligence services. First, the Security Service which deals with all internal security matters including Northern Ireland and reports to the Home Secretary. The Security Service, often known as MI5, is the UK's national security intelligence agency. Since 1909 it has been responsible for countering covertly organised threats to national security. It also provides advice to a range of other organisations, helping them reduce their vulnerability to the threats. Its staff are largely based in their headquarters at Thames House in London. The Service is organised into seven branches, each with specific areas of responsibility, and work to counter a range of threats including terrorism, espionage and the proliferation of weapons of mass destruction.

Next, the Secret Intelligence Service (SIS) supervises all overseas intelligence-gathering and reports to the Foreign Secretary. It operates out of the building located next to Vauxhall Bridge which looks like something you would see in a 'Batman' comic book. SIS is often known as MI6. SIS provides the government's covert capability to promote and defend the national security and economic well-being of the United Kingdom.

Last, we have GCHQ (The Government Communication Headquarters) which gathers intelligence using technical means and services the needs of its intelligence cousins. The headquarters are located in Cheltenham where it has a state-of-the-art building known as the 'doughnut.' It also reports to the Foreign Secretary.

These three organisations are powerful institutions, each with their own agenda, agents, spies, listening equipment, budgets and objectives, all of which are intended to safeguard the UK's internal and external interests. At the same time, I knew that they had no real focus on immigration matters unless they came across an immigration-related organised criminal in the course of their work or they were supporting an NCIS-led operation. Immigration simply wasn't an intelligence collection priority. Our strategy was to seek to change their rules on intelligence collection so that the spy masters would have to support us. We needed to develop an operation that could engage their collective services to support us in attacking the immigration gangs which were acting at home and abroad. Specifically, we had to convince the key player for us, SIS, that they had a vital role in protecting the UK against immigration-related organised crime.

For Operation Maybug we had previously convinced NCIS that they should use their resources to mount an intelligence operation against our UK target. Once we had sufficient evidence against the target in the UK and had identified the routes he was using and the countries involved, we could seek to engage SIS. We needed to use SIS's resources abroad to identify the key racketeers in destination and transit countries. We then needed to convince police in those countries to take action against the main players. The plan was so ambitious that it was almost doomed to fail. We detached an officer from INDIS to work directly with NCIS officers on the operation and this proved to be a success. I worked closely with SIS to identify the racketeers abroad.

Using intelligence gained from surveillance and other activities is more difficult than you might think. If SIS picks up information from a secret source about illegal immigrants being hidden in a lorry coming from Calais to Dover, it cannot simply be given to the police or immigration authorities to act upon. The source of the intelligence has to be protected otherwise the recipient of the intelligence might be able to work out where the information is coming from over a period of time. Should that person be corrupt, then the source might be identified and betrayed to the gang or otherwise harmed. Informers die because they pass on secret information and criminals find out their identity. Therefore there is a layer between the intelligence that is passed on and the people who will use it, and that layer is a unit which takes the intelligence, sanitises it to a point where the source is protected and passes it on to the designated officer on the case who then gets to read the report. Even then, that officer cannot use the intelligence directly. It can only point the way. That officer must collect evidence of criminal activity.

This is the challenge that faces immigration, customs and the police when they want to use intelligence gathered by the Intelligence and Security Agencies. They know the evidence exists but have to provide the proof of criminal activity without referring to the intelligence. But my vision was beginning to become a reality. The target of our surveillance activity was Joginder Singh Kaile, a thirty-nine year old businessman from Southall. We found that over a period of ten years he had smuggled thousands of Indian nationals, crammed into vans or cars which carried them nine thousand seven hundred kilometres across Asia and Europe and into the UK. He took their land in the Punjab as payment for the trip and forced them on arrival to work in his sweatshops, housing them in squalid conditions and squeezing more and more profit out of their cheap labour. Kaile charged ten thousand US dollars for each person who made the journey. Our investigators estimated that he made a profit of nearly three thousand US dollars per person, after expenses. He had become a millionaire. The trail for the illegal entrant started in the Punjab but we identified key traffickers in the Ukraine, Czech Republic, Poland, Belgium, Holland, France and Germany who were a part of the network. Our aim was not just to bring Kaile to justice, as this would have a limited effect on the networks, but also to disrupt the whole of the pipeline and target key criminals in the countries en route to the UK.

Against all the odds, the operation was starting to come together. I set out on a journey to the Ukraine, the Czech Republic and Poland with two colleagues: one was from NCIS and the other was from the F&CO. We needed to convince police in those countries that it would be in their own interest to work with us against the racketeers. It was an enormous undertaking involving the preparation of dossiers in Russian, Czech, Polish and German to show the police exactly how the networks were connected to the key criminals in their own countries. It was sensitive work as our contacts would want to know where we had obtained our detailed intelligence. The dossiers displayed in analytical detail how the criminal networks were not only operating in their own countries but linking with gangs in other countries en route from India. We could not reveal our sources. I would lead our team and present our case at each meeting. The preparation for the trip was intense. We could not afford to make mistakes with the detail and finally we were ready.

The role played by the F&CO, in conjunction with operatives from SIS, in identifying the right person with whom to deal in each country was crucial. Our F&CO contacts carefully planned how we should approach each meeting and briefed us on protocol. The amount of vodka that we had to consume in the course of our work nearly killed us: our police counterparts expected us to socialise after business and the ability to drink copious amounts of vodka seemed to be the key to gaining respect. We had endless toasts in vodka of every description to mutual cooperation but our small team held up magnificently. It was an all-consuming experience.

In the Ukraine, for example, meetings were held in the building that had been used as the Gestapo HQ during the Second World War. The building was an example of the style of architecture known as Ukrainian Baroque. It was a stately home which epitomised luxury and elegance. On entering its ornate doors, you walked up a sweeping staircase that led to the conference room. Large dark oil paintings of stern-looking patricians lined the walls. The conference room was dominated by a long, highly polished dining-table. Small flags of Great Britain and Ukraine were arranged in the centre of the table and intricately carved, ornate chairs with silk seats waited for us. At one end of the table was a huge silver platter which contained glasses filled with vodka. It was ten o'clock in the morning. We were offered coffee but of course the meeting began with toasts to each other in vodka. The majority of the police were former KGB officers who now worked for the Ukraine, rather than the Russian, government. The atmosphere was friendly but we knew that there would be links between the police and the criminals and therefore potential leaks about our operation so our hopes for a successful outcome were not high.

During a break, I needed to go to the toilet. I had to leave the grand meeting room and descend a dimly-lit stairwell that led down towards the basement at the rear entrance. I had an uncomfortable feeling of fear even though I knew nothing would happen to me. It was all too easy to visualise what had happened below in the basement when the Gestapo had occupied the building. When I reached the toilet, which had marble tiling throughout, I found that there was no toilet paper, much to the amusement of my twenty stone guard I had to ask him to get me some. It was obvious to me that the absence of toilet paper was a deliberate attempt to make visitors feel off-balance with a resultant loss of control. Mind games.

We obtained agreements for action and then were invited to an official lunch which started at twelve thirty in another grand mansion. This time there were both police and military officers present and our host was a general.

I looked at the table which had bottles of iced vodka standing sentry along its centre and asked my interpreter what was the best tactic to survive the lunch without being drunk at the end of it. We had meetings with the Minister of Foreign Affairs in the afternoon and I couldn't afford to be dull-witted. She advised me eat the white meat as she called it, or pork fat, to line my stomach and that this would slow down the absorption of the alcohol into my blood stream. There was a catch. The fat was salty and I would therefore want to drink water or beer to slake my thirst. She advised me not to do so as it would quicken absorption. The lunch was torture. There were at least twenty guests and everyone of them proposed a toast. I had to respond to at least five of the toasts which were aimed at us. The protocol was that if the general sipped his vodka, guests did too but if he tossed the glass back and slammed it down with a flourish then so did everyone else. I ate a lot of pork fat and felt queasy but at least I was not drunk. I had previously asked my F&CO adviser if we could just take water with our meal and he had strongly warned me against doing so if we wanted to create the right impression.

Dining in opulence, it was hard to believe that we were only about fifty miles from Chernobyl.[1] We were told not to eat any produce from a market stall and not to eat fish from the river. This human tragedy had happened so close to us. Of course we knocked out all the usual jokes about not needing to wind our watches as radiation would keep them active but I think that we all felt uncomfortable at being so close to radiation that had had such a disastrous impact.

I liked Kiev, with its wide open streets and grand baroque buildings but there was a strong feeling of oppression. I have never seen so many police on the streets. They were everywhere. The city did have a cosmopolitan feel to it but I thought that the people had still not shaken off the tyranny of communism.

We stayed at the hotel opposite the football stadium.

The lobby had just been refurbished and a huge chandelier glittered in the foyer but the bedrooms were dark and utilitarian. There was a commissionaire on each floor who supervised access to the rooms. In communist times she would have been a police or security services informer. I suspected that her role hadn't changed much. The commissionaire on my floor was about fifty years old and grim-faced, barely grunting a 'Dobro Jutro' to me each morning.

After a full day of meetings we were exhausted but still had to attend an informal dinner with members of the security and intelligence services. We were glad to get back to our hotel by eleven o'clock that evening. My colleague from NCIS and I decided to go up to the bar on the top floor of the hotel for a drink and chat about the following day's business. The bar was almost empty apart from four fine-looking women who were chatting to each other. There was a casino. Now I like a flutter. I don't lose much but roulette interests me and so I said to my colleague that we should invest twenty US dollars on the table. He really had no interest. There was no one in the casino but us and so the plan was to lose the money as quickly as possible and get back to chat at the bar. I did not really expect to win but I couldn't stop and won about four hundred dollars in a short time. My colleague eventually encouraged me to return to the bar despite the entreaties of the croupier who had seen all that money go out and nothing come back. We had been at the bar for a short time when two gorgeous looking women came over to us and asked if we would like to buy them a drink. I said that would be fine as long as they wanted a beer: I feared that if they ordered champagne it could set me back hundreds of dollars. They were clearly hookers and, after some light conversation, they got down to business. By this time it was half-past midnight. They said that we could spend the night with them for, guess how much? Four hundred US dollars. That was a coincidence.

With a straight face, my companion asked how much it would cost for two minutes in bed with her, explaining that that this was how long he usually took! I collapsed laughing but the pair of them showed no amusement and said that the price was still the same. Clearly they thought we were a poor investment of their time and they left to continue their hunt. That night I slept like the dead but woke up at three o'clock in the morning with a raging thirst. Sleepily, I went into the bathroom and absent-mindedly poured myself a glass of water from the tap and drank it. Immediately I was wideawake. The residue in the water was brown and we had been told not to drink water from the tap. I groaned. Within one hour I had raging diarrhoea, stomach cramps and was rolling around on the bed feeling very sorry for myself. At first light I got up, found where I could buy Imodium to give me some relief and took twice the recommended dose. By breakfast time I had stabilised my stomach and although I did not feel great at least I was ready for business. We now needed to fly to Prague.

Leaving my room for the last time I encountered my grim-looking guardian who was sitting at her desk. In my poor Russian I thanked her for looking after me, and asked if she had grandchildren. She said that she had three lovely grandchildren. I then asked her if she would buy them a present from me and gave her fifty US dollars. I couldn't believe her reaction to the gift. She started to cry and rose from her chair and hugged me. God knows what would have happened if I had given her a hundred dollars.

I loved the Czechs. The police were up to their ears in their own problems but made time to see us. At our first meeting the leader of the crime team put his gun on the table, glanced at the dossier and asked, 'Who do you want us to get?' It was as simple as that and they kept to their word. We didn't get to see much of Prague at that time but we formed a close working relationship with Prague's crime team. Our business there was swiftly concluded and this time we were expected to consume vast amounts of Czech beer with the team. My liver was under pressure. Our tight schedule demanded that we fly to Warsaw the next day.

The Poles were extremely formal and demanding. There was initially almost a hesitancy to admit that they had organised crime gangs working out of Poland. They reviewed the detail included in the dossier about a key racketeer operating out of Warsaw and questioned us for hours about the intelligence we had obtained. It was a game of cat and mouse as they were probing to discover our sources of information. Poland is a massive transit country for migrants who are seeking to establish themselves in Western Europe and then onwards to the UK. The Poles did not appear to be concerned about the role their racketeer had played in the pipeline until we pointed out his links to domestic crime as well as people smuggling. The Poles agreed to work with us and finally we returned to the UK feeling that we had laid a firm foundation for future action. We had already negotiated with the German and Dutch police so that they could also take action against networks operating in their own countries. We had achieved a great deal in a very short time and I felt really lucky to have had the support of my two colleagues on the five-day trip.

This operation was the result of nearly two years of work: we had started the operation in 2005. However, it was only on our return that the real action really began. Together with NCIS the F&CO and SIS we arranged for the targets in each country to be 'hit' at the same time, or very nearly the same time. The German police jumped the gun on one arrest that left the Czechs furious as they had previously agreed a date. Mix-ups invariably happen, but I was delighted that we managed the whole process so effectively. I pay particular tribute to the work of my colleagues in NCIS and the Secret Intelligence Service. Without their help and the role played by the F&CO my ambitious plan would not have been achieved.

Kaile was arrested at his home in Southall in June 2007. Initially he denied forty charges of breaching or attempting to facilitate a breach of immigration law by supplying false information to support visa applications for people from India who were not EU citizens, between December 2005 and August 2007. We knew that we would need to be painstaking in putting together our evidence to avoid being overwhelmed by Kaile's defence team.

While my team was still working with NCIS to pull the case together, I found that I also had to place another team member at the Home Office Asylum Unit in Croydon to arrange the presentation of evidence in all the files that Kaile was shown to be involved. These files were crucial to the prosecution evidence that he was submitting bogus asylum accounts on behalf of the illegal entrants. We had a deadline to present the evidence to the court so I was dismayed to receive a frantic call from my officer in Croydon who said that she couldn't access the files as the room where they were stored had been declared a health and safety hazard! This was terrible news for me and the police team as the prosecution could fail if our administration was deemed by the judge to be inadequate Two years work would be lost. Kaile would walk free.

I contacted the senior executive officer (SEO) in charge of the filing room and staff and she was implacable. She told me that fumes from the adjacent car park were entering the file storage room and until these were dealt with, her staff refused to enter the room as they were getting headaches and feeling sick. I had no sympathy what-soever with them and told the SEO that we must have the files today and that my officer was prepared to get them. She refused to let her enter the room. When I put the phone down I just stared at the floor with my head spinning with options. I could go to my boss and involve our senior management but we were running short of time. Our evidence had taken six months to produce and exhibit in the correct form and I was satisfied that we had a watertight case. I rang up the police sergeant who was in charge of the presentation of evidence and explained the situation to him. I really had no idea how to break the deadlock. If the room was a hazard, making it safe within our time frame would be impossible.

My colleague on the end of the phone was silent and then in a calm voice said, 'Don't worry, Roger. Tell her I'm sending a team of police divers equipped with oxygen masks to get the files out.'

I just burst out laughing. It was like a Monty Python sketch but I loved him for his practicality. I went to see my boss to tell him about the proposed solution. He was incredulous and laughed at the thought of it. He agreed that we should get straight back to the SEO and tell her what we would do. I told the SEO that we would be sending a team of divers and that they would all need passes for entry into the building at two o'clock that afternoon. The team would enter the room using breathing apparatus and take the files which my officer had placed in one section, and return with them. There was no other option. If she refused to allow us access to the room we would take it further through my Assistant Director and the Police Commander. It was a smoking gun. I said she would have five minutes to decide what she wanted to do and I put the phone down. It was a tense five minutes. The SEO rang back. She said that she had found a way to get the files out without police aid and that they were being brought out as we spoke. My officer confirmed that this was happening and so the evidence was safe. An incredible story, but true.

British Indian Joginder Singh Kaile smuggled thousands of illegals across Asia and Europe to Britain. In court, Kaile pleaded guilty to multiple counts of trafficking. He was sentenced to six and a half years in prison which at that time, was the longest sentence ever given to a trafficker in the UK. Kaile made a huge amount of money from exploiting the misery of illegal entry. As a result of our actions, the networks that he used, stretching from Asia to Europe, were severely disrupted and damaged, at least for a time. He had used a chain of jewellers in the UK to arrange for funds to be moved to and from India. His wealth remained in India and because he had cleverly concealed his titles to land, by using relatives' names, we were never able to confiscate it.

According to estimates from US law enforcers, the world-wide trade in human cargo is now said to be worth twenty billion US dollars a year and no amount of government initiatives will stop it. Some stowaways are paying up to twenty thousand UK pounds to get across international boundaries, which means that fifty people hidden in the back of a lorry can be worth as much as one million UK pounds to the smugglers. Some of the gangs are better at counter-surveillance than any IRA team at the height of the troubles. They expose migrants to deadly risks in the backs of lorries, in sea containers, and even in the wheel cavities of passenger jets. British law enforcement woke up to the problem of people smuggling sooner than most of our counterparts in Europe. We have one of the best immigration intelligence operations in the world and we also have some of the toughest jail terms in Europe. Securing the arrest and imprisonment of Kaile and disrupting the networks really put INDIS on the map and showed just what we could do. This work proved to be a catalyst for allowing the security and intelligence agencies to dedicate more of their resources in the fight against illegal immigration, just as Customs were fighting the drugs traffickers.

Over the next few years I worked very closely with the security and intelligence agencies on a number of sensitive operations which formed the basis for a new and lasting partnership to fight crime. I will never forget those two years nor the people who strove so hard to make it happen.

It was a wonderful example of inter-agency co-operation. INDIS had now grown beyond recognition. We had moved to a new building close to Heathrow Airport, restructured our business to support domestic and international immigration intelligence needs, and had teams working at NICIS and with the security and intelligence agencies. We were fully recognised by our law enforcement counterparts as key players in the fight against illegal immigration. We had come a long way in a short time but there was still much that we needed to achieve.

My role within INDIS changed. I was now responsible for all our intelligence attachments. Our international strategy was now to identify and disrupt illegal immigration before it reached our shores. It was a demanding role that involved travel within Europe and Eastern Europe and it was on one of my many such trips that perhaps fate put me in the right place at the right time.

NOTES FOR CHAPTER TWENTY TWO
1 – The Chernobyl disaster was a nuclear reactor accident that occurred on the 25 April 1986 at the Chernobyl Nuclear Power Plant in the Ukrainian Soviet Socialist Republic which was then part of the Soviet Union. It is considered to be the worst nuclear power plant disaster in history. It resulted in a severe release of radioactivity following a massive power explosion that destroyed the reactor. Most fatalities from the accident were caused by radiation poisoning.

23

MOUNTAINS TO CLIMB

The study of martial arts, particularly karate, has consistently been a part of my life. The benefits of this consistency have been enormous for me in terms of health and happiness. I was extremely fortunate to stumble on Seido Karate during my time in Jamaica. My research then led me to discovering its roots which were linked with the legendary Kancho (meaning Founder) Masutatsu Oyama, of Kyokushinkai Karate. Kyokushinkai was synthesised, from the elements of Goju-Ryu (meaning Hard-Soft Way) a style of karate that originated in Okinawa. Shotokan Karate (meaning Shoto's House) was developed by Master Gichin Funakoshi and included elements of Chinese boxing. At one time, Kyokushinkai was believed to be the strongest form of karate in Japan, emphasising both full-contact fighting and the development of breaking skills.

Kyokushinkai, or the School of the Ultimate Truth, has influenced many of the full-contact style of fighting schools, with realistic combat, physical toughness, and practicality in its 'training' curriculum. The 'knockdown karate' competition system pioneered by Kyokushinkai has also been adopted by many other karate organisations in existence today.

The head of the Seido Karate system, Kaicho Nakamura, was the former right-hand man of Kancho Oyama. Kaicho Nakamura's own background as a fighter of renown is astonishing. He is famous for having completed the one-hundred-man *kumite* (free-fighting) trial: on 15 October

311

1965, Kaicho Nakamura fought one hundred men, one after another, and defeated them all. This was an almost unbelievably difficult feat.

The trial had originated as a result of Kancho Oyama's wish to assess his own fighting abilities. He chose the strongest students in his dojo to fight him, one at a time, and then repeated the process, which took all of three hundred rounds to complete. He defeated them all, never wavering in his resolve, despite the fact that he suffered severe physical injury. Each student had to face him four times over the three days it took to complete the test. Some never made it past the first day because of Kancho Oyama's powerful blows.

Having set the example, Kancho Oyama started the one-hundred-man *kumite* as a requirement for attaining the fourth or fifth degree black belt. He soon found that not everyone had the spirit to attempt the trial. The physical skills could be taught but the indomitable will, courage and determination needed by the contestant to complete the ordeal, prevented all but the most determined from succeeding.

Imagine a fighter battling for one hundred rounds against fresh opponents with no breaks between each challenger. He would not be allowed to wear any head or face protection. He would wear only his gi, a groin guard and a mouthpiece. His opponent would not be allowed to punch to the face but otherwise full-power kicks to the legs, body and head would be permitted. He might knock out an opponent quickly or he might have to fight desperately in an energy-sapping bout. It would be impossible to avoid injury. Just to receive one full-contact kick to his thigh, where the peroneal nerve which supplies movement and sensation to the lower leg, foot and toes is situated, could lead to trauma and injury. It might destroy whole nerve cells resulting in a loss of feeling, muscle control, muscle tone and eventual loss of muscle mass. A fighter could be crippled by such kicks. To enter willingly into such a test needs an iron will. To succeed in the trial without incurring serious injury reflects the highest skill levels. My fighting master, Kaicho Nakamura had a formidable past.

At the time that I joined the World Seido Karate Organisation, I believed that the development of strength and power was paramount. I later discovered that this was far from the truth. Kaicho Nakamura founded Seido Karate after a long inner struggle. He was vilified by Kyokushinkai for speaking unpalatable truths. The World Karate Championship Tournament held on 1 November 1975 would be the catalyst for Kaicho Nakamura to break his ties with Kyokushinkai and set out on a path which would eventually lead me to him.

Kancho Oyama had declared that if Japan lost the tournament he would kill himself in the traditional Japanese manner by committing *seppuku* – ritual suicide using the Japanese sword. At that time, Kaicho Nakamura was the leader of Kyokushinkai in North America and his responsibilities were heavy. Not only was he required to train his American students for the competition but Kancho Oyama had also sent his own Japanese team for Kaicho Nakamura to polish their skills. Additionally, he had to co-ordinate all the teams which would arrive in Japan from Jamaica, Puerto Rica, Trinidad and Tobago and Canada. In addition to these responsibilities, he was ordered to return to Japan to take care of all the preparations for the tournament in Tokyo. On his return, Kaicho Nakamura found that while all other countries had been allowed four members to compete for each team, Japan had allowed itself eight team members. This was manifestly unfair.

Kaicho also found that no arrangements had been made for the foreign teams to train once they were in Japan. Additionally, the pairings for each fight were unfair as the strongest overseas competitors were matched against each other thus greatly reducing the chance of a Japanese competitor being beaten.

The overall judge for the tournament was Kancho Oyama. Kaicho Nakamura and Master Shigeru Oyama were special judges. Their role was to ensure fair play. In reality, many of the contests were anything but fair and Kaicho was ordered to make decisions that favoured a Japanese competitor. His refusal to do so was seen by the Kyokushinkai hierarchy as arrogance. The result of the competition was that Japan gained the top six places but even then Kancho Oyama was displeased as he felt that the Japanese side had done too well: he had wanted Japan to win first place, America second, Japan third and Europe fourth. Kaicho Nakamura was ashamed to be part of such a travesty of the spirit of *bushido* (The Way of the Warrior). He set his mind on a new way forward.

In his own words, 'I decided I would go on alone, or just with those I could trust, on the path I believe in.' Thus *Seido* (Sincere Way) was born out of the crucible of infamy.

Kaicho Nakamura wanted a karate organisation where like-minded people could support each other following the path of sincerity. But he also had a vision of an organisation which would encompass the world. At this time, Kaicho Nakamura had only one club. He wanted a style of karate in which honesty was reflected in hard work, where a student was prepared to respond to disciplined training, and where race and religion were unimportant. An organisation where advancement would depend not only on your fighting ability but also would reflect the development of your character in terms of high moral standards. An organisation where difference does not mean deficit. His decision to leave the Kyokushinkai was heartfelt but the hierarchy turned against him and sought to discredit him. Despite Kaicho's resignation from the organisation, Kancho Oyama issued a letter of expulsion, full of wrongful accusations.

Seido Karate was born in Manhattan in June 1976.

Kaicho received wonderful support and understanding from his students but the Kyokushinkai organisation continued to slander him.

He was also nearly killed when one evening in spring, as he was getting into his car to go home after training, a gunman fired two shots at him. He was wounded in the thigh. Fortunately, the bullet went straight through his leg, otherwise he might have been crippled. Nobody was caught. Who was behind the attempted assassination? Speculation was rife and suspicions abounded but the would-be assassin was never caught. Despite more personal challenges, little by little, stone by stone, Kaicho continued to build Seido into a truly worldwide organisation that had a solid moral foundation and reflected his ideals.

Understanding Kaicho's past history is also a key to understanding why I have followed the Seido path for so long in my life. His ideals reflect the best we can hope to aspire to in our society. But we all have feet of clay and are only human. Many influential students have come and gone over the years. A beautiful concept can turn to dust when the frailties of human nature tear it apart. Over the years, in martial arts generally, I have seen the distasteful side of human nature displayed: confidence tricksters, dojo predators, braggarts, scammers, thieves, and liars. From my years of experience, martial arts seems to be a breeding ground for the worst kind of dishonesty and misdirection. It abounds with false claims promising nirvana but only delivering dust and we lose good honest people as soon as they realise that they have been fooled. Karate competitions which should bring out the best in students often bring out the opposite with displays of egos, disrespect for referees and opponents and tiresome association politics.

The question of honour seems old-fashioned. I am not talking about taking offence at the slightest provocation and striking back, either orally or physically. I think that a sense of honour is an alertness and sensitivity to taking the right course of action when you confront adversity. Exactly what that action is depends on the circumstances at the time.

How would you know if you have acted dishonourably? A sense of shame would be the earliest indication. Good manners and good morals should underwrite your sense of honour. This is why the dojo is so important. It is a place where you can cultivate good manners, patience and be watchful of your own shortcomings. Patience not only with yourself but with others is so important. But doing what you believe to be the right thing will inevitably come at a cost. Our principles will always cost us dearly but I believe that not to take whatever action you hold to be right is to live poorly thereafter. It is dishonourable. These trials help us understand others better and appreciate alternative points of view. From this reservoir of experience, we can often assist our students to cross turbulent rivers themselves.

An incident occurred, in November 1997, concerning the disrespectful treatment of my wife and friends following a karate competition in Kingston Jamaica after which I felt compelled to offer Kaicho my resignation from the Seido organisation. It was a devastating moment for me. I resolved to leave Seido and start alone with students who wished to support me. I agonised over my decision before finally writing to Kaicho to explain my position. I didn't even discuss my intentions with my own instructors, only with Michelle who said that I must do what my heart told me was the right thing. For me, to offer my resignation was the right course of action. I am happy to say that Kaicho persuaded me to not resign but this incident gave me some insight and understanding about what it cost Kaicho to resign from the Kyokushinkai organisation that he had loved so much.

Our Seido Karate organisation in the UK has survived over the past twenty-seven years because of clear principles. The Japanese phrase *Go Gaku Shin* means 'keep your eyes open and learn'. Our organisation has done this. We have not only moved across the years to a more inclusive approach, developing special programmes to better reflect our community, but we have been encouraged to interact globally. Using outside the dojo, the skills developed inside the dojo, is the key to personal development. Not just to empower yourself, although I firmly believe that everything starts with you and that your cultivation of your character underwrites all else, but to give back what you can to others. I have been encouraged by others in my life in so many ways and this in turn spurs me on to seek to widely share what skills I have.

In our modern world, many dojos are based on a competitive structure – students compete against each other to raise fighting level skills. Whilst this is laudable, it can encourage aggression and imbalance. It is for our instructors to ensure that we not only teach the physical side but also ensure that the meditative side is fully explored. The thirst of a first degree brown belt for his or her black belt is understandable but it must not represent another goal, aim or trophy to be hung on the wall. Our Seido organisation should encourage us to focus as much on harmony and balance in the dojo as it does on producing strong and powerful students.

Breaking 150lbs. of concrete with an elbow strike.

Black belts are no more than advanced students. Their technique is not yet refined and they execute technique to the level of *jutsu*, which is mechanical understanding.

At around the fourth degree level, having practised for some twenty years or more, the student should be practising *waza* where *waza* is intuitive skill that surpasses simple physical competence. Moving to fifth degree level, the student should seek to embrace *ryuku* which is a level where the physical and mental senses merge with a wider understanding and harmony between the body and the mind. It would be far better in many ways if we did not have an outward manifestation of rank. After all, you only have to enter a dojo and look around you to recognise levels of attainment, and I sometimes feel that the belt system reinforces the concept of ego, making us goal-oriented. Seido Karate tries to compensate for this by asking all students trying for a black belt rank to return to *shoshin*, or 'beginner's mind', and wear the plain and simple white belt before and during the grading.

Our ranking system seeks to award titles to those persons who progress along the path of physical, mental and spiritual understanding but these things cannot be learned from a book. Students must carefully study under their seniors and seek to master their art, however long the journey, recognising the burden of imperfection. The dojo should firstly be a place of spiritual advancement which allows students to recognise their faults and weaknesses and seek to build a solid moral foundation. Every action within the dojo is a struggle against the self. All opponents remind us of our faults and it is in the struggle that we give ourselves a chance to grow. Any place designated as a place to try to develop yourself in balance, both physically and spiritually, can be a dojo. The Seido dojo should represent a spiritual waterfall that embraces and empowers us.

I have taken many promotions over the years in order to attain my current rank of sixth degree black belt. All of those promotions, except the first one in Jamaica, have been taken with Kaicho Nakamura as the examiner. At every level you must fight for your belt. This is most important. As we grow older, it becomes harder to maintain high levels of fitness. If we are not careful, we can provide a stream of excuses about why we cannot meet the demands of the promotions. These excuses are simply unacceptable. When you fight, you continually face your own fears and have to deal with them. Facing your fears makes you stronger. I have seen students of every condition, including students with cerebral palsy, fight for their belts with the incredible support of their peers to get them through the promotions.

Many of you reading this will have little idea of what happens at a Seido Karate promotion so imagine that you are the one who is taking your black belt promotion under Kaicho Nakamura at our HQ (Honbu) in New York. You have been training for nearly six years, two to three times each week with me at my dojo in Kingshill, near High Wycombe. You started out as a beginner[1] with the rank of tenth *kyu* but you are now an advanced brown belt holding the rank of first *kyu*. You know that that it is a great honour to be invited to take your first black belt under Kaicho Nakamura in New York. You know that gradings normally take place over a four week period and test not only your basic technique, but your knowledge of basic and advanced free-fighting techniques, basic and advanced Seido self-defence techniques and *kata* which is a series of pre-arranged fighting moves against imaginary opponents. Additionally, you will be required to demonstrate your fighting skills over a two hour period. This will test your fitness, stamina and spirit. You know that the key to a successful promotion is sound preparation which is aimed at improving your aerobic and anaerobic capacity. Fortunately, you began to lay down the foundation for your promotion four months previously and you are now in peak condition. Your technical skills are also of a high standard. You are ready for the challenge.

Your fellow students wish you luck and give you a party on the last training session at your dojo. They all hope for your success. The expenses for the journey to New York, accommodation and training, are high but your club has contributed financially to your trip. You appreciate their help very much. You would not be where you are now without the help of so many other students, many who have become firm friends over the years. Your family has seen you develop over the years from a teenager with many personal issues to a confident young man who has matured in so many different ways through his training. They are fully supportive of your quest.

It is time. On a Sunday in September you arrive at Heathrow's Terminal Four in time to catch the British Airways flight that will depart for John F. Kennedy airport at eleven o'clock in the morning. The flight is uneventful but your mind is restless, constantly turning over scenarios that you might face in the days ahead. On arrival at JFK airport, you pass through the passport formalities and get the bus into Manhattan. This is your first trip to New York and so you are impressed with the skyscrapers you see as the shuttle bus takes you over the Brooklyn Bridge and drops you near your hotel after eleven hours travelling. You are tired but wired. This is the eternal city so you find a nearby restaurant, have dinner and then go to bed. Sleep doesn't come easily.

At eight o'clock in the morning you turn off the alarm and turn over in bed. It seems that you have slept for only a couple of hours. You will need to be at Honbu at eleven o'clock so that you can register, warm up and then take Kaicho's midday class. Your mind is full of thoughts about the grading and you feel concerned.

You leave your hotel and walk down towards Honbu which is located at 61 West 23rd Street near the corner of 6th Avenue. You can see the Seido flag waving in the breeze above the entrance to Honbu. You feel those familiar butterflies in your stomach and you are apprehensive about how your first day will go. You open the door and take the lift up to the second floor. Students are already in the dojo and you can hear the sound of 'Osu'[2] as they make their bows towards the Shinzen[3]. When you leave the lift, you put down your kitbag and make a deep bow towards the Shinzen showing your respect and appreciation of being at Honbu.

You are immediately greeted by the receptionist at the front desk who shakes hands with you and says that you are expected. He also says that there are quite a few other candidates coming from abroad to try for promotion and you feel easier at hearing this. You complete your registration and then proceed to the locker room to get changed. As you enter the dojo you are struck by the light filtering through the large plate glass window bouncing off the long sweep of the honey-coloured lacquered floor. Your eyes turn towards the Shinzen, and you make another deep bow and say '*Osu*'. Students who are warming up turn to watch you enter. You notice the racks of weapons on the walls on your right side, the kick bags, other training aids and the floor to ceiling mirrors lining the dojo on your left. The dojo smells fresh and there are flowers next to the Shinzen. You feel strangely calm as you change into your gi. Other students greet you in a friendly manner as you leave the locker room and go back into the dojo to warm up.

The dojo starts to fill up with students. You greet a few previous acquaintances, glad to have the opportunity to feel more at home in Honbu. There are now some fifty students waiting for Kaicho to enter the dojo. A senior black belt calls out, 'Line up,' and students spring into action, finding their places in their ranks. You are not sure about exactly where you should stand wearing your brown belt with its advanced tag but friendly hands guide you to your place. The class becomes silent as Kaicho enters the dojo and a loud '*Osu*' thunders out. Student bow towards him to show their respect.

Kaicho has dark hair, a thick neck and broad shoulders that radiate power. His eyes are piercing and appear black.

You notice his calloused hands. His gi is immaculate and almost glows white. The black belt around his waist is so worn that it appears tattered. His gaze sweeps down the lines of students and then rests on you. It feels as if you have been physically struck but he smiles and beckons you to join him at the front. You bow and come forward. He speaks your name and tells the students that you are from Jun Shihan Roger Thyer-Jones' dojo in England. He welcomes you to Honbu. He then gestures for you to kneel in front of him and asks you to remove your advanced Brown Belt which you do. A senior Black Belt hands him a plain white belt and he asks you to stand up. He then ties the white belt around your waist. You know that this signifies the start of your promotion as the custom is that you should now act as if this is the first day of your training. Kaicho gestures and you return to the line but you are no longer at its front. You join all the beginners at the back of the dojo.

The training regime at Honbu kicks in. You take early morning class at 7.30 a.m. under the watchful eye of Jun Shihan Walter who teaches a strictly traditional class emphasising excellent basics. Sometimes there is a fighting skills class after this from 8.30 to 9.00 a.m. You take your shower and then head off to the nearby diner for a full American breakfast. After breakfast, you rest for a while before returning to the dojo at 11.00 a.m. to practise until Kaicho's class at 12.30 p.m. At 1.30 p.m. there may be a conditioning or free fighting class. You are starting to feel the demands of the day by now. The classes are intense and you drip with sweat . You do push-ups on your knuckles and, even with toughened skin, they start to feel bruised. You are under scrutiny throughout the class so there is little opportunity to relax. In the fighting class the punches and kicks to your body take their toll. After lunch, you try to get some rest as you know that you have to be back in time for 4.30 p.m. in order to limber up for Kaicho's 5.30 p.m. class. Kaicho usually mixes up his classes using conditioning training, technique development and kata practice. He is unpredictable and tests your concentration throughout the class. He pounces on errors and rarely misses them.

At 6.30 p.m. you take Kaicho's fighting skills class which is non-stop, emphasising movement, speed and power development. Kaicho tells the students that if they feel faint they should just sit down until the faintness passes and then rejoin the class. You get to work out with a variety of students, ranging from lightweight to super-heavyweight. Often Kaicho will switch the emphasis of the class and say that you can only point-fight, which means exchanging techniques with very light contact but at a fast pace.

By 8.30 p.m. you are completely exhausted and then remember that this is only day one of your promotion. As you have travelled from abroad, Kaicho will condense the four-week promotion usually taken by Honbu students into one week for you so that the cost of living in New York is kept as low as possible. You complete your final bow of the day and leave the dojo. Every muscle in your body aches but you have started on the path and now must condition your mind to keep your standards high.

The days follow a similar pattern with classes varying in content and intensity. Twice each week there is a Seido Meditation class. On Tuesday evening you go up to the other dojo on the next floor of Honbu. The dojo is dark. There is one large white ceremonial candle burning in its holder in front of the Shinzen. Its flickering light makes large shadows. You line up in one of the four long lines of students who stand silently facing the Shinzen. In your hand you hold a seiza bench that has been specially made for meditation. Kaicho enters the dojo from a side room and you all make a deep bow towards him. He gestures for the students to kneel down in rank order and you do so. Kaicho invites the class to follow him in pre-meditation drills that calm the mind. You settle into your posture, monitor your breathing and listen as the big ceremonial drum sounds its bass note three times. Each drum beat signifies the unity of the mind, the body and the spirit and reflects the Seido principles of love, obedience, and respect.

A haunting flute starts. The flute's notes rise and fall like the tide ebbing and flowing on a sandy beach. You half-close your eyes and focus inwardly. The seniors slowly walk up and down the kneeling lines of students holding the *keisaku* which is a stick used to strike the acupressure point a few centimeters above the shoulder blade. You find yourself becoming drowsy and unable to concentrate. You request the monitor by placing both hands together near your chest. The monitor stops and you bow to each other. You place both hands on the top of your left knee, palms down and the monitor strikes you three times echoing the drum beats. You repeat this process on the other side of your body and then return to the upright position. You bow to each other and the monitor moves down the line. After thirty minutes the sound of the flute fades away and the drum beats three times again to signal that meditation is over. Slowly you rise. Your legs are numb and you feel pins and needles as the blood flows fully through them again. You now start *kinhin* which is walking meditation.

Kinhin begins by properly positioning your body and slowly moving forward starting with your right foot, almost gliding across the floor. You time your breathing, inhaling a breath as you raise your heel, exhaling as you slide the foot forward. As you walk, you feel how your weight is distributed at all times. You feel as if you are floating across the dojo floor. After a circuit of the dojo a handclap indicates that you must speed up until once again you come to rest in four lines in front of the Shinzen. At this point, after the formal bows, the meditation session is over. You feel relaxed yet invigorated. Your mind is clear.

Kaicho then asks all the students to sit down comfortably in front of him on the mats. He stands before a chalk board framed in the glow from a small spotlight. There is silence as he chalks Japanese calligraphy on to the board. He writes the English translation underneath. He then talks about an aspect of life on which we should reflect. At this time, he produces a book that was given to him by a friend in Japan. The contents of the book moved him. It concerns a Japanese lady without arms or legs since the age of three. It tells of how she overcame the negative pressures of society, faced unbelievable hardships but married and raised two children. The pages detail how she perfected her calligraphy and as a seamstress, produced fine garments and dolls. She died in her mid eighties.

Kaicho reflects on how easily we can be dissuaded from keeping to our chosen path. How minor excuses jump up to prevent us from moving forward. He uses training in karate as an example. The excuses can be: 'I can't train because I don't have enough time; I have an old injury that pains me; it's difficult to get to the dojo as I live so far away; we don't do any new material and I am bored; I'm too old, too frail, too poor' etc. Kaicho reminds us that continuity is the key to development. The aim is simply to train and not to look for rewards. To take what comes, but be consistent. He refers to the lady in the book. He asks us how this lady was able to overcome so much hardship with so few physical attributes to help her in daily life? The answer is that her strong spirit shone brightly in the darkness that surrounded her.

Kaicho continues, saying that it is easy to be strong and highly focused when you are in good health, but what about when one tiny virus makes you as weak as a child? Kaicho says that the spirit of the lady in the book is an example to all of us about what we can achieve in adversity. We grow when we have to struggle. We have a better understanding of others when we have endured hardships ourselves. This is the true meaning of our training in Seido Karate: to develop a non-quitting spirit in all circumstances. The dojo echoes as the students say a loud *'Osu'* acknowledging this key point. You reflect quietly on your own life and the reasons why you are now here. The day ends.

Wednesday. You feel tired as you kick back the bed clothes, grab a banana, slurp a soft drink, get dressed and head for the early morning class. You know that this evening at 6.00 p.m. you will accompany the other eighteen candidates, together with senior instructors, to the Manhattan School of the Blind. Seido is running successful programmes for blind and partially sighted students there. After your training session, you will return to the dojo where you will demonstrate your knowledge of the Seido syllabus. The day unfolds and soon it is evening and time for the school for the blind. You meet up with the other candidates in reception and then the senior instructors line up all the students. You put on your blindfold. You know that this is an important part of your promotion. To experience what it is like to have an impairment will help with your understanding of people who have such difficulties. As you walk in New York, blindfolded at rush hour time, you know that this is an experience you will not easily forget. Mostly, you feel highly vulnerable as you cross the busy streets while holding on to the student in front of you.

You arrive at the School of the Blind where you will now take class with blind and visually impaired students. Everything seems strange to you and you have no idea of your surroundings. Helpful hands guide you to your spot in the dojo. The instructor at the front of the class welcomes you on behalf of all his students. Once again, you feel nervous as you have no idea what you will be asked to do. Your mind seems overloaded and it becomes more and more difficult even to remember basic parts of the Seido syllabus. You have a real fear of falling and you are constantly concerned about hitting someone close to you as you execute your techniques. You are often disoriented and sometimes cannot hear what the instructor is saying. You know that you are required to act but don't know what action to take. You just stand there until someone tells you what to do. You feel stupid. One hour and a half passes and the class is finally over. The instructor tells the class to remove blindfolds but before you do so he asks you to think about all the feelings you have just experienced and to relate them to others with impairments. He asks you to appreciate the effort it costs a blind student just to get through the day in New York, perhaps crossing roads or using the subway. The light floods in as you take off your blindfold and then exchange observations and emotions with the other students. It is an experience that has had a profoundly positive effect on you.

But the evening is far from over. You make your way back to the dojo and climb the stairs up to the third floor where you wait until you are invited to enter the dojo. Kaicho's black belt class is just finishing and over sixty black belts of all ranks have been training together. It is an impressive sight. You are invited in and all eighteen candidates line up facing the rows of students who are now seated in the chairs opposite you in rows from 8th degree black belt downwards. Kaicho is seated behind a desk in front of the students and looks on impassively. He splits the candidates up into groups. He then asks each group to demonstrate *kata* or self defence. Some groups have to complete their task with their eyes shut, some have to execute moves painfully slowly and some in the normal manner. Over one hundred pairs of eyes are watching each move and you know that every mistake will be noticed. You will soon be exposed if your technical ability is found to be weak. Time seems to stand still but eventually this part of the promotion is over. Kaicho seems pleased with the standards although he has spoken sternly to some candidates when they have repeatedly made the same mistake. You leave the dojo and socialise with the other candidates discussing how the day had unfolded. You feel that you have done quite well so far and go to bed tired but quite content. Unfortunately, your brain seems to spin at a fierce pace as you review the day and think about what lies ahead. Sleep is hard-won but eventually comes.

Friday is the last day of your formal tests before the fighting part of your promotion which will take place on Sunday morning. You know that on this evening you will have to discuss your essay in front of Kaicho and all the black belts. The essay is an essential part of your promotion and is different for every rank. The aim of the essay is for you to discuss your progress in life in an open and honest manner. For many students even writing a formal essay presents formidable challenges while public speaking brings fear into many a heart. The essay you have written is available to all the black belts to read and they want to have a good insight into your character. Kaicho puts a high value on this part of the promotion saying that it reflects the highest principles of Seido Karate. This is not something to take lightly.

After more tests you line up together with your group and Kaicho ask you all to sit down. Each student then rises and speaks about his or her essay. At the end of each talk, Kaicho asks the black belts if there are any questions about it. Those questions can be penetrating and expose a lack of candour or a desire to cover up a key part of your background. Kaicho can get angry if he feels that you are not being honest and many a student has been prevented from proceeding further in the promotion at this point. It is nerve-racking. On the other hand, as you listen to the trials and problems of your fellow students you feel that you are closer to them and understand them better. This is indeed the human face of karate.

It is your turn. You complete your bows to Kaicho and all the seniors and compose yourself. You give your name, age and occupation and tell Kaicho in which dojo you study and for how long you have studied. You then discuss your essay and talk about many aspects of your life and those who have supported you on the path you have chosen. You gain confidence as you speak. Kaicho listens intently to you. His eyes never leave your face. He signals that you should stop and asks a perceptive question which you answer honestly. Two black belts have questions for you. Kaicho asks your instructor, Jun Shihan Roger, to speak in support of your promotion, which he does. It's over. Kaicho signals for you to sit down. Your mind is blank and you smile weakly at students sitting near you before you focus on what the next candidate is saying. Later, you reflect on what you have said and how you answered the questions. You are unhappy about some aspects of your explanations but feel that at least you spoke in a straightforward manner and from the heart.

Sunday morning finally comes. In many ways it is the day you welcome most as all you have to do is fight. You know that you are a good fighter but when you train at Honbu you find yourself working out with fighters who are well above your skill level. Some of them have been on the competition circuits for years and have been champions. The Jamaican fighters are particularly strong, fast, and fearless. You will have to fight a wide range of black belts in order to gain your belt. At 5.00 a.m., you rise from your bed, shower, dress, and grab your kit bag. You don't feel hungry and your stomach is churning but you know that you need to eat something. You grab a banana as you leave the hotel and walk down the street to the dojo. Manhattan is quiet at this time of the morning, with just a few yellow cabs cruising the streets.

The morning is cold but the sky is clear and blue. You set off for Honbu. When you arrive there, students are already entering through the door. You smile at some of the other candidates you know and exchange a few remarks. Your stomach is still churning as you enter the locker room and find a place to change into your gi. You smell the sharp tang of liniment and leather. You see some students wrapping their hands with a bandage to protect their knuckles and hear the crackle of gis being shaken out of kit bags before being worn. You tie your white belt around your waist and pull on the belt ends resolutely. You check your fighting equipment and put on your foot protectors and gloves, keeping your helmet and gumshield in your hands. You leave the locker room and make your way upstairs, past students who are warming up on the first floor. You can almost smell the tension in the air. You wonder if you

Mike Knight and I have made many trips over the years to study at Honbu and have remained staunch friends.

should go to the toilet again and empty what is left in your bladder but decide that you will be fine.

You bow and enter the dojo on the third floor which is full of students. Some are already fighting as they warm up with each other. There is a buzz in the room. You find a corner where you can stretch out and start your warm-up routine. Joints are being loosened and you can hear the snap of the canvas of karate suits as students practise their kicks. All around you, there are candidates watching, thinking, picturing how to handle the expert fighters, conserving energy and becoming more and more silent. The dojo is now full of black belts. It is nearly 6.00 a.m. There is total silence as Kaicho enters, together with the most senior black belts. A voice whips out, 'Line up,' and the thunderous sound of *'Osu'* hits the air as students quickly find their positions. All the candidates are together at the back of the dojo. The formalities begin. So many seniors to bow to. You just want it to start.

Kaicho lines up all the candidates in lines three deep and opposing each line is a line of black belts. *Senseis* (fourth degree black belts) are in charge of each group. You will have to fight all the black belts in front of you and then, once your group is finished, you will move down the line to the next group of black belts and start again. This will go on for nearly two hours.

Kaicho climbs a double-sided ladder that is used to reach and replace light bulbs. He sits on top of the ladder with a whistle in his hand. He now has a bird's-eye view of the fighting and will control the fights from his perch. He tells the candidates to face their first opponent. You will fight for one and a half minutes. No punches to the face will be allowed and Kaicho insists that good control must be exercised. He doesn't want to see any serious injuries. You feel nervous but calm inside as you face the black belt opposite you. She is tall, has blonde hair and is good looking. She smiles sweetly at you. Kaicho says, 'Begin.'

You have thought about your strategy to cope with each fighter. You are of medium build, light and quick on your feet. You use both kicks and punches well and also like to unbalance your opponent with sweeps to his legs. You know that there are four main categories of fighter: the elusive fighter who attacks and retreats, moving in and out of range very quickly, cuts angles so that he isn't hit and uses a lot of combinations and fakes; the aggressive fighter who attacks first and attacks relentlessly relying on power to win and who doesn't like to retreat; the counter-fighter who almost never attacks first, shields or parries counter-strikes but wants his opponent to come forward and responding instantly to weak or over-committed attacks; finally there is the shadow fighter who likes to win at all costs, breaks the rules of the game and plays mind games with his opponent, trying to psych him out and hit him when he is off-guard, even looking for ways to cheat, and talks and uses body language to intimidate his opponent. You know that a top fighter must master all four fighting styles. First and foremost you must know yourself before you can understand others. You incline more to being an elusive fighter who likes to counter your opponents after they have committed themselves. At least you know what you need to do to improve your skills and this fighting test represents a great

Michelle and I with our sons (left to right) Alex, Andrew and Gareth
and daughters-in-law Jo (daughter Gracie May)
Caroline (Caroline later gave birth to Annabelle
in November 2010) and Lisa.

opportunity for your to measure yourself against fighters of all kinds of skills, body shapes and sizes.

A whirlwind of punches and kicks assaults you as she attacks you from every angle. She is not smiling now and as the first punches rip through your guard, you grunt as you feel her power. A lighting fast kick nearly knocks off your helmet and the Sensei supervising the fight stops it until you have fixed it back in place. You are breathing hard.

Your thoughts drift back to advice given to you by one of your seniors. He reminded you that, above all, you should remember that everyone will be there for you. They will help and support you as well as test your resolve. You smile just as the first bout comes to a close.

The bouts seem endless. You are determined that in each fight, no matter how good your opponent, there will be at least one time when you will go on to the attack even though you know that it will sap your energy. The fighters respect you for trying, even though at times you show little in the way of power. The fights settle in to a rhythm and you are so glad that your fitness preparation was sound, otherwise you would be in no condition to carry on. You are now near the end of the lines and mentally let down your guard thinking that the promotion will be over soon. Suddenly a side kick knocks you to floor.

Your opponent is one of the top fighters at Honbu. He picks you up and then knocks you down again. He is not injuring you but you are winded each time you hit the floor. After you are knocked down the third time, you feel sorry for yourself and your mind starts to tell you to quit. You remember one of Kaicho's lectures, *'Nana Korobi Ya Oki,'* which means if you get knocked down seven times then get up eight times. You get up and hear encouragement from other students as you fight on. The bout ends and you move on to the next fighter. You hear a distant voice shout, 'Last one,' and as you begin the bout, you decide to throw your heart and soul into the last fight until you have nothing left.

Like so many of the other candidates, you forget that you are fighting in groups of three or four and will still have another three men or women in your group to fight. At least one of your opponents is twice your size and the last opponent is one of the best fighters in the dojo. You fight on in a blur, kicking and punching with grim determination, soaking up the blows to your body. You feel empty, both physically and mentally. You hear, 'Yame,' which means 'stop fighting', and the two hours are over. You line up with the rest of the candidates and try to stand as tall as you can. You remove your fighting equipment. Every part of you seems battered but you have survived.

Kaicho and his senior black belts stand before you. You hear your name called out and you walk forward towards the Shinzen and Kaicho. You stop and make your bows. Kaicho asks you to kneel and remove your white belt which is sweat stained. Your gi is also soaking wet. You kneel and hold the belt in your left hand. Kaicho gestures for you to stand up. Every bone in your body seems to groan as you do so. He leans forward and ties a black belt around your waist which signifies that you are now a first degree Seido black belt. He shakes your hand and offers his congratulations. You then move down the long line of black belts waiting to congratulate you, shake your hand, pat you on the back or even hug you, if they are friends. It is only as you make your way around the lines of black belts that emotion wells up inside of you. Familiar faces pass by amidst smiles and tears. You appreciate all those people who supported you, realising that today happened as a result of your family, instructors and fellow students believing in your ability and giving so much without expectation of any reward.

It is over. After the celebrations with your friends, you return to your family and loved ones. A week of your life has sped by and yet you have learned so much about yourself and others during that time. You are not the same man that left the UK. You have so much to give back to others.

With the help of Michelle and so many fine instructors we have built a strong UK organisation which should survive long after I am gone. We have excellent leaders of all our dojos and good communication. Having a structure to support you, not only physically but mentally and spiritually, is very important and Seido Karate has provided this support for me over the last twenty five years, but having people who love and care for me despite my weaknesses and faults is the height of good fortune and I deeply appreciate this.

As I write this I am sixty three years of age. I try to train every day and I have my own well-equipped studio in my house to facilitate this. Of course it gets harder to keep in shape as you get older but I accept no excuses. My body is made for hardship and will cope extremely well. I am not as fast or as supple as I was thirty years ago. I am fortunate that I can still test my skills at karate, judo, and unarmed combat against great exponents of these arts. Sometimes I do well, sometimes I don't. What matters is that I continue to cultivate a strong spirit as giving up easily is unthinkable. This non-quitting attitude that you should cultivate in the dojo can then extend into your everyday life. As I have said, I have learned that the most important approach to life is to be consistent in what I do, and training in Seido Karate has given me uncountable benefits. My hope is that some of you reading this autobiography will be inspired to find your own path and stick to it through thick and thin without seeking rewards.

I think that mentally I have climbed many mountains in my life. I know that my nature is that once I have reached the top I will always find another mountain to climb but I am content with this. I know that it is the journey, not the destination, that is important. I also appreciate more and more the value of family and friends and how the loss of loved ones can have such a lasting impact on our lives.

NOTES FOR CHAPTER TWENTY THREE

1 – A beginner in Seido Karate holds the rank of tenth *kyu* and wears a plain white belt. *Kyu,* meaning 'grade' is a designation signifying a level of achievement below black belt. The colour of the belt worn by *kyu* grades becomes darker as you progress towards black belt.

2 – 'Osu' is a contraction of the Japanese phrase *Oshi Shi No Bu.* It is a word that has a variety of meanings and is used as a greeting when bowing and addressing others. It is also used as a reminder for students as it implies patience: benefits from training only come with long, constant practice. When used in class it creates energy as students strive to do their best. It is an important part of training.

3 – 'Shinzen' is the spiritual heart of the dojo. Often there will be a traditional miniature wooden temple set above calligraphy that has a special meaning. In our Seido style, that calligraphy means *'Seido Jukku'* or 'Special Place.'

24

WHEN IRISH EYES STOP SMILING

I made a life-changing decision. I decided that I would take early retirement from the Immigration Service at the age of fifty-five. On 31 March 2005, I officially left the job. I wanted to be able to spend more time with my family, visit my mother and our cottage in Ireland and also to focus on expanding my martial arts interests.

I knew that early retirement would mean that we would not be financially so well off, but I was confident that I could develop the self-protection side of teaching martial arts which, together with my pension, would provide us with a comfortable existence. Another reason for leaving the job was that I had seen more and more friends and colleagues suffer stress-related illnesses and even die over the past two years from cancer or heart attacks. Our work in intelligence was becoming hugely demanding and I was carrying a very heavy portfolio of responsibilities. I knew that life would become increasingly difficult and we would be asked to take on more work with fewer resources. I did not want to leave the Service in a coffin.

Once I had made my mind up to leave, I looked forward to the challenges ahead and particularly to visiting Ireland and seeing my mother.

Mother was born on 21 April 1914 in Lisahully County Fermanagh, to Henry and Mary Fannon. She was one of eight children and her brothers were Jack, Fran, Harry and her sisters, Mary, Sadie, Beck, and Aggie. At school she was bright and quick. She told me that she knew she wasn't cut out for the farming life as once, when she was left in charge of the farm, her parents returned to find the ducks eaten by foxes and the farm in disarray. What she was cut out for was helping people and, at the age of fifteen, she won a scholarship to Edinburgh to study to be a nurse. Nursing at that time was very exacting and she was the only Irish girl on the nursing course. Away from her own home, and having to cope with the strict demands on a student nurse, must have been very hard for her.

During the war she nursed the sick and wounded. She was present at Dover during the Dunkirk evacuation, Operation Dynamo, treating some of the ten thousand soldiers who had suffered horrendous injuries, on their return to England. More than three hundred thousand troops were evacuated from the long stone and wooden jetty at the mouth of the port of Dunkirk by the Royal Navy and a flotilla of small boats. The aim of the operation was to rescue a fighting force. The wounded, who could not be moved, were to be left behind. This left the doctors with a difficult choice. Who should be left and who should be evacuated? Who should stay behind to care for those not evacuated? For those who were left, capture was inevitable and death a possibility.

It is hard to imagine what life must have been like for Mother and the other medical staff coping with the stream of the sick and the wounded on their arrival at Dover but no doubt this included long hours working in terrible conditions and surrounded by bloodshed and carnage. You have to be a special person to deal with such conditions and medical staff are often unsung heroes and heroines who just do their job without expectation of reward. They are quite remarkable people and I am proud that my mother was there to give what help that she could.

Mother didn't want to discuss the details of that time with me and I think that she had created a special place in her mind where she could take refuge and block out the terrible sights that she must have encountered. It was her ability to retreat into her private world which allowed her to cope with anything that life threw at her afterwards. Sometimes I could see her retreat into her special place when she needed to be away from the world. She became oddly distant and erected a barrier around herself. Late on in life she found herself able to share private thoughts with Michelle but this would not happen often.

At various times of her life she worked as a children's nurse, theatre sister, and dental nurse, each time dedicated to helping others. She was an attractive woman and at one time was engaged to two different suitors! She broke off both engagements when she met my father, Phillip Thyer-Jones, a dashing Welshman who was in the RAF at the time. He swept her off her feet and they married on 14 June 1941 in war-torn Britain. Mother said that her bridal dress was made from the silk of a parachute and they looked a very handsome couple indeed.

I believe that Mother must be a candidate for sainthood as my Aunt Molly often said that it needed the patience of a saint to live with Dad. Mother, like so many women, was the glue which held our family together and she often made sacrifices to ensure that my brother, Mike, and I had the best of life. Dad didn't want to die in hospital. Mother said that she would nurse him at home to the end. Again this was a brave decision as nursing a dying man is a most difficult and demanding task, especially a man such as Dad. It must have been heartbreaking for them both and I will never really understand, nor fully appreciate, all that she had to do to make him comfortable in his last days. I think that it must have been a great relief when Dad died as he was not the man he had been and suffered great pain right up until the end.

After Dad's death on 5 March 1973, she coped well with her grief, eventually leaving our flat in Crooms Hill and moving to live in a flat in Blackheath. She lived there comfortably until she again moved to Bromley, to live near my brother Mike and his wife, Barbara, and their children. Mike bought the flat for her and, initially, she loved it there and made friends in the area. We used to see her often. She was devastated when Mike split up with Barbara, leaving her for another woman. This hit Mother very hard indeed as she just could not believe that Mike would commit adultery. She had held him in such high esteem. It crushed her spirit and she felt that she needed to distance herself from the problems that inevitably follow such situations. She decided to move back to Ireland. Her family were there and Aunt Molly and Uncle Fran, her closest brother and sister-in-law, had moved over to Belleek some years before. Mike said that he would sell her flat in Bromley and buy a house in Belleek for her, which he did.

I never wanted her to leave England, where she had her sons and grandchildren, without first living in Belleek for a trial period of six months. I knew that if she moved, she wouldn't see her grandchildren for long periods as it is never as easy as you think to visit relatives who are far away, despite good transport. I think that she just wanted to run away from Mike's broken marriage and the heartbreak of seeing Barbara left with the children. It was an escape route for her but I felt that it was the wrong decision. She left for Ireland and went to live in a small house in Belleek, a small village in the north west of Ireland, twenty five miles from Enniskillen. She lived with her sister, Aggie. Unfortunately, she clashed with her over finances: Mother was generous and would spend freely to eat and keep herself comfortable but Aggie would try to save every penny she could, including switching off the heating in the winter. They appreciated each other's company but Aggie's drive to save money used to madden me and I even got the electrician to move the thermostat as high up the wall as possible just so Aggie couldn't turn off the heating in winter. My action was to no avail as Aggie simply used a stepladder.

Over the years, Mother's health deteriorated and, after a series of mini strokes and an incident when she fell out of bed and lay prone on her bedroom floor for hours until Aggie found her, we arranged for her to move into the nearby Shannagh Nursing Home. We knew the manager and the staff there and the standard of care was excellent. We would try to visit Mother as often as we could and she was always in good spirits, never had any complaints and always praised the nursing care she received. She was admired by the staff as a kind and gentle woman. Very slowly she deteriorated and Mike and I were told that she was dying. We went over to Ireland and spent two weeks with her and lost count of the number of times we were told that it was almost her time.

Strange things happen in Ireland. One afternoon, I was with my Aunt Una in Mother's room while she was sleeping. Una got up from her chair and went to Mother's wardrobe. She opened the door and looked at the clothes hanging there. She returned to the bed and asked me, 'What are you going to lay your Mother out in?'

I was shocked. I had not even thought about how to dress her once she had died and anyway she was still alive. Una, practical as ever, said that there was no suitable blouse for her in the wardrobe. She could be laid out in her suit which was fine, but a pretty white blouse was needed to go with the suit. We would need to go to Slavins department store in Ballyshannon to choose a proper blouse It seemed an almost surreal conversation but, after Mike came to take over from me sitting with Mother, Una and I drove to Slavins.

Of course Una knew the assistant there and she explained that Mother was slipping away and we needed a suitable blouse. I was shown two or three blouses and the merits of how she would look in each one were discussed. I felt that I was in the middle of a comedy sketch but eventually Una decided to take the three blouses back to the Shannagh and see which one best suited Mother. No payment was required until after we had selected the right blouse. We returned to the home, where my Aunt Molly had arrived, and a lively discussion started about the merits of each of the blouses. Mother continued to sleep throughout the discussion. I thought that it was disrespectful, and said so, but Una and Molly told me not to be so stupid. Finally, a white blouse was selected and put on a hanger together with the suit in which Mother would be laid out. Mike and I had to return home for the weekend and attend to pressing matters before coming straight back to Mother's side. Mother's condition was stable and the doctor had now told me that she could continue in this twilight state for many days more.

With Mother on her 90th. birthday.

A day after I arrived home, on 7 February 2006, Mother died. After spending so much time by her side, I was sad not to have been there, but there was nothing I could do.

Funerals take place fast in Ireland and my cousin, Patsy McCauley, is one of the best funeral directors I have ever known. He is a superb organiser with a deep sense of respect and reverence. He knows how a funeral should proceed if it is to properly respect the dead. A man like Patsy is invaluable at a time of mourning and we left all the funeral arrangements to him.

Mother had her funeral mass in the Catholic church in Belleek where many of our relatives are buried and there is real family history in the graveyard. I was proud that two of our sons, Gareth and Andrew, were coffin bearers. Nothing gives you a stronger sense of family than to carry the coffin of a loved one. I gave a eulogy in the church and our niece Alison Longhurst spoke personally about Mother to all those who attended the lunch afterwards in the Carlton Hotel in Belleek.

How can I sum up Mother's character? She always had a soft spot for anyone in the caring profession and admired dedication in others. Her nature was soft and gentle but she showed strong determination in keeping our family together. She was a caring mother who loved her family and friends. She was a fine-looking girl who grew into a beautiful woman. She spent the majority of her life helping others. No higher tribute can be paid to her. I miss her. She would have loved to have made the age of ninety-two. I rarely heard her say an unkind word about anybody and she would always congratulate you in success and support you in failure. My own special memory of her is when we took her to the Manor Hotel in Enniskillen for her ninetieth birthday. We had a birthday cake made and this was brought out in ceremony with candles burning on it. We sang 'Happy Birthday'. Her comment, typically, was, 'Arrah, I don't want any fuss' and that is how she lived her life, with as little fuss as possible.

After her death, I found a letter written by her to Mike and me. The letter said that in the event of her death she wanted us to know that she thought that we were two wonderful sons. She praised her daughters-in-law and grandchildren. She passed on her love to her surviving sisters, 'Aga' Beck and Sadie, sister-in-law, Una, and brother, Harry. She said that her best friend had been her sister-in-law, Molly Fannon. That is the sort of woman she was, always thinking of others even in her last hours. She had beautiful blue smiling Irish eyes. Now, sadly, they are forever closed.

25

DOGS ON THE RUNWAY

'Don't you dare die on me.'

Blood was gushing out of the cut on the right of his forehead. His lips were blue and his face was deathly pale. I had turned him over onto his back and tilted his head by lifting his chin. I bent close to him with my cheek against his lips. I couldn't detect any breathing.

'Don't you dare die on me,' I shouted again.

Dave had also reacted quickly and was kneeling at his side. He had laced his fingers and found Richard's chest bone. He began to rock forward compressing the heart so that we could pump the blood around the body.

'Don't just bloody stand there, call an ambulance,' I shouted at the gawping Lufthansa attendant and then sealed Richard's mouth with my own and tried to breathe life into him again.

A crowd gathered around us; spectators ghoulishly watching as a stranger's life was held in the balance. Dave was pumping Richard's heart. I was breathing into his lungs. I started to feel nauseous.

Time stood still.

Breathe, pump.

Breathe, pump.

Richard's mouth was still blue. I could feel no sign of a pulse. I shouted at him again but I don't remember what I said. I felt a tap on my shoulder.

'I am a doctor. Shall I take over?'

I nodded and he prepared to relieve me just at the

moment when the paramedics arrived with their life-saving equipment. Dave and I stood up as the paramedics gave Richard oxygen and attached the crash pads to his chest.

Crash.

The voltage ripped through his body and he convulsed. The heart monitor still showed a flat line.

'Don't you give up on us Richard,' I shouted. 'Don't you dare give up.'

Crash.

This time the monitor flickered and showed that his heart had restarted. Tears ran down my face and I turned to look at Dave who was equally emotional.

The paramedic team moved as an efficient unit and, in a very short time, Richard was taken from the airport building and into the waiting ambulance. He was being taken to a nearby private hospital. We had no way of knowing if he would live or die.

I took stock of the situation. I was covered in Richard's blood which had soaked into my suit, shirt and tie and I had blood on my hands as well. Dave was dishevelled. I turned to the check-in desk where the Lufthansa representative who had denied us boarding was standing with his manager. I told the manager that I was angry about the way his employee had handled matters. His intransigence had resulted in my colleague almost dying in front of him. Unfair, but I was past caring. The manager gave me his business card and told us that when we wanted to return to the UK we should just let him know and he would make arrangements for our return flight.

Dave and I sat down at an airport café, ordered two strong coffees and two large brandies before we started to make calls back to the office to let them know what had happened. The mobile phones were hot as we placed calls to the UK and the British Embassy in Bonn. The office had to let Richard's wife know what had happened. She had to cancel her operation. The support network was as busy as a beehive. Nothing was too much trouble. It was heartening to see how many people were pulling together to ensure that Richard got the best care possible. We cleaned ourselves up in the men's toilet and took a taxi out to a hotel next to the hospital. We had a shower, changed our clothes and set off to visit Richard. So many questions went through my head. He was alive when the paramedics took him but he had stopped breathing for what seemed like a long time, almost four minutes, I thought. Had we done enough to prevent brain damage? What sort of shape would we find him in? My stomach knotted and I just didn't want to think about the possibility that he would not survive.

I stood outside the door of the intensive care ward. I couldn't see in but I knew that Richard was there. I slowly opened the door. He was alone. He was lying in bed dressed in a white hospital gown. His grey hair which was usually immaculately well-groomed, was dishevelled. His face was pallid. He was surrounded by medical equipment. His eyes were shut but his mouth was open. He seemed to be in a light sleep. His chest rose and fell regularly. I felt very emotional. He was still alive. Tears gathered at the corners of my eyes. A nurse said that we could speak to him for a short time but we were not to tire him. Dave and I stood watching him for a while. It was six o'clock in the evening, nearly five hours after that dreadful moment when he had collapsed.

Richard slowly opened his eyes and looked across at us as we approached his bed. He seemed confused and butterflies fluttered again in my stomach. He licked his lips. I approached the side of his bed. He turned his head slowly to look at me.

With some effort he clearly said, 'My dear boy, I understand I have you to thank for saving my life. I also understand that you had the most unpleasant experience of having to breathe into my mouth. What a good job for you that I had that large gin and tonic.'

I burst out laughing, as did Dave. I could have hugged Richard if he hadn't been so enmeshed in an intimidating network of tubes. He said that they had given him drugs to make him sleepy and so that he wasn't at his best. He said that his mind was fine. He then told me that he thought that he had collapsed as a result of over-anxiety and the fact that he had previously had a triple heart by-pass! I could have passed out myself when I heard this news. We had been under extraordinary pressure over the preceding days and he had not once mentioned his medical condition. When I asked him to explain, he said that his operation had been some time ago and his heart was sound and had not caused him the slightest of trouble until now.

If only those dogs on the runway had not been there.

Richard recovered well and Michelle and I subsequently visited him and his wife at their home. We never spoke of the incident again.

Dogs on the runway. Were they chance, destiny, divine will, karma, kismet, predestination, fortune, or fate? Each and every action we take will have a corresponding result. Each individual action, even the smallest and most insignificant, is full of consequences. However tiny a spark may be, it can burn down a haystack. Yet tiny good actions bring hope and give comfort, just as little drops of water will eventually fill a big barrel. My philosophy of life is summed up in Lao Tsu's[1] poem penned two and a half thousand years ago and shown on this book cover. But my favourite poem, which will give hope to people in dark places, is by Robert Service.[2] Always have just one more try.

NOTES FOR CHAPTER TWENTY FIVE

1 – Lao Tsu was a philosopher of ancient China, best known as the author of the Tao Te Ching of philosophical Taoism.

2 – Robert Service was born in England in 1874. He commenced a life of adventure which he recounted in songs, ballads, rhymes and poems which are famous across the world. He caught the spirit of the wanderer in us all.

The Quitter

When you're lost in the Wild, and you're scared as a chil
And Death looks you bang in the eye,
And you're sore as a boil, it's according to Hoyle
To cock your revolver and . . . die.
But the Code of a Man says: "Fight all you can,"
And self-dissolution is barred.
In hunger and woe, oh, it's easy to blow . . .
It's the hell-served-for-breakfast that's hard.

'You're sick of the game!' Well, now, that's a shame.
You're young and you're brave and you're bright.
'You've had a raw deal!' I know - but don't squeal,
Buck up, do your damnedest, and fight.
It's the plugging away that will win you the day,
So don't be a piker, old pard!
Just draw on your grit; it's so easy to quit:
It's the keeping-your-chin-up that's hard.

It's easy to cry that you're beaten – and die;
It's easy to crawfish and crawl;
But to fight and to fight when hope's out of sight —
Why, that's the best game of them all!
And though you come out of each gruelling bout,
All broken and beaten and scarred,
Just have one more try – it's dead easy to die,
It's the keeping-on-living that's hard.

Robert William Ser

The Quitter

When you're lost in the Wild, and you're scared as a child,
And Death looks you bang in the eye,
And you're sore as a boil, it's according to Hoyle
To cock your revolver and . . . die.
But the Code of a Man says: "Fight all you can,"
And self-dissolution is barred.
In hunger and woe, oh, it's easy to blow . . .
It's the hell-served-for-breakfast that's hard.

'You're sick of the game!' Well, now, that's a shame.
You're young and you're brave and you're bright.
'You've had a raw deal!' I know - but don't squeal,
Buck up, do your damnedest, and fight.
It's the plugging away that will win you the day,
So don't be a piker, old pard!
Just draw on your grit; it's so easy to quit:
It's the keeping-your-chin-up that's hard.

It's easy to cry that you're beaten – and die;
It's easy to crawfish and crawl;
But to fight and to fight when hope's out of sight –
Why, that's the best game of them all!
And though you come out of each gruelling bout,
All broken and beaten and scarred,
Just have one more try – it's dead easy to die,
It's the keeping-on-living that's hard.

Robert William Service